Good Humor, Bad Taste

Humor Research 7

Editors

Victor Raskin
Willibald Ruch

Mouton de Gruyter
Berlin · New York

Good Humor, Bad Taste

A Sociology of the Joke

by
Giselinde Kuipers

Mouton de Gruyter
Berlin · New York

Mouton de Gruyter (formerly Mouton, The Hague)
is a Division of Walter de Gruyter GmbH & Co. KG, Berlin.

♾ Printed on acid-free paper which falls within the guidelines
of the ANSI to ensure permanence and durability.

Library of Congress Cataloging-in-Publication Data

Kuipers, Giselinde, 1971—
    [Goede humor, slechte smaak. English]
    Good humor, bad taste : a sociology of the joke / by Giselinde
Kuipers ; [translated from the Dutch by Kate Simms].
        p. cm. — (Humor research ; 7)
    Translation of : Goede humor, slechte smaak with revised
material and added chapter.
    Includes bibliographical references and index.
    ISBN-13: 978-3-11-018615-4 (hardcover : alk. paper)
    ISBN-10: 3-11-018615-2 (hardcover : alk. paper)
    1. Dutch wit and humor — History and criticism.   2. Wit and
humor — Social aspects.   I. Title.   II. Series.
    PT5346.K8513   2006
    306.4'81—dc22
                                                                2006010029

ISBN-13: 978-3-11-018615-4
ISBN-10: 3-11-018615-2
ISSN 1861-4116

Bibliographic information published by Die Deutsche Bibliothek

Die Deutsche Bibliothek lists this publication in the Deutsche Nationalbibliografie;
detailed bibliographic data is available in the Internet at <http://dnb.ddb.de>.

Translated from the Dutch (except for Chapter 9 and Appendix 2) by Kate Simms, To the
Point Translations, Baarn, the Netherlands.

Cover design: Christopher Schneider, Berlin.
Printed in Germany.

For my sisters, Wendelmoet and Margit

Acknowledgements

Many people have contributed, both directly and indirectly, to this book. I am very grateful to all the people who agreed to be interviewed by me, or to participate in the survey. This research would have been impossible without their willingness, and enthusiasm, to indulge my rather bizarre request: to discuss their sense of humor with me.

Joop Goudsblom, my advisor, or *promotor* as this function is so aptly called in Dutch, has been a great help and inspiration to me ever since I started my life in Academia. I hope that some of his constant dedication and attention to clear writing and clear thinking shows in this book.

Kate Simms has been of invaluable help in the latest transformation of this book: she did a wonderful job in translating the original Dutch book and correcting the new chapters and sections. It was a pleasure to work with someone who took my sentences so seriously.

Most of the research was done at the Amsterdam School for Social Science Research at the University of Amsterdam. I still look back on my years at "the School" fondly and nostalgically, both for its sociable atmosphere and its wonderfully stimulating intellectual climate. I owe a great debt to the many people with whom I discussed my ideas and who read (parts of) the book during my years at the University of Amsterdam: Erik Bähre, Marieke Bloembergen, Talja Blokland, Jaap Dronkers, Jeffrey Goldstein, Bart van Heerikhuizen, Marcel Hoogenboom, Dienke Hondius, Theo Meder, Bowen Paulle, Jan Rupp, Bert Schijf, Abram de Swaan, Jo Swabe, Bonno Thoden van Velzen, Jojada Verrips, Frank Wiendels, Nico Wilterdink, and Cas Wouters. I have also benefited greatly from the international community of humor scholars. I especially want to thank Christie Davies and Victor Raskin for their support from overseas

My research in the United States, in 2003-2004, was made possible by a Talent grant from the Netherlands Organization for Scientific Research (NWO), for which I am very grateful. NWO also generously funded the translation of this book. I want to thank Jeroen Jansz, Peter Neijens, and Patti Valkenburg at the Amsterdam School for Communication Research for their help in securing this grant and enabling me to leave for a year.

At the University of Pennsylvania, I have enjoyed the hospitality of both the Annenberg School of Communication, and the Department of Sociology. I want to thank Amy Jordan and Kathleen Hall Jamieson at the Annenberg School, and Elijah Anderson, Vida Bajc, Randall Collins, David

Grazian, Jay Hodos, Ross Koppel, Jenn Larimer, Daniel Maman, and Erika Summers-Effler at the Sociology Department. Jennifer Beer has been a wonderful host and key informant, who greatly enhanced my understanding of Americans in general, and Philadelphians in particular. I also want to thank Salvatore Attardo and Victor Wan-Tatah for their help in arranging the interviews in Youngstown, Ohio.

In the writing of the American chapter, I have benefited greatly from the many discussions on cultural differences and cross-national comparisons with my colleagues at Erasmus University, Pauwke Berkers, Susanne Janssen, Alex van Venrooij, and Marc Verboord.

I am grateful to the editors of *Moppentoppers* at Endemol Studios, who allowed me to participate in the selections, where I found many of my interviewees. I also want to thank Reid, Geleijnse, and van Tol for letting me use their Fokke and Sukke cartoons to shock Americans, both in the American survey, and again in this book. Patrick Chapatte was very generous in letting me use his cartoons in the survey.

Finally, I want to thank all my friends and family for their support, company, and good humor. Three of them deserve special mention, both for being wonderful friends, and for their contribution to this book. When Suzanne Kuik and I started our PhDs, we shared not just an office, but all our ideas, doubts, and enthusiasm. It a great loss both for me, and for scholarship, that she is no longer in Academia, but the sharing of ideas, doubts, and enthusiasm has never ended. I also want to thank Jeroen de Kloet for our ongoing conversations, from either side of the post/modern divide, on the vicissitudes of life, academic and otherwise. Our conversations have grown increasingly nomadic over time, yet they always feel close. I hope they will they wander on indefinitely. Finally, Peter Zuithoff not only was an indispensable help because of his statistical knowledge, but also has been the most loyal of friends throughout the years.

As its previous incarnations, the English version of this book is dedicated to my sisters: to Margit, whose sense of humor I have seen develop over the years with a mixture of sisterly and scholarly interest; and to Wendelmoet, who always is the first, and sometimes the only one, to laugh at my jokes.

Contents

Chapter 1
Introduction: Jokes, humor, and taste

The importance of a shared sense of humor is made obvious by its absence. It is almost impossible to build a relationship with someone who never makes you laugh, who never laughs at jokes you make or even worse: who tries really hard to be funny but insists on telling the wrong jokes. Very few things are more painful than an attempt at humor that is not appreciated by those listening.

To tell the right joke at the right time requires considerable cultural knowledge. Someone who doesn't laugh when others do or who laughs when the rest are silent, exposes himself as an outsider: he reveals his lack of awareness of codes, habits, and rules. He doesn't belong. In social relationships, humor has the role of measuring mutual understanding and signaling good intentions. When a joke fails, listeners usually feel like rejecting the joke teller, and often do.

What counts as "good" humor differs from group to group, from person to person, and from moment to moment. The extent to which people differ in their opinions of what is funny is sharply illustrated in a form of humor prominent in day-to-day interactions: in joke telling. The joke is a humorous genre about which opinions are extremely mixed. There are true joke lovers – proverbial uncles at parties producing enough jokes, one after the other, to last the whole evening – but also self-declared adversaries. Certain groups welcome jokes with great enthusiasm while others reject the telling of a joke with demonstrative silence; the latter group sees joke telling as tasteless and vulgar.

Judging jokes goes further than expressing personal style or taste. Sense of humor is connected to social milieu and background. Not only are there individual differences in how humor is appreciated but there are also differences between men and women, between people with different educational advantages, between old and young, and of course differences between people from different cultures and countries. What people think is funny – or not funny – is strongly determined by how they were brought up and the company they keep.

This book has to do with the relationship between sense of humor and social background. As the starting point for understanding and plotting these social differences in sense of humor, I will be looking at how people think about one specific humorous genre: the joke. More precisely: I will be looking at the standardized or "canned" joke: a short humorous story, ending in a punch line, which the teller usually does not claim to have invented himself. Dutch, the language in which most of this research was originally carried out, has a specific word for this genre: *mop*. In English, "joke" can refer both to this specific genre and more generally to something said or done to amuse people. However, even though there is no separate word in English for the specific genre, the joke was clearly recognized as being separate by the Americans I interviewed.

It may perhaps surprise the reader that I chose this, of all genres. The subject "humor" is capable of suggesting something profound and of prompting people to contemplate human nature, the importance of creativity, or the connection between suffering, humor, and detachment, but the joke evokes many fewer grandiloquent associations. Jokes are amusement more than anything else, without many pretensions or profound purposes: they are meant to make people laugh and no more.

The joke is perhaps not a particularly chic genre but it does evoke emphatic reactions. As I did my research, I interviewed people who considered telling jokes to be "the acme of humor", "just part of any good night's fun", and even: "the essence of togetherness and pleasure, a reason to laugh till you cry". But I also talked to people who denigrated jokes as "a form of spiritual poverty", "tiresome things, enormously disrupting to conversation". One of my informants stated very decidedly: "Jokes that's not humor". In saying these things, people are also stating implicitly what humor means to them: what they consider funny, hilarious, corny, far-fetched, vulgar, or banal. They are verbalizing a decision about good and bad humor. But just behind the scenes, ideas are lurking about what a good conversation entails, what an enjoyable evening looks like, what being sociable means, and more generally: how people are supposed to interact with each other. Judgments about humor are directly connected with ideas about what constitutes pleasant and unpleasant communication.

Researching jokes

This variance of opinion itself makes the genre of the joke a suitable starting point for research into differences in how humor is appreciated. Research into preference for and aversion to jokes leads to more general questions about humor: why do some people love certain forms of humor while others can't stand them? Which subjects are preferred joke material and which are not? Why do people consider something funny, amusing, hilarious or, rather, corny, feeble, or vulgar? What do people mean by "sense of humor"? How do people differ in their opinions on this? And what are the consequences of such differences in humor style?

In order to answer these questions I conducted interviews, I did a survey of humor styles, and I collected a large number of jokes. The research on which this book is based was carried out mostly in the Netherlands. However, the final chapter presents the results of a similar, though smaller, study in the United States. In the Netherlands, I spoke extensively to seventy Dutch people about jokes and humor. First, I talked to thirty-four joke lovers, people who knew and told a lot of jokes. These were acquired through newspaper advertisements and through the grapevine, but primarily gleaned from people participating in the selection for the Dutch television program *Moppentoppers,* a program aired by RTL4, a large commercial TV channel. *Moppentoppers* (the name is a contamination of *toppers*, which means approximately the same in English, and *moppentapper*, a rather jocular word for joke teller) was a highly popular joke-telling contest for amateur joke tellers.

I also interviewed four editors of joke books. After that, I interviewed thirty-two "ordinary people" about their sense of humor: men and women, young and old, of different educational and professional backgrounds, joke lovers and joke haters. All these interviewees, under fictitious names, will be cited frequently in this book. The group of thirty-two was a sample taken from a group of 340 Dutch people who had filled in a questionnaire about jokes and humor in 1997/1998. In addition to this, I collected many thousands of jokes: I found them on the Internet, in joke books and magazines, in archives, and they were told to me by friends, acquaintances, and people whom I interviewed.

Differences in the appreciation of jokes touch upon three of the most important social distinctions in the Netherlands: gender, age, and particularly class. In the Netherlands, like in other Western countries, it is often said that class no longer plays a role of any importance. Classical distinctions between high and low culture are said to be fading; people can freely choose from a great diversity of "lifestyles". That educational level and social milieu played such a huge role in appreciating humor surprised me too. My questions about jokes, humorists, and humorous television programs seemed to lead automatically to the subjects of vulgarity and good taste, high and low culture, common and elitist humor. The discourse about humor in the Netherlands turned out to be imbued with references to class.

Five years after I did these interviews in the Netherlands, I carried out a similar, though much smaller, study in the United States: I interviewed twenty-eight people and 143 people filled in a questionnaire similar to the one used in the Netherlands. Not only did this enable me to compare Dutch patterns of humor styles and social background with American humor styles, it also gave me an opportunity to include national differences in the comparison. Moreover, the American study functioned as a cross-cultural validation of the approach to humor and social background I had developed in the Dutch study: it turned out that, in a different cultural context, the approach and the concepts still worked, even though actual social distinctions in the US were markedly different.

Jokes and humor

Jokes are – as all humor is – meant to amuse, to make people laugh. Ever since antiquity, many superior and inferior thinkers have reflected on humor, and there is but one thing upon which they all agree: humor is a pleasant experience, often (but by no means always) accompanied by laughter. Humor is not solely amusement; it can bring people closer to each other, embarrass, ridicule, cause to reflect, relieve tension, or put into perspective serious affairs. However, if people do not like the joke, humor cannot fulfill these other functions competently. Humor can fulfill a great number of functions, but the first goal of the joke is to provoke mirth, amusement, and preferable laughter.

The joke is but one form of humor. In addition to jokes, many other humorous genres and styles exist, varying from slapstick to doggerel to cabaret critical of society. To investigate social differences in sense of humor, it seemed most sensible to me to focus on one genre. It is simply not possible to allow all styles and genres sufficient space in a single book. It is also questionable whether one can make meaningful generalizations about such divergent genres as jokes, cabaret, revue, stand-up comedy, clowns, TV satire, sitcoms, humorous talk shows, let alone cartoons, regular columns, trick cigars, fake turds, clowns' noses, or the humor in advertisements, on signboards, or carved into toilet doors. And then these represent only standardized humor: spontaneous jokes like those made every day fall outside these categories. Therefore, I sought to limit my scope.

After serious consideration, I chose the joke, one of the most widely distributed and most recognizable humorous genres in the Netherlands and throughout the world. It is basically a short humorous text with at its end an unexpected turn or dénouement, the punch line. Usually jokes have the form of a story, but riddles are also considered to be jokes. These have, as jokes do, a clear punch line and are based frequently on the same themes. What happens in a joke generally follows a standard pattern: things often take place three times. There are standard formulas for the telling too: "A man walks into a bar..."; "A Dutchman, a German and a Belgian..." or their American counterparts, "A Polack, an Irishman and a ..." Themes, settings, and personages are largely standard as well: a dumb blonde, a woman at the doctor's, a man in a bar, a fly in the soup, three persons on the Eiffel Tower, in an airplane, or on a desert island – all personages and situations the good listener immediately associates with jokes. Some of these characters have a more national flavor: in the Netherlands the dumb character is usually Belgian, the little boy outwitting adults is called Jantje (Johnnie), and Jewish stock characters Sam and Moos (short for Samuel and Moses) will be out walking in the Kalverstraat, Amsterdam's main shopping street. However, the same jokes, featuring different characters, can be found in other countries around the world, from America to India or Chile.

The strong standardizing of jokes has to do with the fact that jokes are orally transmitted. Jokes are written down, for instance in joke books, but the majority of the jokes contained in these derives from the oral culture of storytelling. Such oral genres often have standard formulas and themes: this makes them easy to remember and repeat to others. In addition, new punch lines can be built into an existing pattern. Everyone who tells a joke is dipping into an enormous, pre-existing, repertoire of jokes. A joke teller will then never – at least almost never, and then very seldom rightfully – claim that he thought up the joke himself. Not only the joke itself is at issue in joke telling, but also the art of telling it: whether or not someone knows how to "present" it.

This verbal transmission means that jokes grant researchers a view of the role, so difficult of access, that humor plays in normal, day-to-day interactions. Jokes are not the domain of professional humor producers, but are mainly told in everyday situations by "ordinary people". Jokes differ in this from other standardized humor usually taking place on paper or on a podium. Comedy often is a rather one-sided form of communication: the role of the audience is limited to laughing or not, laughing right out loud or less enthusiastically – where in humor on paper, radio, or television the humorist does not even get to hear whether this happens. However, the teller makes direct contact with his audience in telling jokes. Also, the division of roles is not standardized: different people gathered together can tell jokes in turn. Jokes thus provide the opportunity to look at humor as a mode of communication.

The joke is a preeminently social phenomenon. Jokes belong to everyone: they are not thought up by any one person, but are told again and again and continuously redesigned in the interaction. A joke is a joke only if it is repeated: only at the moment of repetition does a joke become a joke, a "social event" instead of an individual creation. This too is one of the reasons why I chose the joke: research into cabaret or other humor whose author can be clearly indicated would quickly have become a history of important names and conflicting artistic movements. In research of this nature, I would also have run the risk of placing the emphasis on creation instead of communication. Jokes are what Emile Durkheim ([1895]1964) has referred to as *social facts*: phenomena that cannot be reduced to the level of individual decisions and motivations.

The consideration that finally determined my choice for the joke is how people think *about* jokes. As I have already mentioned: the joke has very definite advocates and opponents. In general, however, the joke's status is low. This means that the joke forms a good basis for this research: it is precisely the "low" and controversial genres that evoke explicit reactions and thus make visible social distinctions. Explicit judgments about the joke have a lot to do with the fact that joke appreciation is often couched in terms of good and bad taste. "Taste" does not usually point to matters of life and death but rather to mundane things like preferences for interior decoration, clothing, or television series. And yet, in judgments having to do with taste, preference or aversion is often highly present and deeply felt. Social boundaries are sharply delineated by what seem to be trivial matters, in which "tastes differ".

Given that this is mostly research into my own society, throughout the research I was very much aware of these opinions on good and bad taste. I have never been particularly tempted to tell jokes (in spite of my prolonged contact with them, I have never become a virtuoso joke teller) and in my social milieu I seldom hear them. This "anthropological impulse" also spurred me on to choose the joke as my research subject: researching something you don't know well often produces more insight, even into what is very familiar and trusted, than researching something with which you are intimately involved. In choosing jokes, I was not choosing an unknown subject but a "strange" one, nevertheless, to those in my own circles.

Humor as a social phenomenon

Thinking about humor has always been predominantly the domain of philosophers and psychologists, and more recently of linguists. While humor is preeminently a social phenomenon, social scientists have only dealt with humor research sporadically. The scientific background of the majority of humor researchers has influenced the questions they have asked about humor. Philosophers see humor to a large extent as something intrinsically present in a text or an event. The question then quickly is focused on what "the substance" or "the essence" of humor is: what are the distinguishing characteristics of "humor", "the laugh", or "the comic"? (Morreall 1983, 1987). Within psychological research, the emphasis is strongly placed on humor as an individual matter: the confrontation between an individual, with specific moods, distinguishing personal characteristics, aspects of character and interests, and a joke (e.g. Martin 1998; Ruch 1998). Linguists, finally, have tended to focus on the formal characteristics of the humorous text: what distinguishes jokes and other funny texts from serious ones? (Raskin 1985; Attardo 1994, 2001)

In this book, I want to look at humor primarily as a *social* phenomenon: a form of communication that is embedded in social relationships. For this reason I have also chosen a working definition of humor in which the social aspect is prominent: I see humor as "the successful exchange of joking and laughter". Humor in this definition is viewed as an exchange involving a number of people. This communication can be more or less successful; there is only question of humor if the joke "succeeds". An unsuccessful exchange does still contain an aspiring joke – an attempt to make people laugh – but this is not successful humor: no one laughs, smiles, or otherwise acknowledges the joke.

While humor also can be unintentional, I will be looking primarily at conscious attempts to make people laugh: jokes, performances of comedians, television comedy – all of these socially stylized invitations to laughter. The ideal reaction to such a joke is always a laugh. Everyone who tells a joke hopes that it will be laughed at. The joke tellers I spoke to said without exception that the attractiveness of telling jokes lies in the fact that people laugh at them, "that people fall off their chairs laughing". "That the canteen resounds with laughter. The more people laugh, the more fun you have telling them." "What's fun about telling jokes? If I go to a bar, the moment I come in, everybody starts laughing. That's the nice thing about telling jokes."

The explicit mention of laughter in this definition may be something of a provocation in current humor research, where humor and laughter are generally considered separate and partly unconnected phenomena. Not everyone who appreciates a joke expresses that by laughing, and there are many forms of laughter that are not responses to humor (Douglas 1975; Provine 2000). Still, everyone who makes a joke hopes for laughter as the result; and everyone who hears a laugh assumes that something funny has happened (and will also want to know "what's so funny?").

As the sociologist Rose Coser wrote: "To laugh, or to occasion laughter through humor and wit, is to invite those present to come close." (Coser 1959:172) Laughter signals the acceptance of this invitation. As so often happens with invitations, acceptance of the invitation is often interpreted as an acceptance of the inviter at the same time. Thus, humor and its counterpart and reward, laughter, are among the strongest signals of social solidarity and togetherness.[1]

Therefore the laugh is a fundamental part of the way people *perceive* humorous communication. It is the expected, intended, and coveted reaction of any joke teller. Laughter is the idealtypical expression of the emotion of amusement. As such, it cannot be ignored as a social phenomenon and a form of communication in any study of humor. But there are of course other possible reactions: these range from smiling and grinning to complicated (but culturally coded) reactions such as half-exhausted sighing at a corny joke, or verbal expressions of appreciation. When I was living in the United States, I was rather puzzled at the prevalence of verbal acknowledgements of jokes: "That's so funny" in addition to, or even instead of, laughing.

The description employed bypasses the crucial question about humor: what is it that makes people laugh? If people try to get other people to laugh by using a joke, how do they do that? Ever since Plato and Aristotle, people have asked themselves these questions but it is very difficult, if not impossible, to answer them conclusively and definitively. From the perspective chosen here, this is not necessary either. Here we are concerned not with the essence of humor, but with its social functions and meanings. Thus, even though the question how humor works, and what mechanisms are central to it, will emerge several times in the course of this book, most extensively in Chapters 7 and 8, this book is not an attempt to construct a theory of the workings and mechanisms of humor.

Humor has peculiar contradictory meanings: a joke can be an invitation, as Coser states, but it can also put people off and exclude them (Bergson [1900]1999; Billig 2004). Humor brings people together but it can also emphasize and augment differences in status. Humor can shock, insult, hurt, and consecutively be used as an excuse ("it was just a joke") but nevertheless a sense of humor counts as a positive feature. This multiplicity of contradictory functions has a lot to do with the fact that humor is "not serious". Something that is said in the guise of a joke should not be taken literally (Bateson 1972; Mulkay 1988). Because of this, the same joke can have different functions and meanings at one and the same time. Signals like laughter and smiling, as well as verbal cues of humorous intent ("Have you heard the one about...") separate humor from ordinary, serious communication. This so-called *framing* separates playing behavior from serious behavior; it separates what actors do on stage from what is done in the "real world"; and it separates humor from seriousness.

The different functions of humor often intersect and can hardly be separated in concrete situations (Palmer 1994; Ziv 1984). A regularly occurring event such as telling an ethnic joke – for instance about the Turkish minority in the Netherlands – can be an attempt simply to amuse, as well as an expression of a shared negative attitude regarding a specific ethnic group. Perhaps a joke of this type is also an attempt to acquire status or to bring up in conversation the sensitive subject of migrants. If there are Turks present, it may be an attempt to shock, insult, or exclude them. Among Turks and Dutch people who know each other well it can, instead, be a way of showing that they are above such sentiments. One and the same phenomenon can therefore have a diversity of functions for different persons or in different situations; for separate persons it can, moreover, have another function than for the group or society as a whole.

The polysemy of a joke makes it impossible to say with certainty which function it fulfills or what the joke teller meant: humor is by definition an ambivalent form of communication. "The" function of the joke or humorous genre can thus not be firmly established. What's more: even "the" function of a single joke about Turks in one, specific, social setting generally cannot be established firmly. Quite probably even the person telling a joke does not know for sure why he's doing it, let alone why he chose that joke. The only thing he will probably know for sure is that he wants to make people laugh.

If humor is seen as a social phenomenon, in addition to that communicative aspect two other aspects are of special importance. Firstly: differences in appreciation of humor are for a large part socially and culturally determined. What people think is funny varies from culture to culture and from group to group: even within one culture there are differences in taste. Even though many scholars have commented on the cultural variability of humor, comparative research on humor is almost absent.[2]

Secondly, humor often touches upon social and moral boundaries. Jokes often deal with taboos or "painful subjects"; this means that social and moral boundaries are often transgressed to some extent (Douglas 1966, 1975). Humor, however, also marks social boundaries: it is a powerful means of pulling people together and, in doing this, automatically shutting other people out. Sometimes this takes place directly, by laughing at people, but it can also be indirect: taking place through shared standards of what is funny and what is not, or because the joke includes a reference that not everyone understands. The laugh makes group boundaries clearly visible and palpable: he who laughs belongs, he who does not laugh is excluded.

Humor is a form of communication, a question of taste, a marking of social boundaries. These three aspects determine the social functions and meanings of humor, and these aspects will serve here as guidelines for an exploration of the sociology of the joke. These subjects lie at the cutting-edge of humor research and sociology: within social theory, taste, communication, and social boundaries are important themes. Two of these, the connection between humor and social boundaries, and the role of humor as a form of communication, are important themes in the existing research in the social sciences into humor. The third – the connection between humor and taste – has hardly been investigated; thus in this book I have tried to establish a connection between humor research and theories about taste and taste difference in the social sciences.

Humor and taste

Anthropological research into humor also shows a clear connection between humor and culture: the documented humor from cultures far distant from our own in time and place often seems coarse, strange, absurd, or simply unintelligible to us (Apte 1985). The impossibility of understanding someone else's humor has much to do with cultural knowledge: people do not understand each other's jokes because they fail to understand crucial references. Additionally, cultural background affects cultural boundaries, and that also affects sense of humor: something that is funny in one culture can be shocking, embarrassing, or even repugnant in another.

But mostly, cultural differences in sense of humor are also connected with culturally determined differences in style. For instance, the difference between British and American humor has been summarized as the contrast between understatement and overstatement. This difference lies not in the themes or subjects of the joke but rather in the general tone or attitude: it is possible to conceive two completely different jokes about similar subjects, and with similar techniques, but with a completely different presentation, tone, and purport. Such differences, which reflect more general notions of what good and bad humor are, are matters of *style*. Style differences of this sort are difficult to verbalize; they are more subtle but more crucial than the more obvious differences in subject choice or language use.

Not only among cultures but also within any given culture, huge differences exist in what people find funny. Within the Netherlands there is, for instance, a cultural difference between city and countryside, between the college and non-college educated and between young and old. These cultural differences are reflected in humor: the highly provocative stand-up comic Hans Teeuwen is thus for the young while the late Toon Hermans, who often seemed more a clown than a comic, and whose humor ranged from the absurd to the sentimental, is preferred by those who are older. André van Duin, a comic from the music-hall tradition, known for his impersonations of rather bizarre characters, is the popular humorist while Freek de Jonge, a critical comedian from the slightly moralist Dutch *cabaret* tradition, with his dense, poetic style, and fast and chaotic presentation, appeals more to intellectuals. (Short descriptions of Dutch humorists and television programs mentioned in this book are provided in Appendix 2.)

The differences in humor between different groups within Dutch society, just as the differences between cultures, can to some extent be clarified by differences in cultural knowledge and sensitivity to certain boundaries. Most cultural differences within the Netherlands are, however, also a question of style. This is, for instance, the case for André van Duin, the most prominent popular comedian in the Netherlands. Probably very few people in the Netherlands have difficulty understanding him, he does not antagonize people by transgressing boundaries, and no one doubts his professional skill. And yet there are many people who don't like him. Differences in the appreciation of van Duin are questions of style, of taste: his humor is a close or less close match with what people expect of good humor.

"Style" and "taste" are connected concepts: both have to do with esthetic preference for and aversion to something. Each concept can be used both in the evaluative and the descriptive sense: someone who "has style", has good style; someone "with taste", has good taste. There are, however, differences: taste primarily has to do with judgment and appreciation while style implies a more active role: it can be linked to both appreciation and creation. Someone with a certain taste *likes* a certain style. Taste has to do with "what people see in something" while style has to do with "how people do it".

The social formation and determination of taste is one of the classical themes in sociology (e.g. Bourdieu [1979] 1984; Gans [1974] 1999; Veblen [1899] 2001). Sociologists tend to speak of "taste" rather than "style" when describing how social background relates to esthetic appreciation. This reflects and reproduces a distinction between consumption and production of esthetic preferences, which does not make much sense when discussing joke telling and humor, where appreciation and creation are intimately connected. In this book, I will therefore often speak of "humor style" rather than "humor taste". However, the main theoretical inspiration of this book comes from sociologists studying taste, most notably Pierre Bourdieu.

The central proposition of sociological studies of taste is that they can be used to demarcate social boundaries (Lamont and Fournier 1992; Lamont 1992, 2000; Lamont and Molnar 2002). It is preferences for mundane things such as furniture, books, paintings, clothing, television programs, and hobbies that come to have exceptionally strong symbolic meaning. Choices of this nature can and do evoke vehement and emphatic reactions. Taste, just as humor, is felt to be something extremely personal and spontaneous, but it also serves as a way of establishing whether or not people are on the same "wavelength". In this way, these taste differences function as a direct social delimitation, not just between cultures, but also between groups within one culture.

Cultural differences within one society are not completely independent of one another. Although different groups within Dutch society have to some extent their own values, norms, ideas, and symbols, differing from those of other Dutch subcultures, taste and style are defined and formed in relationship, and even in contrast, to tastes and styles of other groups (see Kuipers 2006a). Youth culture, for instance, often includes a more or less conscious rejection of the adult culture (Hebdige 1979; Willis et al. 1990). Class culture as well is often partially based on rejecting the taste, behavior and lifestyle of other classes. The higher middle class has always tried to distinguish itself from the culture of the lower classes. "Taste" is one of the weapons used by the higher classes in doing this: the power to define the preferences of other people as less valuable than one's own.

That taste is a way of distinguishing oneself – a means of distinction – is the central proposition of *La Distinction* (1984). In this book, Pierre Bourdieu shows that esthetical preference, therefore taste, is strongly connected to class. Not only the art form people appreciate, but also what they prefer to eat, how they furnish their houses, what they prefer to photograph, is connected with their class position. Taste is not just a way to distinguish oneself from others, it also reveals one's status. The preferences of the college educated are socially more valued than those of the non-college educated. Their taste has more status because *they* have more status, and vice versa: they have more status because of their taste. Taste of the higher circles very quickly becomes the legitimate taste. Taste is then, in Bourdieu's words, a form of symbolic capital: the status of certain groups is automatically equated with the status of their esthetical preferences.

In *La Distinction*, Bourdieu distinguishes two different sorts of capital: cultural and economic. Class, and thus taste, is connected with possessions and wealth: economic capital. Beside this, there is the influence of cultural capital: the education one has had and, connected to this, one's knowledge of "high culture". These two forms of capital do not completely coincide. There are people with a great deal of cultural but very little economic capital – penniless but very cultivated intellectuals and artistic persons – and the *nouveau riches* with a great deal of money but the "wrong" cars, clothes, hairdos, and holiday destinations. The esthetical preferences of these two groups do not completely coincide: people with more economic capital are often somewhat more conservative; people with more cultural capital are often somewhat avant-garde. These are all "legitimate" tastes: they are not shared, however, in all high circles.

This relationship between taste and status is also the motor behind the trickle-down effect (Fallers 1954; Elias [1939] 1978): the mechanism by which many tastes, styles, and preferences diffuse through a society. People attempt to distinguish themselves from others in a positive sense by acquiring tastes and styles with higher status. The effect of this is that this taste or style diffuses further and further downward in the society, after which those in the upper layer seek something else to distinguish themselves. The drive to distinguish oneself is thus an important source of cultural change.

Since Bourdieu's theory of cultural and economic capital was developed, in the France of the 1960s, class systems have eroded considerably in most Western countries. Social hierarchies have become less strict, social mobility has increased, and other social distinctions, such as age or ethnicity, have become more influential. As a result of this, relationships between taste cultures are less clear-cut than Bourdieu's theory might suggest (cf. Holt 1997, Peterson 1997). Rather than "trickle down", processes of emulation and distinction may lead to elements of working-class and youth culture "moving up" (e.g. blue jeans, pop music), or to taste groups combining high and popular tastes (Peterson and Kern 1996). Additionally, processes of distinction and emulation may not be limited to one society, leading to incorporation of foreign, cultural elements into taste cultures.

That taste is a means of distinction, does not however, mean that people necessarily allow themselves to be led by the need to be different or better than others in their preferences for humor, art, or television programs. Neither is it so that assuming the taste of people with higher status, the legitimate taste, solely arises from the drive to imitate. Taste is more than an imposed attempt to belong somewhere; taste happens automatically. "Each taste is experienced as natural – and it is practically that, as habitus – which amounts to rejecting others as unnatural and consequently bad." (Bourdieu 1984: 56) Variations in taste and style, according to Bourdieu, are the *embodiment* of social distinctions, they are "symbolic re-creations of actual differences". Esthetic judgments are inevitably intertwined with social distinctions.

Taste is an integral part of what Bourdieu calls the *habitus*: embodied culture, culture that has become part of people's most automatic reactions and preferences. *Habitus* is culture worn in, as it were, to the body. This includes not only esthetical preference or aversion, but also how someone speaks, how someone moves, how someone sees himself and others. All these things are formed by culture and social position. What someone finds humorous is also part of habitus: the reaction to humor is almost a reflex – you either laugh or you don't. But at the same time the reactions – as will become apparent from this book – are strongly connected to social position: different people laugh at different things.

And yet "sense of humor" is not only linked to status arising from cultural and economic capital. Bourdieu and other sociologists of taste described primarily how taste differences mark class boundaries. Next to these, there are other, different, important social distinctions such as age, gender, religion, regional or ethnic background – all these distinctions are generally connected with taste and lifestyles, and thus: humor style.

Making the appropriate jokes and knowing which jokes to laugh at are always skills held in high esteem. A good sense of humor also is a way to distinguish oneself *within* one's own social group. The ability to tell jokes well is also a form of capital; the only thing is that it does not have the same value in every situation. Having "a sense of humor" always goes together with social status, but not by definition with economic or cultural capital.

A good sense of humor, the ability to make, share, and appreciate the right jokes is always symbolic capital. But still, the humor of the groups with the highest status is not everyone's idea of the funniest humor. I will try in this book to classify not the lifestyles but the humor styles: the differences in "humorous habitus".

The context of Dutch humor

A study of a country's humor inevitably becomes something of an ethnography of that country. This book, although primarily a book about humor, will probably reveal much about the Netherlands. The final chapter, while intended mainly as a cross-cultural validation of the approach developed in the first nine chapters, will also shed light on American culture.

To approach a country through its humor is to produce a rather unusual image of that country. This study highlights the backstage areas of private interactions with family and friends, the minutiae of everyday communication, and the subtle distinctions and judgments that people make about others. It is also so that the jokes I collected and discussed with my informants give a view of the Netherlands that may differ from the official "frontstage" image of the Netherlands. Like jokes around the world, Dutch jokes are mostly concerned with the sensitive areas in Dutch culture and society.

This book not only looks at Dutch society through the lens of humor, it looks at *differences* in humor. This focus on social differences highlights cultural rifts and distinctions within Dutch society. It wasn't until I did a similar project in the US that I realized there was something particularly Dutch about Dutch respondents, despite their great differences.

This Dutchness, and commonality within Dutch society, may need a short introduction here. Given the book's focus on class differences, probably it is important to note that the Netherlands is a fairly egalitarian society, even by Western European standards. Traditionally, the Netherlands had hardly any nobility, and no upper class to speak of. Ever since the seventeenth century, Dutch society has been solidly middle class, with the elite consisting of merchants and bankers rather than counts and princes. The country did not become a monarchy until the nineteenth century, after the defeat of Napoleon. The Royal Family, though very prominent in jokes, has never had much real power and has always worked hard to cultivate a normal, accessible, and middle-class image. Social mobility is relatively high and traditional indicators of class inequality such as elite universities and a very uneven distribution of income are not present in the Netherlands (Dronkers and Ultee 1995). The class difference in sense of humor found in this study is by no means a reflection of the Dutch self-image. Like Americans, Dutch tend to think of themselves as part of a classless society, making references to social class slightly taboo.

Currently, the Netherlands is one of the most secularized countries in the world. Until recently, religion significantly influenced all domains of life; witness the characteristic "pillarization": Catholics and the various protestant denominations each had their own churches, political parties, and leisure activities (Lijphart 1968). A remnant of this system can still be found in public television: each of the old "pillars" has its own broadcasting corporation. In general, the various cultural revolutions of the past fifty years seem to have hit the Netherlands harder than other countries: the Netherlands has not only become one of the world's most secularized, and one of the world's most permissive countries (Kennedy 1995). This shows in Dutch humor, which has changed very quickly since the 1950s, becoming more transgressive and explicit than in other countries.

Another characteristic of the Netherlands that may be important to keep in mind is its ethnic composition. The Netherlands had a large Jewish minority until the Second World War, when a large percentage of Dutch Jews was deported. Apart from the Jewish community, the country was ethnically very homogeneous. It was only after 1970 that the country gradually became more mixed, with the arrival of migrants from the (former) colonies of Surinam and the Netherlands Antilles, and guest workers, mainly from Turkey and Morocco. However, at the time of this research, even though migrants had become the target of many jokes, for the most part they did not take part in Dutch joke culture (this is changing quickly, see Meder 2001). The former guest workers in particular did not speak Dutch well as a rule. Thus, the Dutch research addresses class, age, and gender differences, but not ethnic differences. The sample simply did not include enough members of ethnic minority groups to say much about ethnicity.

A final aspect of Dutch society that may need some introduction is its humorous tradition. Although the research dealt primarily with jokes, to create a larger perspective for the appreciation of jokes, informants also were asked about comedians, humorists, comic television shows, and other standardized forms of humor. This was done both in the interviews and in the surveys, both in the Netherlands and in the United States.

The Dutch humorous tradition aptly illustrates the Netherlands' position in the world. All the main comic genres have foreign names: cabaret, revue, sketch, stand-up comedy, sitcom. However, each of these imported genres has acquired a highly Dutch flavor. The main humorous genre in the Netherlands is called *cabaret*, which has emerged from the French tradition of café entertainment (Ibo 1981). Nevertheless, Dutch cabaret generally consists of long performances in a theater setting rather than in a smoky cellar or café; one person is involved, doing humorous monologues, which may be combined with songs, poetic monologues, social satire, and social critique. The best known representatives of cabaret are the late Wim Kan, Freek de Jonge, and Youp van 't Hek, celebrities who will be mentioned many times in this book.

Many comedians have a rather ambivalent view of the "cabaret" label because of its association with intellectualism and elitist social critique. The late Toon Hermans, whose humor lies somewhere between the clownish and the poetic, explicitly rejected cabaret. More absurdist comics like Brigitte Kaandorp or Herman Finkers are not completely comfortable being called *"cabaretiers"* either (Hanenberg and Verhallen 1996). Younger performers like Hans Teeuwen or Theo Maassen often move back and forth between the cabaret tradition and the faster and shorter "stand-up comedy", imported from America and the UK in the 1990s. This Anglo-Saxon tradition is faster and more densely packed with jokes: the Dutch version of stand-up comedy does not leave much room for poetic musings or social satire.

Until the 1970s, there was a strong tradition of popular performance, variety shows called *revue*: a combination of sketch comedy with other traditional, vaudeville disciplines like dancing and singing. André van Duin, the favorite comedian of most joke lovers, comes from this *revue* tradition, which was superseded in large part in the 1970s by television comedy. Television is now one of the main sources of comedy. TV comedy shows clear American and British influences, with most comedies following the sitcom format. Other genres on Dutch television are transnational too and include candid-camera shows, talk shows presented by comedians, and sketch comedy.

Different TV stations in the Netherlands target different audiences. RTL4, which aired *Moppentoppers*, is the largest commercial network, with popular shows and comedies aimed at large audiences. However, some of the public broadcasting corporations also aim for popular success. André van Duin had a variety show aired by TROS, one of the public broadcasting corporations, before joining RTL4, and the (formerly) socialist broadcasting corporation VARA has a long tradition of producing successful sitcoms. The most explicitly intellectual or highbrow broadcaster is called VPRO. Over the years, this corporation has produced many forms of slightly experimental and avant-garde humor, ranging from the political satire of van Kooten and de Bie to the absurdist sketch comedy of *Jiskefet*.

The design of this book

This book consists of three parts: following upon the introduction, one part deals with differences in the appreciation of the genre and another with differences in the appreciation of separate jokes. These two parts are followed by a chapter describing the American research into social background and joke telling.

The first part is called *Style and social background*. This part deals with the question of where differences in appreciating the joke as genre arise. To begin with, Chapter 2 summarizes the coming into existence of the genre. I go into the history of the joke and try to connect this with the development of other humorous genres. There follow three chapters centered around the question of why people like the joke as a *genre*. In Chapter 3, I connect social differences in appreciation of jokes to differences in communication styles. Chapter 4 deals with the relationship between the appreciation of jokes and other forms of humor. In it, I contend that the appreciation of the genre of the joke is connected as well to differences in humor style: ideas about good and bad humor. Chapter 5 addresses humor styles in day-to-day life: here humor styles and communication styles are connected.

In the second part, entitled *Taste and quality*, the attention shifts to the content of separate jokes. Not everyone thinks every joke equally funny, or every subject equally suited to the making of a joke. But perhaps every joke is not equally funny, and differences in the appreciation of jokes are also a question of quality. I begin this part with a chapter about the repertoire: about the jokes being told at this moment in the Netherlands. Chapter 7 deals with the question of what a "good joke" is. In the last chapter of the Dutch study, I look at variations between groups in the appreciation of separate jokes. The content of the jokes is consciously placed after the chapters dealing with differences in the diffusion of the genre as a whole; if jokes are primarily told in certain social groups, this will also have an effect on their content.

The final part of this book is called *Comparing humor styles*. This consists of Chapter 9, which presents the results of the American study and compares these with Dutch humor styles. Some theoretical implications of this study are discussed in the concluding chapter.

While the book is not so much about jokes as about judgments *about* jokes, jokes are regularly quoted. Some of these will perhaps strike the reader as hurtful or shocking. This is intrinsic to jokes: humor always touches on social and moral boundaries. The fact that I quote a joke does not mean that I appreciate it or even approve of it; it means only that it illustrates or supports my arguments appropriately.

In writing this book, I consciously chose to make my own voice heard occasionally. In writing about tastes it is almost impossible not to reveal something of your own judgment. No matter how hard I try, my descriptions of elite humor will always sound more sympathetic than my descriptions of a typical sexual joke. This has played a role not only in the descriptions but in the whole research process. I am deeply persuaded of the fact that because I did the research and all the interviews personally, this has influenced the book. The central concept of this book makes this almost matter-of-course: the interviews with persons who shared my taste and conversational style went more smoothly. I simply did not always succeed in laughing at the jokes my informants told me; I could not always tell them jokes they thought were funny either. In research into humor a first-person perspective is not only honest, or difficult to avoid in collecting material, but also useful. The judgment of humor cannot be disconnected from the person judging. Both in conversations with the interviewees and in exposing myself to the humor, my own role and judgment formed an important research resource.

The judgment of whether something is funny or not is spontaneous, automatic, almost a reflex; people laugh almost without reflecting. This goes for someone investigating humor too. Sense of humor thus lies very close to self-image. My informants often found it strange and not entirely pleasant that I was trying to connect something as personal and spontaneous as humor to social background: a scientific approach to humor seems to make its authenticity dubious. Resistance was particularly focused on my attempts to connect humor to class. While interviewees seemed quite ready to reflect on masculine and feminine humor, on the rough humor of the young and the respectable humor of the old, on the differing humor of believers and nonbelievers, and even enjoyed expanding on differences between people from different parts of Holland or the United States, the discussion of humor and class obviously made them ill at ease. Here a researcher encounters double resistance. Neither the Dutch, nor the Americans, like to talk about class differences. Both societies are believed to be meritocratic and individualistic; this does not sit well with the notion that your parents' professions influence who you are. Thus, people do not easily admit that their own behavior might have something to do with class, and they are more wary still of making any statement whatsoever about the class of others.

To indulge in a sociological analysis of humor is not to opt for unqualified pleasure. Not only is this opting to strip something we hold dear – our sense of humor – of its magic, the serious tone of science is also hard to combine with the frivolity of the subject. A scholar dealing with humor must quickly mount an adequate defense against the lethal accusation of not having a sense of humor. Analyzing humor is, after all, not always easy to combine with appreciating it – let alone creating it. This is not meant as a funny book. It is a book about jokes and not in itself any funnier than other books in the same genre: social-scientific monographs.

Part I. Style and social background

Chapter 2
The joke: Genesis of an oral genre

All over the world, people tell each other funny stories and anecdotes. The form of these stories and the subjects they deal with vary. The aim of people telling such stories is always the same: to make someone else laugh. To elicit laughs, one can invent one's own funny stories but each culture also has its own freely available repertoire of fun that belongs "to everyone": communal anecdotes, freely told and retold, that no one would dare to assert he had thought up himself. In the Netherlands, this repertoire consists primarily of jokes, a genre that has expanded during the last two centuries to become the most important orally transmitted humorous genre in the Western world.

Rigorous Darwinian principles govern orally transmitted genres such as the joke. Funny stories that no one likes do not survive; they simply are not retold. A joke that no one likes any longer is snuffed out the moment insufficient people retell it. Joke books can sometimes keep corny jokes alive a little longer, but they simply defer their demise. No one buys a book with jokes that are no longer funny. Thus purely bad jokes do not exist; at most, some superannuated jokes may still be limping around.

This applies to all orally transmitted genres, not only jokes, but also riddles, urban legends, songs and children's games. Oral literature is dependent for its survival upon people thinking that something is worth transmitting to another, who in turn thinks it worth passing on to someone else, who then tells it to someone else again, who then does the same, until enough people have heard the joke or story to ensure that it stays alive. This means that the joke can justifiably be called "a social fact": a cultural expression of a whole society, or of specific groups who appreciate the genre.

Even though the Dutch joke repertoire belongs to everyone, not everyone has the same affinity with the genre. Some people never hear or tell jokes, while others know hundreds. In the first part of this book, the central question is why some people appreciate the joke *as a genre*. Before this question can be answered, we must know what the genre amounts to: what are jokes? How do they come into existence? How are they spread? However, I will begin with the most-asked question about jokes: if jokes do indeed belong "to everyone", to all the Netherlanders but to no one in particular – who makes them up?

The joke as oral culture

Who makes up jokes? Anyone who has ever told a joke – almost everyone – will have wondered about this question. Particularly jokes already doing the rounds within hours of a disaster or a scandal cause a great deal of surprise: how can it be that jokes are already circulating about an airplane crash, a sunken ferry, a terrorist attack, an exploded spaceship, or the death of a princess and her lover within a day of these events?[3] Where did these jokes come from?

This can probably best be answered by saying that jokes are not made up but that they come into existence in the course of many interactions. People busy producing a joke are seldom aware of doing so. Professional joke writers do exist, but the majority of jokes is not purposefully invented but grows slowly from a spontaneous remark into a real joke. I imagine a joke coming into existence a bit like this: someone says something funny: a rapid-fire remark, a well-aimed witticism, an apt description or an appealing play on words. One hearer retells this – on the condition that it is not too context-dependent. If the teller is modest, he will mention the original maker of the funny remark, but he may not even be aware that he did not make it up himself. Then someone will tell this funny story on another occasion, and then again, and then again, and so we go round and round until the moment comes when the original joker and the context have been totally forgotten. Meanwhile, ingredients from the local joke culture have begun to trickle in. The words to the what-is-almost-a-joke are placed in the mouths of established joke personages – a blonde, a Belgian, a woman at the doctor's or a man in a bar. It is relocated to standard joke situations: a desert island, Main Street, a bar. Thus, the original anecdote or one-liner is embedded in the pattern a culture has for humorous narratives.

This means that someone busy producing a joke seldom knows he's doing it. The first person simply makes a remark; the second tells about the witty remark "somebody or other" made yesterday or pretends he thought it up himself; the third and subsequent tellers repeat an anecdote they've heard from someone else and slowly but surely a new joke germinates without anyone involved being aware of having contributed.

This is most obvious for jokes that come into existence in reaction to an actual event. One of the jokes in the questionnaire, for instance, dealt with the accident in which Diana Spencer and her lover Dodi Al-Fayed died, in 1997, several months before I distributed the survey.

> Diana and Dodi are sitting in the car arguing. Their dinner that evening was disappointing and they still want something to eat but can't agree on what. Diana wants to go get Chinese food and Dodi wants shoarma. The chauffeur is sitting there listening and he's just about had his bellyful of the bickering in the back seat. He turns around and says: "If you can't make a decision, why not the drive-in."

With jokes like this, it is possible to state with a great degree of certainty that it is new, since it only makes sense in a highly specific context. Also, it is certainly an exclusively Dutch joke, since the original Dutch version (skillfully adapted by my translator) has a reference to the exclusively Dutch tradition called "eating out of the wall" (*uit de muur eten*): fast food, mostly deep-fried variation on sausages and meat balls, dispensed from small coin-operated windows in the wall.

Nevertheless, I have never heard people claim to have invented such jokes themselves. In 1996, I actually attempted to trace the source of a joke about the Belgian child molester Marc Dutroux.[4] In the Dutch-Flemish joke cycle about this scandal, there was one particularly famous joke, based on a play on words concerning Dutroux' name and a children's song.[5] This joke must have been invented specifically to refer to this event. I asked everyone who told it where he had heard it, hoping to get some inkling of the ditty's distribution, but it spread so rapidly that I quickly gave up. In spite of the fact that practically everyone in the Netherlands eventually had heard it, I never heard anyone claim it as his. Of course, with the rise of the Internet such an effort has become even more complex. Jokes about the attacks on the World Trade Center in New York on September 11, 2001 spread so rapidly, often across national borders, that any attempt to track them would be impossible (Kuipers 2002, 2005).

The Diana joke, like the Dutroux joke I tried to trace, is definitely tailored to this situation. However, most disaster jokes are not really new. Many Dutroux jokes I had already heard as sick jokes about Hitler (generalized jokes about sadism and random cruelty) or, more topically, about Michael Jackson, also accused of pedophilia. Some jokes about 9/11 were recycled jokes about the explosion of the Challenger Space Shuttle in 1986. Jokes are recycled more often than new jokes are invented: existing jokes are continually adjusted to a new situation. This applies not only to jokes in reaction to current affairs. Over time, almost all jokes now in circulation have been adjusted a number of times to social shifts.

This variability is characteristic of orally transmitted genres. A joke is public property and thus everyone is free to change or add elements to it. Such changes are most easily observed in ethnic jokes targeting groups with specific characteristics. In the Netherlands, as time went on, the same jokes about stupidity, with the same punch line, were told about German immigrants, maids, farmers, Belgians, Surinamese immigrants, and, most recently blondes.

There are few really new jokes. Most jokes that people tell have existed in one form or another for many years or even for many centuries. Researchers have been able to trace jokes, or, more accurately, their basic punch line, back to seventeenth-century jests (Neumann 1986: 22–24; Röhrich 1977: 22–28) or even to jokes from classical antiquity (Baldwin 1983: 59). Most jokes are probably not that old. It is certain that a repertoire of "basic punch lines" exists, some old, some more recent, to be reshaped again and again into jokes with new casts in different situations.

This repertoire is transnational. Variants of most of the jokes told in the Netherlands circulate in other countries. The sociologist Christie Davies found exactly the same jokes about stupid people in India and Columbia as in all sorts of West European countries, only with other targets (Davies 1990, 1998a). Not only the themes but even the punch lines and the situations could be exactly the same. A recent example of the international spread and adaptation of jokes is the blonde joke (see also Oring 2003, 58–70). The dumb blonde jokes that appeared in the Netherlands 1990s I first heard in the late 1980s as American jokes about blondes, but also about a more specific group: fraternity girls. These jokes were rapidly converted to the "blonde jokes" which would take the whole world by storm. In the Netherlands, these jokes usually explicitly refer to the protagonist as a *dumb* blonde. After the introduction of these jokes in the Netherlands, many jokes about Belgians were also converted into blonde jokes. In England, the blondes have been converted into Essex girls, adding a class element to these jokes, Essex being associated with working class culture (Davies 1998a: 182–187). It says a lot that the British, who, more than any other European nation, are preoccupied with class, have given these jokes a class connotation. Apparently, each society adjusts jokes not only to the local stereotypes but also the local preoccupations.

With all its local adjustments and supplements, the joke has evolved into a global genre. The whole world can access the same repertoire of punch lines, personages and situations and roughly recognizes the same pattern for a funny story. Even before the Internet, jokes with the same pattern and punch line could be found all over the globe. Notwithstanding this, not all jokes are told everywhere. The regional differences lie not only in the specific interpretation one gives to a joke, as in the English transformation of the blonde joke, but also in the selection made in each culture from the global joke repertoire. Davies sees the presence of jokes with certain themes as indicating the cultural meaning of these themes (1998b). Jokes about stupidity are the clearest example of jokes that have caught on all over the world, and Davies links this to the rise of modernity and the resulting imperative of rationality. He refers to stupidity jokes as "jokes from the iron cage", in a reference to Max Weber's metaphor of the iron cage of rationality (Davies 1990).

However, Davies also cites examples of joke categories that migrated to new countries through translation but did not catch on. Jokes about "dirty peoples" seem to catch on in the United States, the Netherlands and Germany but not in France and the United Kingdom (1998a: 166–176). Davies sees the importance of hygiene in these different countries as the explanation. He shows how these jokes have been imported, mostly in translated jokes books. However, in neither France nor the UK, the "dirty peoples" jokes never actually spread outside of these translations. The critical moment for a joke is when it leaves a joke book and enters the oral circuit. A joke is only a joke if it is retold.

The spread of the joke

The success of a joke is always dependent on the people telling it. However, jokes are not exclusively passed on by word-of-mouth. While every joke teller maintains with complete conviction that everything depends on the "presentation", that a joke on paper is not funny, that it is then a mnemonic device instead of an occasion for a laugh, jokes nevertheless have been written down from the moment that people began to write. The oldest known joke book dates back to the fourth or fifth century after Christ: the *Philogelos* or Laughter-lover (Baldwin 1983).

While oral transmission is the natural medium of the joke, jokes on paper can, indeed, be funny. I regularly have to laugh at a joke I have read. The interviewees have told me that they regularly had to laugh right out loud at jokes on the questionnaire I circulated. However, they often said that they had also told the jokes on the list to others, copied the list and handed it out or fastened it to the notice board at work or circulated it at a party. A joke can work well on paper but everyone feels the need to return the joke to the sphere where it belongs: social interaction.

This does not negate the fact that little books containing humorous stories have formed a significant portion of literary production since the rise of the printing press. In the sixteenth and seventeenth century, "prose jest-books" were produced, which can be compared to present-day joke books (Brewer 1997; Dekker 2001; Verberckmoes 1999). These books constituted one of the first forms of "mass culture". Inexpensively produced joke books still appear in huge editions as always.

There has therefore always been a market for written jokes. In disseminating jokes in writing, the rules for oral literature obtain; in many joke books, reference is made to the social context in which these jokes should be told. For these books too, it remains true that no one can claim the joke as his own property; jokes are stolen from others without scruple. I have spoken to various Dutch compilers of joke books and columns and they tell me that they get their jokes from English, German or American books. As one editor explained: "Yes, I just gave one of my secretaries a large stack of those little books [in English and German] and underlined the ones she I wanted her to type over."

The uninhibited copying of jokes from other sources partially explains the large international diffusion of the genre and the repertoire. Jokes in joke books do not, however, adequately reflect the whole joke culture. As Davies has demonstrated, only a portion of translated jokes actually finds its way into oral joke culture. In some joke books, I saw little correspondence with jokes I was being told. Additionally, a great deal of censuring takes place in joke books and columns: the language is cleaned up and certain joke categories are even completely excluded. In the Netherlands, this self-censure affects practically all jokes referring to ethnic minorities. Explicit sexual jokes and sick jokes are not deemed appropriate for publication either. Editors of joke pages I spoke to notice the operation of self-censure: many jokes are not even sent away to be included in joke columns. This censuring makes written sources a weak reflection of the oral repertoire.

Therefore, jokes do not spread internationally only through books; these contain solely a censored selection from the repertoire. Many jokes circulating internationally are not published anywhere. A good example of this is the "holocaust joke" - sick jokes about the persecution of the Jews (later I will quote a number of examples). Exactly the same jokes about this subject circulate in Europe, North and South America and even Israel (Dundes and Hauschild 1987). These jokes are not deemed publishable in any of these countries. The wide international transmission of exactly the same jokes, at least prior to the existence of the Internet, must thus have been oral. Another joke category that is not published but is present internationally is the "attitude joke" (Kuipers 2000), in which people are incited to murder or maltreat a certain group. The clandestine aspect of these joke categories ensures that, except in closed circles, they are almost never told and thus are spread almost exclusively orally.

This seems to be changing with the Internet. Jokes are being spread in large numbers through the Internet and they travel significantly larger distances than ever before. Self-censure hardly plays a role. Sometimes vehement discussions take place about the allowability of certain jokes, but mostly, consensus seems to exist that anything should be possible. The Netherlands, as far as that goes, is a noteworthy exception: postings of racist jokes often lead to intense discussions and in some cases even to calls to the anti-discrimination complaints bureau. People in the Netherlands seem more sensitive to ethnic jokes than people of other nationalities. The primacy of freedom of expression backed up by American Internet supremacy is not always endorsed on the Dutch-speaking portion of the Internet (Kuipers 2006b).

The Internet as a medium escapes a number of traditional dividing lines: the boundary between public and private diminishes significantly and the distinction between oral and written is blurred. While, in principle, it all takes place in writing, the language use and directness of the communication often more nearly resemble the spoken word. It is quite possible that oral genres like the joke will change significantly under the influence of the Internet.

The new medium has, in any case, very largely upped the tempo at which jokes diffuse through the world. This is true of all the technical innovations: printing, radio, television, long-playing records, cassette tapes and telephone as well have probably hugely increased the rate of circulation of orally transmitted genres. Nevertheless, not one of these technical innovations since the time of the first printing press has yet succeeded in wiping out the oral transmission of these genres, even though the death of the joke has been announced many times. The fact that many jokes transgress boundaries dictates the need for the seclusion of the private sphere. And besides: jokes are too strongly connected to the art of telling, the pleasure of listening and the atmosphere of an evening of joke telling.

The genesis of the joke

The joke has become a global genre: everywhere in the world, humorous anecdotes are poured into the joke mold. Everywhere in the world, humorous stories with a clear punch line are told and everywhere in the world these stories are located in bars, on desert islands and at the doctor's. In this section, I will try to trace the development of this genre: how has this specific pattern of humorous stories developed? The joke's history can be retrieved only from written sources. The problem with joke books has already been mentioned: they are heavily censured though unpublished collections do exist that have undergone only self-censure. What is more, you never know for sure if these jokes are actually told. When tracing the form of the joke that is not so important: regardless of content, it is possible to see into which "mold" punch lines have been poured over time.

The joke as we know it seems to be a relatively new genre: probably the genre is approximately one hundred and fifty years old. Wickberg (1998) and Röhrich (1977) date the origins of the joke in the nineteenth century: they connect the origin of the joke with modernity. Röhrich points to the fleetingness and changeability of the genre that he contrasts with the long-standing continuity of precursors such as the "jest". He calls the joke the genre of "present-day, modern, industrial society", belonging to "metropolitan surroundings" (1977: 10).

The dating of the genre is dependent on how it is defined. If "humorous story" is understood by the word "joke", the joke is many thousands of years old. The pattern presently called "joke" is subject to more stringent demands then those of a simple story that makes people laugh: there must be a punch line, recognizable personages and settings, and the composition too must conform to certain demands. The joke seems to me to be a more tightly standardized genre that its precursor, the "jest". A well-documented Dutch example of the "jest" is the collection of humorous "anecdotes" of the seventeenth-century Dutch lawyer, Aernout van Overbeke (Dekker and Roodenburg 1997; Dekker 2001; Roodenburg 1997; van Overbeke 1991). Van Overbeke did not concern himself much with genre conventions we distinguish: anecdotes, jokes, funny stories, witticisms, funny incidents, both self-made and heard from others; stories with and without punch lines are all mixed up together. Other form conventions of the joke only sporadically occur in van Overbeke's work, such as the thrice repeated event, the building block of the modern joke: a man goes to the doctor or visits the pub, and then again and he then does exactly the same thing again, building up an expectation that can be dashed the third time.

The Dutch word "*mop*", denoting only this specific genre, has only gotten its present meaning since the nineteenth century. The *Dictionary of the Dutch Language* places the oldest mention in 1875. Of course, the fact that the term is new is not a decisive factor in dating the creation of the genre of the "*mop*". In English a separate word has never been coined for the "*mop*", but English speaking areas still have the same phenomenon and they distinguish it as a genre. The coining of the new word in Dutch does, however, point to a need that had to be met.

The determining difference between the modern joke and anecdotes, jests, and stories from before the nineteenth century is the punch line. The main demand made of the joke by modern joke tellers is that it have a denouement at the end that puts all the preceding in a different light. Books of jests show that back then this was not demanded of humorous stories: the denouement is usually followed by a number of lines containing a moral, a further elaboration or even what is presently a most grievous sin: an explanation of the punch line. In addition, many jests have nothing at all like what we call a punch line: they are simply a story that – as far as we are concerned – babbles on and then stops just like that. That would be unacceptable at present. The punch line is a must for a joke.

How did this pre-modern, story-telling jest without a punch line give birth to the modern joke? Wickberg and Röhrich see modernization as crucial in the transformation of the jest into the joke. Modernizing influences changed old, relatively unchanging, oral genres into a fleeting, sharp genre easily transplanted from one context to another. In general, the burgeoning urban culture of amusement following in the wake of industrialization played an important role in this transformation from old to new genres. About halfway through the last century, a new amusement genre was born: "the first completely urbanized amusement appealing to a large audience of a new proletariat and lower middle class" (Senelick 1981: 2). In England it was called music hall, in America vaudeville and on the continent cabaret or revue (Ibo 1981; Senelick 1981; Slide 1994; Stein 1984; Wickberg 1998). All these types of vaudeville were not exclusively for the lower social classes but they offered low-class, not highly refined amusement (Stein 1984). Even though a gentleman on a wild night might frequent vaudeville, the ladies of the bourgeoisie definitely did not.

Humor played an important role in vaudeville. While song, dance, magical tricks and juggling were also included, a large proportion of the performance consisted of sketches, comic songs, monologues and jokes strongly standardized as to form and content. In these genres that had so recently blossomed, new themes, types and forms of performance devel-

oped quickly as did new theatrical, musical and humorous forms. Vaudeville probably has played an important role in "urbanizing" the jest. Peter
Bailey describes how traditional song culture was transformed within the
context of the music hall into a genre of humorous music hall songs called
swell songs:

> It marked a shift away from the leisurely narrative of the ballad tradition to
> a more episodic or situational representation. . . The text was now less liter-
> ary or poetic, and comes off the page poorly, relying as it did on perform-
> ance *and* reception to detonate the changes that lie in the compressions and
> ellipses of its otherwise unremarkable language. . . The swell songs ex-
> ploited a range or cues that drew the audience into active recognition of its
> own various social selves, it directly exploited the sympathies and distances
> within and between them. As a genre, its form can only be satisfactorily de-
> fined in terms of performance and use. (Bailey 1998: 123–4)

What Bailey describes here is also applicable to the joke, even though the
joke has been less professionalized than the song. Vaudeville, music hall
and cabaret probably have set the tone for new standards in humor as well.
Nineteenth-century, low-class amusement was a setting in which the old
oral genres could be transformed into urban, fleeting, contextless, genres,
that were use than content-defined. In short: *modern* genres.

The change in form of the joke into a more pointed and sharp genre is
also in keeping with a change in all humor since early modern times: the
increasing language-dependence of humor. In the joke, the humor is based
on a sudden shift in perspective, brought about by the joke's last sentence.
While the situation or the character of the joke also contribute to the
amusement, the ultimate laugh is consistently caused by the punch line: a
cognitive shift, essentially brought about by language, not by situation or
character. This is easy to see in jokes on a theme also very popular in the
jests: stupidity. In jokes about Belgians, the magnification of the stupid
behavior of the Belgian never directly provokes the laugh: the laugh always follows upon the punch line, upon an oral rendering of stupid Belgian behavior. In contrast, jest, and most early modern humor, is more like
the humor of clowns – nowadays a "childish" sort of humor – where the
laugh is directly provoked by stupid behavior: falling over one's own feet,
doing things backwards, inside out or upside down. In jokes, the emphasis
is on the word not on the action.

Anton Zijderveld has described this development as the intellectualization of humor: a more general cultural process in which "all human im-
pulses and emotions" – thus also play, amusement and humor – "are sub-

jected to an increasing degree to cognitive capacities" (1982: 42). The shift from action to word fits well in this process; the punch line is firstly a "cognitive" technique of humor, a change in perspective that can operate relatively detached from the affective content of the joke. This intellectualizing of humor is part of a broader civilizing process affecting humor (Elias 1978, 1982; Zijderveld 1982).

In the sixteenth century, the clergy, the humanists and other moralists began a civilizing offensive against the laugh. Johan Verberckmoes (1999) has beautifully described how one tried to tame and discipline the "wild lack of restraint" inherent in the laugh. As this process continued, all those things capable of causing a laugh – jokes, jests, theater plays, satire – were increasingly restrained, refined and civilized (Thomas 1977; see also Burke 1978). The simple transgression of a boundary, doing or saying something that was not allowed, referring to a taboo – humor techniques still very effective in the Middle Ages and early modern times – began quickly to be seen as too coarse, too unrestrained and too little refined. Boundary transgressions and taboos were increasingly obscured, "packaged" in humor techniques. This greatly increased the importance of oral, intellectual humor techniques that did not rely on the emotional content of the joke. Perhaps the humor theory of Sigmund Freud ([1905]1976), with its emphasis on humor technique as a means to mislead the censor, can then best be understood as reflecting a given moment in time, the culmination of a development of continuously increasing coercion to obscure the affective content of jokes through punch lines, plays on words and other cognitive tricks and techniques.

This is not the place to go deeply into the history of humor. I am discussing these two developments, civilization and intellectualization, particularly because they shed light on the present genre of the joke. It is not only the form of the genre that is connected with these processes but also its present low status. The criteria of refinement and restraint, the standards set by these processes, have ultimately turned against the joke. The joke has increasingly found itself on the side of wildly exuberant, unrefined humor: humor that is *not* civilized and not in the least intellectual. This has brought the joke "low". Within the already not very elevated domain of humor, the joke is probably the genre with the lowest status.

The status of the joke

Thus, in the course of past centuries, many changes have taken place in the design of the genre of the "short humorous story". The genre has become more pointed and concise, it has had to conform to new standards of content and the punch line has become a necessary ingredient. As time went on, in the Netherlands the genre even acquired a name of itself. It is not only form and content that have changed but the way in which the genre is perceived too. The social status of the joke (jest, pun, pleasantry, anecdote) has sunk lower and lower. The history of the joke is not only the history of the advancing intellectualizing and standardizing of a genre but, simultaneously, a history of gradual status decline of a cultural form

The status of orally transmitted genres is not very high. In the modern Western world, other edifying and entertaining media have taken over many of the functions of the old oral culture (Reijnders forthcoming). From the time of the rise of the printed book, the art of telling stories has perhaps not, as so many had expected, disappeared, but it has been discredited to some degree. The death knell has sounded a number of times for oral culture. Folklore is justified again and again as the savior of the old heritage. In spite of all the expectations to the contrary, oral genres remain very vigorous. The *mop* has arisen as a new genre, as has the urban legend.

Orally transmitted genres are connected more and more often with groups having little status or power: with "the folk", as is evident from the name of the discipline that has paid the most attention to oral literature, folklore. This (not completely accurate) association with not particularly dominant groups demonstrates that orally transmitted genres do not count as very important or respectable.

The joke has a double status problem: not only are jokes orally transmitted but the joke is also a *humorous* genre. Humor has always had a somewhat doubtful status: everyone loves its but no one sees it as completely respectable. Humor is always classified with the "lower" forms of amusement and diversion: it counts as exuberant, licentious, folksy, popular, superficial and frivolous.

It says a lot that humor is often enjoyed in combination with other "animal pleasures". Joke pages appear nowadays especially in men's magazines such as *Playboy*. The name of the Dutch national humorous art form, the cabaret, still calls up associations outside the Netherlands with dingy nightclubs, dissipated amusement and scantily clad women. That is, indeed, the context from which the cabaret arose. The association of food with humor has diminished with time but the carnivals of the Middle Ages, much of the symbolism of which was food-related, were occasions to laugh and gorge oneself sick (Pleij 1979). The association of humor with alcohol is undiminished and taken for granted and the pub still counts as the most natural environment for the joke and the guffaw. Humor is a frivolous, easy and particularly: a physical type of amusement (Bakhtin 1984; Verberckmoes 1999).

Ever since early modern times, clergymen and other moralists have attempted to restrain this physical, superficial phenomenon. The consequences thereof were not only the already mentioned increased civilizing of humor and laughing but also an increased separation of "high" from "low" humor (Brewer 1997). In the seventeenth century, Herman Roodenburg (1997: 126) writes, "social and esthetic standards began to coincide. . . Under the influence of the newest codes of civility, the elite was no longer allowed to enjoy low comedy in all its physicality." Differences in status began to be more and more clearly delineated within the domain of humor – just as within other forms of amusement.

Since those times, high humor distinguished itself from low humor, as it still does now, in three ways. Humor can escape the epithet "low" by becoming humor with a message or *moralizing* humor, humor with an esthetically responsible design or *refined* humor, or humor without much exuberance or *civilized* humor. But, since then, even cultivated humor has had to live to some extent in the shadow of "real" art. Only very recently has the profession of cabaret artist begun to be seen as respectable; humor is beginning to emancipate itself (Dekker 2001). As a consequence, there are increasing distinction *within* the domain of humor: the low status of the joke and other lower forms of humor is delineated even more sharply than formerly.

High and low humor

"High" and "low" are polysemic concepts in the domain of humor as they are everywhere. The fact that a cultural phenomenon has low status can mean that it principally manifests itself in low-status situations but also that it only appears in the presence of persons or groups with a low status. However, in a process of cultural 'trickle down', this means that its status in absolute terms continues to decrease: originally popular in higher circles, but with the passage of time taken over by persons from lower strata, whereupon those in higher circles turn their backs on the cultural product as a means of distinguishing themselves (Elias 1982; Fallers 1954).

Originally, the low status of the joke and its precursors seems mainly determined by the situation. Slowly but surely, the telling of standardized humorous stories actually began to disappear from higher circles. Only in the twentieth century does the joke seem to have sunk definitively: in the interim the joke has reached such a low status that the higher classes hardly ever tell jokes. The following chapters will provide thorough evidence for this assertion (at least in the Netherlands). I will attempt here to trace this process of sinking.

As far as one can determine, "jests" were told and performed everywhere around 1600: they were popular with the elite but also circulated among the common folk (Roodenburg 1997: 114). One famous collector of anecdotes, van Overbeke, was a lawyer and spent his time in the highest circles. "Popular culture includes gentlemen", concludes Brewer (1997: 97) in his discussion of sixteenth and seventeenth century *jest-books*. Both Roodenburg and Brewer observe, as mentioned, that in this period the gap between high and low humor began to widen. High humor had to be refined and civilized: two demands very difficult to observe in an orally transmitted genre often having a plot that was by no means subtle.

In the eighteenth century, one more criterion for good humor was added to those of restraint and refinement: authenticity through personal inventiveness. This gave rise to new objections to humorous stories, used against jokes even to the present day: they are not self-made. The earliest reference I know where this objection is made concrete is in a Dutch etiquette book from 1735, with the amazing title *The book of ceremony comprised of civilized custom, courtesy, ceremonial and cultivated civilities. An instructional aid for everyone, in strict accordance with his gender, birth, status, fortune, servants, profession, riches, state, relationship to others, etc., in the etiquette of behavior with the object of making himself beloved and happy in this world.* The writer of this book severely disapproves of telling jokes not invented by the teller; jokes must "spring in a fluid fashion from the stream of conversation, because without the self they are pusillanimous, arid and lack of the spark of life" (van Laar, quoted in de Man 1993: 107).

These exhortations began to be heard at the moment that the bourgeoisie, under French influence, started to define humor more and more as *esprit*, which corresponds roughly with English "wit", German *Witz* or Dutch *Geest*. All of these terms used for humor arose in the eighteenth century. They place humor firmly in the domain of the intellect, in contrast with earlier terms which tended to categorize humor in the domain of play and unseriousness (English "joke" is related to the French word for play, *jeu*, as well as a Dutch word for lying, *jokken*) or emotion (*humor* is derived from a word used to describe the bodily fluids creating temper and temperament).

This influence of French humor styles leads not only to an increasing linguistic component to humor. It also led to an emphasis on originality, creativity and ready wit. Venting another's felicitous phrases in the face of this demand for individual creativity amounts to an admission of weakness. One must demonstrate one's own scintillating spirit through inventive witticisms and refined plays on words.

The criterion of authenticity is directly connected with the intellectualizing already mentioned. While the ascent of the punch line fits this development well – the punch line, after all, emphasizes cognitive humor – the joke on other fronts falls far short if intellectuality is desired. The criterion of intellectual refinement thus disadvantaged the joke. The increasing emphasis on wittiness, nimble-mindedness and the art of conversing also demanded civilized humor. "Esprit" does not connote a guffaw or clandestine references but restrained, disciplined little smiles. The fact that, in all its refinement, the joke could be rather sharp, points at most to an even more effective restraint on affect.

The most compelling report of this eighteenth-century humor is not provided by scientific research but by a film: *Ridicule* (France, Patrick Leconte 1996). This film beautifully sketches the French cult of wittiness. It concludes, very aptly, with a Frenchman who, after his escape from France after the Revolution, devotes himself to learning English *humour*, a term that only conquered the continent in the nineteenth century.

This piling up of objections to the jests and anecdotes led thus to a decline in status of the humorous narrative. The joke does seem to have become more and more a genre for low and licentious *occasions* but not necessarily for low and licentious people. The joke is, for instance, regularly mentioned in the context of university student culture, a phase of life in which members of high circles experimented with the lower aspects of life. An important part of the only nineteenth century "informal" joke collection in the Netherlands that I am aware of, that of the doctor Cornelis Bakker (Meder 1999, 2000), also comes from Leiden's university environment. Jokes from this collection shed a very surprising light on the respectable nineteenth century: behind closed doors one could be fairly foul-mouthed. This last collection in particular makes apparent how the joke in the nineteenth century must have been a clandestine genre and thus unavoidably: a genre for "indecent" events in "decent" environments.

Until the middle of the twentieth century, a joke could quite easily be "civilized": maybe not chic but not exclusively vulgar either. The boundary between high and low humor was to some extent drawn *within* the genre of the joke, while it is difficult to establish how much consensus there was for this. In spite of increasing objections to the joke – not refined, not authentic, not restrained – it gains more and more in visibility towards the end of the nineteenth century, both in low and more bourgeois environments, as written culture strongly expanded.

The status of the joke can be illustrated by its place in twentieth century popular press in the Netherlands. From the beginning of the twentieth century until the 1950s, almost every self-respecting illustrated magazine had a joke page or even a joke supplement. Until the 1970s, there was a genre called the "family magazine", meant for the respectable middle classes, and presumably made defunct by the television. Of the four important Dutch family magazines *Panorama*, *Revue*, *De Spiegel* [The mirror] and *De katholieke illustratie* [The Catholic Illustration], only the Protestant *Spiegel* lacked a joke column. These joke pages were usually at the back, in the light-hearted department, but they were not placed on the children's page. Jokes in these magazines were presented as a civilized form of amusement, among the reports of world situations, the photograph series, the recipes and the knitting patterns. In addition to these joke presumably meant for the middle classes, there were also jokes in really popular magazines such as *De Lach* [The laugh], which combined jokes and cartoons with risqué pictures of ladies in bathing suits that became skimpier over time, until *De Lach*'s demise in the early 1970s. The joke, in short, was presented to the populace through many venues, some rather vulgar and others decently middle-class.

Within the family magazines, the aim of these jokes was clearly to amuse the readership in a civilized and refined way. Illustrative of this objective is the description of the editor of *Revue*'s joke page in 1954:

> Those of you who have already enjoyed his jokes in *Revue* can imagine his characteristic, mysterious smile. Herman Focke. . . is not the man for flashy fairground amusement. . . He sketches his little jokes with a subtle pencil or quick stroke of the brush and captures the gist, which usually causes a fine but especially pleasurable smile to light the face of the reader. (*Revue* 1954, issue 5)

The criterion of authenticity is trickier with jokes, but the other two demands, civilization and refinement, were adequately met, according to the quote: no "flashy fairground amusement" means no uncivilized humor.

And the "fine smile" points to refined humor. Remember that the targeted audience was not the elite who had gone to university – these magazines most likely aimed at the broad middle group – and this was, of course, a specific sort of joke, a "decent" joke. What this quote does indicate is that the joke *as a genre* had a significantly wider range than it does at present, the possibility for "civilized jokes" existed and this is now almost a contradiction in terms.

Not until the 1960s did the joke begin to visibly lose ground. Jokes disappeared from the more proper magazines at a great rate. Nowadays in the Netherlands, jokes are only still published in children's magazines such as *Donald Duck* and men's magazines such as *Playboy* and *Aktueel*. Of the more mainstream magazines, only the Dutch version of *The Readers Digest* continues to publish decent jokes (but this magazine is attempting to keep alive the atmosphere of the 1950s in any way it can). So it is only towards the middle of the twentieth century that the joke concluded its trickle down. Until that time highly cultured objections to the joke built up steadily but the genre stood its ground, in the guise of the indecent events of decent people, in the margins of high humor, in pubs and at parties and even in one of its decent facets: right at the center of middle-class "entertainment culture".

What happened after the 1960s that decline of the joke's status? In the course of the following chapters, I will work out the answer to this question slowly but surely as I discuss the objections of the highly educated against and the arguments of the less educated for jokes. What happened to make it impossible for the highly educated to appreciate a joke nowadays, even in low-status settings? Where did this rejection of the whole genre originate?

I will close my description of the slow demise of the joke's status, however, with an eyewitness declaration from the period during which the joke definitively disappeared from "decent" environments. Rinus Ferdinandusse, former editor of the prestigious intellectual weekly *Vrij Nederland*, and also the editor of the most successful Dutch joke book of the past 25 years, told me:

> Jokes? At that time they were a dying race. We had been enriched in the sixties; we were all heading for a newer and a better world. All the humorists from the Tuesday evening radio entertainment program were disappearing, retiring. . . . So then I thought, what we must do is collate a standard book with everything that's left of this disappearing culture.

The thousand worst jokes in the world (De duizend slechtste grappen van de wereld), which had many reprints after its first edition in 1972, thus began as a memorial for a disappearing genre, much like folklore a century earlier. A rescue operation was not in the least necessary though, as became apparent later. The joke pulled itself together and found a different niche. The "decent joke" though really died in the process; decent citizens went of in search of other entertainment.

Conclusion: Changing criteria for judging the joke

This chapter was meant to do two things. Firstly, it was meant to sketch a profile of the joke as an orally transmitted genre, a mold into which to pour jokes so that they could later be passed on orally. Secondly, after introducing the genre, this chapter was meant to introduce an important ingredient of the argument to be followed in the rest of the book: the fact that the joke is a low status genre. The status of the joke, or any other humorous genre, is determined by criteria for good humor and objections to bad humor. This is exactly what the whole book is about. "Taste" amounts to nothing more that: criteria for what is good or beautiful and objections to what is bad or ugly.

This chapter sketches the historical origins of three criteria of taste that have become increasingly important in judging humor. The first criterion, intellectual refinement or quick-wittedness, is connected with a process of the increasing "intellectualizing" of humor. The second criterion, restraint or civilization, is connected with the continuous tightening of the fetters on affect and, as such, influences not just humor but the laugh as well. The third, authenticity, in demanding that humor reveal something essential about the teller is less easily connected with a single sociological process. "Individualizing" would not be a bad candidate and neither would "psychologizing". The increased emphasis on the criterion of authenticity or originality in humor seems to be of more recent date than the other two. I think that it was precisely this criterion that finally, definitively, sunk the genre.

It is at the concurrence of these three criteria that one finds what Bourdieu (1984) calls the *esthetic disposition*: a distant, restrained and cerebral view of art and of other things subject to esthetic judgment, like humor. According to Bourdieu, this disposition characterizes the esthetic outlook of persons with legitimate "good" taste. This is the disposition essential to an appreciation of modern high culture. Beauty, in this vision, is not a question of direct sensual experience but a more distant and especially a more informed enjoyment of an "acquired taste".

This disposition demands a large degree of intellectualizing: the experience of beauty is almost completely subjugated to understanding. In modern times, to esthetically judge high culture, one needs knowledge. A great deal of affective restraint is also required: Bourdieu's esthete actually looks down a little on things meant to elicit a direct, emotional response, unless this is negative, because that could be turned into a distanced, positive, appreciative reaction. The last demand, authenticity, is always the decisive criterion in art. The criteria against which people measure humor are therefore akin to those established for other esthetic frames of mind – even though emotional reactions to beauty are less visible, less physical and less restrained than the laugh. This probably means that humor will never completely belong to the "elevated" arts: even the highest humor will always be a bit "low".

Chapter 3
Joke telling as communication style

"I'm one of those ones who's got a joke on the tip of his tongue all the time. I just finish telling one and out rolls the next. My family and friends are always saying 'Hans, come on over here and tell us a good joke.'" Hans Wagenaar, a forty-year-old factory worker whom I met at the *Moppentoppers* selection, is characteristic of the thirty-four joke tellers that I talked to: a jovial, talented raconteur with a reputation among those close to him as a joke teller and as the life of the party.

While these joke tellers were all proud of their extensive repertoire and kept track of it on beer coasters, in notebooks and even in computer databases, they saw telling jokes primarily as a social event: "If I'm sitting with six or seven others in a group and everybody's telling jokes, then every man jack of them can come up with four to six good ones. One of the guys will've told one and that gets the others itching to tell theirs, and off we go. We'll be sitting there just chewing the fat when all of a sudden someone tells a joke and then everyone gets into the act." While Wagenaar admitted that he liked the attention he got from telling jokes – "I always like the feeling of being the center of attention for a while" – he saw telling jokes primarily as social enjoyment. As he said: "There's always a high point at a birthday get-together and that's when it's always really nice to tell a few. It's part of being together. Spontaneous. Among friends."

Like all the joke tellers I spoke to, Hans Wagenaar loved joke *as a genre*, and joke telling as something he does with other people. For this reason, he found it difficult to say which jokes were best: "I don't really have a huge preference. I like them if they're well told and reasonably up-to-date. You can't really say I've got favorites, like: I crack up at a Belgian joke or jokes about Turks or Surinamese or any other, racist jokes or whatever, that doesn't make any difference to me. If a joke's put together right and it's funny, I get a good laugh out of it, no matter what it's about."

Joke lovers like Wagenaar take the floor in this chapter. Their views will be contrasted with people with no interest in jokes and even people with an aversion to them. All these people have one thing in common: they have an opinion about the joke as a genre. This opinion usually has to do with joke telling as a social activity. All of these people distinguish within the genre between better and worse jokes. Even a rabid joke hater will laugh at a really good joke once in a while, and even the most enthusiastic joke lover singles some jokes out as corny, coarse or incomprehensible. But a judgment of the genre precedes a judgment of any single joke. And that initial judgment is strongly connected with social background.

Joke telling and social background

Since the survey made clear that jokes are appreciated as a genre, I will start with the survey results. Respondents to this questionnaire, 340 people from all layers of the population, judged a number of humorous television programs, entertainers, writers and presenters and 35 jokes.[6] The jokes, which are listed in Appendix 1, were very diverse in character, varying from Belgian jokes, absurd riddles and other relatively innocuous jokes to the explicit ethnic and sexual jokes.

Statistical analysis showed that judgments of the jokes from the list were strongly connected. Correlations between the appreciation of jokes were usually significant, which means that if someone liked one joke, he usually liked most of the rest too. Moreover, a factor analysis – a method for finding patterns in groups of data – of the jokes also suggested that the respondents' evaluation of jokes in the questionnaire were linked. This factor analysis resulted in a two-factor solution. The first factor was one on which all jokes load, and thus correlates perfectly with the average rating of the jokes for each respondent. The second factor indicates that respondents also distinguish between jokes. This factor can be interpreted as a scale of offensiveness to innocuousness of jokes: racist and sick jokes have the lowest factor loadings, absurd jokes and wordplay the highest. Table 1 shows the relationship between these factors and various social background variables. A table with the factor loadings for these two factors can be found in Chapter 7 of this book.

Thus, variations did exist in how the jokes were evaluated. As becomes clear from the factor analysis, some respondents showed a preference for more or less transgressive jokes. The second part of this book deals with differences in the evaluation of separate jokes. The main conclusion to be drawn from this analysis here is that, in addition to judging separate jokes as more or less funny, people also value jokes in general. The differences within the genre as a whole were less noticeable than the similarities: if someone liked the offensive jokes, chances were high that he would also appreciate the cleaner specimens.

Table 1.   Factor analysis of joke appreciation: relation with social background
(N=340) [7]

	Factor 1: Joke appreciation	Factor 2: Innocuousness
Mean appreciation of jokes	1.00**	.01
Mean offensiveness of jokes	-.20**	.42**
Mean knowledge of jokes	.25**	-.15**
Age	-.05	.48**
Gender	M > F *	n.s.
Income	-.09	.10
Educational Level	-.19**	.00
Cultural Capital (N=248)	-.31**	.07
Economical Capital (N=248)	-.11	.07
Class (N=275)	.16***	-.09
Education appropriate for profession (N=275)	-.21**	.02
Education appropriate for profession partner (N=148)	-.29**	-.11
Education appropriate for profession father (N=283)	-.11	-.04
Education appropriate for profession mother (N=87)	-.09	.07

* p < 0.05
** p < 0.01

As can be seen in Tables 1 and 2, appreciation for the questionnaire jokes
was connected to education and gender: men liked the jokes more than
women; those with lower education thought them funnier than the highly
educated. Other social characteristics, such as age, regional background or
religion were not connected with the evaluations. While gender was relatively easy to operationalize, class is less easily defined. Table 1 shows that
while a relationship was found with education, income was not related to
how the jokes were evaluated. The table also shows the relationship between joke appreciation and various other measures of class: the EGP scale,
a five-layer classification of class widely used in sociology (Erickson,
Goldthorpe and Portocarero 1979) as well as the education most appropriate for the present profession, based on a measure of the Netherlands Statistics Bureau (CBS 1992). Both these measures are based on the respondent's description of the present job, and thus account for mobility after
graduation. All these scales show a similar tendency: the higher one's

status, the less one's appreciation for jokes. Finally, I have included a measure that distinguishes between the cultural and economic capital attached to people's jobs (Ganzeboom, de Graaf, and Kalmijn 1987), showing that the aversion to joke telling is mostly related to high cultural rather than economic capital.

The easiest as well as the most objective measure of class is educational level. Since the various measures of class point in the same direction, I will use this for the remains of this book. The Netherlands has an a fairly hierarchical educational system, distinguishing between vocational and (more prestigious) general education both on the secondary and highest level. However, the main distinction – both in everyday language and in its social consequences – is between the so-called "lower educated" (*lageropgeleiden*) and the "higher educated" (*hogeropgeleiden*), the latter being those with either higher vocational (HBO) or university (WO) education. For convenience, I refer to these groups here as "less highly educated" versus "college educated" or "more highly educated".

Table 2 gives the average joke evaluation per educational level and gender. This table clearly shows a relationship between joke telling and these social background variables, and it also shows the gender distinction to be more pronounced in the lower educational levels.

Table 2. Evaluation of the jokes in the questionnaire, broken down according to educational level and gender. (On a scale of 1 to 5)

	Men	Mean Women	All	SD	N	Gender difference
1. Primary	3.01	3.13	3.00	0.47	7	n.s.
2. Lower vocational (LBO)	3.52	2.77	3.29	0.61	25	**
3. Secondary vocational (MBO)	3.32	2.91	3.16	0.63	92	**
4. General secondary (MO)	3.15	2.92	3.07	0.65	60	n.s.
5. Higher vocational (HBO)	3.07	2.76	2.96	0.63	92	*
6. University (WO)	2.89	2.71	2.84	0.56	54	n.s.
All	3.17	2.83	3.04	0.63	330	**

* $p < 0.05$
** $p < 0.01$

To explain these results, it would perhaps seem obvious to say that women like humor less than men or that the more highly educated have less sense of humor than the less educated. These thoughts would be in keeping with existing stereotypes about humor: the idea that women have no sense of humor; and the somewhat less poignant stereotype that common people are high-spirited, happier and more gregarious. The ratings of the comedians, entertainers and humorous television programs do not, however, corroborate these stereotypes. I did not find any gender or class differences in evaluations made of all the entertainers/comedians and television programs. Different groups do not like humor either to a greater or lesser degree, but they like different types of humor.

Jokes and gender

The differences between men and women, the highly and less highly educated were still more obvious from the interviews than they were from the questionnaire. Of the 34 joke tellers, 31 were men. Despite my avid search for female joke tellers, I was unable to find more than three. Only one of these I contacted at *Moppentoppers*, the other two I only found after a long search, while men generally came forward on their own. Apparently telling jokes is a rather unusual activity for women. All three of the women interviewed, moreover, were part of a Dutch subculture in which it is perhaps less unusual for women to tell jokes; one was Jewish, another was "Creole", i.e. African-American from the former Dutch colony of Surinam, and the third was only sixteen. To some extent, Jews, Creoles and children have their own joke cultures separate from the Dutch mainstream.[8]

All the interviewed joke tellers, even the women, saw joke telling as something primarily done by men. Jokes, my respondents assured me again and again, are part of a "man's world": the pub, the harbor, the soccer club, the billiard club and "boys' nights out". Joke tellers told their jokes mainly to other men, heard them from other men and preferred masculine company as the ambience for these activities. Most men also thought that you had to be "careful" with jokes if women were around. "If there are women around that I don't know, I won't start telling jokes. It's a question of respect" said Otto van der Meijden (40, wholesaler). 48-year-old welder Matthieu Cnoops told me: "I always try to be more civilized to women than I do to men."

If jokes are told in a woman's presence, language is censored. Gerrit Helman, a 26-year-old logistics manager tried to explain "With a woman around, you've gotta watch your language now and then. Yeah, I don't know how to say it, but it's definitely different" [laughs]. (GK: "Do you think less is permitted with women present?") "It's just something you don't do. I don't know if it's permitted or not but you don't do it." Particularly with sexual jokes, one has to watch out in the presence of women. "I'd say the more erotic genre wouldn't be something you'd get into with the girls around. There's always a little voice in your head saying you've gotta make a good impression" (Frits Eldering, 26, wholesaler). I personally witnessed how problematic it is to tell jokes in the presence of a woman during the interviews. I had to go to great lengths to convince people that I was hard enough to hear certain jokes. Many joke tellers only consented to tell me certain jokes "because I was doing research". Even then they admitted, sometimes even blushing, that it was embarrassing to tell me a certain kind of joke.

Half of those interviewed expressed the opinion that it wasn't appropriate for women to tell jokes at any time. Egbert van Kaam, a 34-year-old working at traveling fairground, stated that women who told jokes "tore the crowns from her own heads" because "joke telling was not something a lady did". Otto van der Meijden was somewhat more diplomatic in saying: "when women tell jokes it's very confronting". Jacob Hitters (53, architectural draftsman) said: "it's pretty coarse, isn't it, a woman sitting there telling a joke?" This counts even more strongly for sexual jokes. As Egbert van Kaam said: "If a woman tells two dirty jokes, a man starts thinking she'll jump in the sack with anyone". This disgust felt when women told jokes was not generalized: the other half of the joke tellers did not object to women telling jokes and some even expressed the hope that women would eventually get around to telling more.

The three female joke tellers were quite conscious of the fact that telling jokes could damage their "reputations". "A woman has to be aware of what genre she's dealing with", said Chantal Wijntuin (45, social worker*)* for instance. "Number one, there's the sense of shame. Number two, it's not something women do, you know how that goes. You take a real nosedive as far as the guys are concerned. Okay, I hear a joke. A real filthy joke. Believe me, I wouldn't be gross enough to go and repeat it to just anyone. Nope, they'd be sure to say: 'yikes, that one's got a real foul mouth'."

In addition to restrictions for women connected to decency and decorum, some interviewees mentioned another impediment: women *cannot* tell jokes. They start with the punch line, laugh before the end, are too shy, too cautious or too proper: in short, they get it all wrong.

> Actually, women can't tell jokes because they never go to the pub. I have a lot of difficulty laughing at women because they're so awfully decent. (Evert van Roden, 68, retired professional entertainer/ joke teller)

> It strikes me too that if once in a while a woman tries to tell a joke, she can't remember it. She starts off with: "yeah, how did that go again?" Or:

> "yeah, yesterday my husband told a really great joke, now how did it go?" Or, and this happens quite a lot, they say: "I don't if I've got this right but..." (Huibert Busser, 42, personnel manager)

> A whole lot of women aren't any good at jokes. You want to know why? Maybe they don't really believe in it; maybe they've got their doubts; maybe they're even a bit embarrassed or something. That's it I guess: you've gotta be completely convinced" (Alfred Kruger, 61, sound technician)

Women often agree with this: the interviewed women themselves stated that they often couldn't tell a joke. ("I always start with the punch line." "Halfway through, I forget where I'm headed.")

In the eyes of the joke tellers, jokes are a man's business and, as in so many matters featuring masculinity and femininity, tied up with ideas about honor and shame (Bourdieu 2001). Men can win admiration for telling a joke while women run the risk of being disgraced. In spite of diminished differences in power between men and women, differences in standards for masculine and feminine behavior still exist and these also cover the domain of humor and the telling of jokes. This does seem to be shifting: younger interviewees were less disapproving of joke-telling women. However, they too said that they most often told their jokes to other men. Sex roles seem persistent here too.

The interviewees who had filled in the questionnaire were generally quite aware that the joke was a man's genre.[9] During these interviews, it became apparent that even women who had given high marks to jokes often didn't tell them themselves. They chose to be listeners. Sofie Gooijer, a 37-year-old homemaker and part-time administrative worker, told me that she always let her husband tell jokes for her. If jokes were being told and she knew an appropriate one, she would whisper the details into her husband's ear so that he could tell it. Another couple had a similar division of labor. The wife of 49-year-old janitor Jaap van Noord said: "Jaap is the joke teller; I give him hints." Women who like jokes usually like them from their role as audience, not as performer: they laugh at jokes told by men.

In the group of thirty-two interviewees, twelve explicitly told me they didn't like jokes at all: nine of these were women. In addition, there were six women who didn't mind hearing a joke now and then "as long as it stayed within bounds". The objections that these women had to jokes can be loosely divided into three categories. To begin with, jokes were "predictable" and "stale". Telling jokes was "exaggerated" or "forced": the joke teller wanted "attention" more than anything and was "trying to be funny".

The objection mentioned most often was that the jokes were "impersonal": the teller did not invent the joke himself. Anke Vermeer, a 52-year-old freelance writer, thought jokes evinced "spiritual poverty" for this reason. Almost all the women interviewed said that they preferred spontaneous, self-created jokes and humorous stories about real happenings. As will become apparent, these objections resemble those made by the highly educated.

The seventeen interviewed women from the sample unanimously confessed that they could not remember jokes. In recent years, many women have told me, in almost precisely the same terms, that they "always immediately forget" jokes. Given the fact that women are supposed to listen to men's jokes, this seems efficient: they thus become the everlasting audience. This widespread inability to remember jokes is not only characteristic of women but also of many highly educated persons. I suspect this is partially due to a lack of interest but mainly to lack of practice. As I have discovered meanwhile, you don't remember a joke by simply listening to it but by telling it over and over. The telling of jokes is not only a preference but also a skill that can be learned: a competence for which men win more esteem than women.

Jokes and class

People are usually aware of the connection between gender and joke telling. This is much less so for class differences. The majority of the interviewed joke lovers came from the working or the lower middle classes; only two had had higher vocational training. High school sophomore was the highest educational level obtained by twenty of the interviewees. If I told the interviewees that the educated, like my university colleagues, didn't tell many jokes, they were quite surprised. They derived from this that university employees didn't like humor or that they were boring and serious. Joke telling to them was more or less the same thing as humor. "Maybe laughing a bit more would do them good", said Jaap van Noord. And Claudia van Leer (62, homemaker, lower vocational education) said: "I guess they don't have much fun. They've been sitting with their noses in the books for so long that I guess real life just passes them by." Only two of the joke tellers were aware that the preference for jokes had something to do with class.

The reactions of the more highly educated in the sample were more varied but usually they were aware that jokes were more popular in "other circles". Most of the highly educated seldom heard jokes: "I must say that I'm very seldom in circumstances where I hear jokes or tell them", said 56-year-old high school teacher Cornelis Blom. This was also true of persons who had rated jokes from the questionnaire reasonably high, such as Louis Baldé, a 50-year-old English teacher: "I sometimes love to hear them but I don't really ever get the chance. And I remember them abominably badly. I might hear five and, of those, I'd be lucky to remember one." The most remarkable exception was a 52-year-old medical doctor, Kees van Dokkum. Of the college-educated, he was the only one who was genuinely surprised when I told him that the questionnaire had demonstrated that the highly educated liked jokes less. He said: "Is that so? I would've thought that they'd understand things more quickly. That surprises me. Obviously they've decided that jokes are below them. Amazing. Yes, it's a deliciously relaxed form of humor, you don't even have to think hard, and you can just have fun. And then that's frowned on. A Calvinistic throwback maybe."

Other highly educated interviewees only heard jokes incidentally. And they were not complaining. In spite of the fact that I had tried to select from the questionnaire a sample of just as many people who liked jokes as those who didn't, the majority of the more highly educated interviewees (nine out of fourteen) was negative about jokes. The first reaction was usually disinterested ("I actually never hear jokes"), but as I probed more deeply, most went on to call jokes irritating or even embarrassing. More highly educated respondents described jokes as "crude", "vulgar", "simple", "easy", "predictable", and "a forced way of getting a laugh" (Rob de Laat, 42, team manager in an electronics installation company) and typical of "laborers and neighborhood pubs" (Lotte van der Lans, 84, homemaker, university). Two typical comments:

> Joke telling is really only passing the baton. I would say that thinking the joke up yourself is a degree higher. (Ton Linge, 61, retired editor)

> If I run into someone at a party who's really into jokes, then I try to escape pretty fast. There's no way you can have a normal conversation with somebody like that. I don't mind if someone tells a joke now and then, you know, to fill a crack in the conversation, but if it's joke after joke and that's the level, I usually try to disappear quickly. (Corine Steen, 40, marketing researcher)

Jokes clearly do not have a very high status for these educated respondents. All these reactions are rather explicit expressions of class distinction; jokes are associated with the "lower classes"; the telling of jokes of this sort is seen as "bad taste", and "of a lower level". It is clear that someone who tells a joke in surroundings like this tends to disqualify himself.

That is not to say that a joke is never told. The objections were not usually aimed at an incidental joke but at real "joke telling": the committed exchange of jokes that takes up a great deal of time. In spite of the objections, an absolute prohibition does not exist. Jokes can be tolerated in certain situations, and an ironic presentation is always a good way to deflect eventual disapproval. Generally though, telling jokes is seen as somewhat tasteless and embarrassing behavior.

The people most aware of this in the group of interviewees were the upwardly mobile. They were not in the least surprised when I suggested that telling jokes had something to do with class. In total, I spoke to six of them and they all had personally experienced the fact that their present friends or colleagues did not much like or accept jokes told at their parents' homes. Three of them didn't like jokes at all anymore, in contrast with their parents and siblings. Roos Schuurman, a thirty-year-old teacher whose father does administrative work, even said: "My university education has spoiled me for jokes." When I asked her if she ever heard jokes, she told me about the joke volleys at family parties:

> There are always a couple of uncles who take up sides and pitch jokes back and forth. Yes, a couple; now and then a real volley takes place.
> *Do you like it?*
> [Silence] Hmm. Yeah. I don't mind. No, not really.
> *But that doesn't sound very convinced. Do you like it when that happens?*
> Yeah, well, not really. I don't like family parties very much. No. I like watching them tell jokes – they enjoy it so much and sometimes I can laugh too and then it's funny enough. So I don't feel that I'm too good or anything. But no. I can't really get into it anymore... I don't much mind when it happens though.

Three others who were upwardly mobile said that they liked jokes when they were at their parents' places, but that they knew that they couldn't very easily tell them to their friends, colleagues or partners. Thus they changed register, making quick-witted retorts to their educated friends and telling jokes to family. Nevertheless, sometimes an uneasiness could be felt. This is apparent, for instance, from this segment of my interview with Sybren Boonstra, a 36-year-old lawyer, in which, even before the interview actually began and before I had mentioned anything about class difference, he said that his friends and acquaintances had "too much education" for jokes:

Do you ever tell a joke?
Yes, sometimes. But we often have the idea that we don't, we don't exactly come from the part of town [laughs] where jokes are created. When I'm with my family, then there's a lot more people who tell jokes, you know. I like that. If I can remember one and the conditions are right, I'll tell it too.
One?
Yeah, I don't tell a whole lot in a row, I can't remember that many anyway. I might be lucky enough to remember one. But it's also a bit of a social setting – you know, a setting where jokes don't – they really don't have much of a place.
What do you mean? Not at work?
No. Not at home either. And not in my circle of friends either. I don't know how to say it exactly. It happens now and then, but...
Why is that, do you think?
[Silence] I think most jokes are pretty insipid anyway [laughs]. And that most people there are too highly educated for jokes. They just aren't keen. [Silence]
There aren't a lot of people who would dare to say that.
No. No, you're right. But I think that's what's behind it. Jokes are looked at as something for, you know, dumber people; I don't know how to say I very well. Like this, sort of: "it's just not done".

Boonstra identifies more with his parents' environment than Schuurman does, even though both express some ambivalence about the different environments in which they find themselves, a split that occurs often in people who have climbed higher on the social ladder (Brands 1992). All of the upwardly mobile had discovered exactly the same thing; joke telling among the highly educated was not only unusual, it was also "not done".

Gender roles and class cultures

The contrast between gender difference and class difference is striking: people show themselves to be much more aware of differences between men and women than of differences between people of different educational levels. If what is being discussed is masculine or feminine humor, clear standards and rules apply; there are standard phrases and established truths about the lack of humor in women, about off color jokes told "when out with the guys", about women who can't tell a joke, about honor and disgrace, about ladies (who never tell jokes) and sluts (who laugh at dirty jokes).

The lack of conscious standards and rules for and even the lack of awareness of class differences – especially among those with less education – points to a cultural difference. People are often little aware of their own culture: people in a joke culture do not often realize that telling jokes is taken for granted much less in a different culture and similarly those not inhabiting a joke culture are not always aware of the humor of others. The people most confronted with these cultural differences have a foot in each culture – the upwardly mobile.

Telling jokes is much more a part of the culture of those less highly educated. This distinction does not precisely coincide with a traditional division between white-collar and blue-collar work: the cultural boundary in the Netherlands seems to run between working class together with the lower middle class (or those with primary and some secondary education) on the one hand and the upper middle class (the highly educated) on the other hand. Class cultures within one society are, however, not independent: to some extent they are shaped in contrast with one another. The upper middle class generally tries to distinguish itself culturally from the lower classes (Bourdieu 1984). This is apparent from what was said above about jokes by the more highly educated: they are condescending about the humor of those with less education, call it "vulgar" and are slightly pained when confronted with it.

The more highly educated are more knowledgeable about the culture of those with less education than vice versa. To distinguish yourself from something, you have to know something about it. The asymmetry in knowledge about another's judgment of jokes, as more generally knowledge of another's tastes, is connected to social status. Tastes with higher status are, by definition, more difficult to access than lower tastes: not only are they screened off because they are more difficult but knowledge of what judgments are actually being made is kept off bounds for others. Still, the highly educated reject joke telling based on inaccurate knowledge. Their image of joke tellers is stereotyped and inadequately elaborated – just clear enough for contempt.

The joke tellers also expressed a similar negative stereotype about the highly educated but their image of the highly educated was vaguer still. Hans Wagenaar, who was introduced at the beginning of this chapter, said:

> They [people who have gone to university] simply have other things on their minds. Not that they never tell a joke, but then it will turn out to be a little anecdote about how someone failed or, you know, what went wrong with this or that company, that sort of thing. I don't think that they hear or tell normal jokes. I certainly don't think they do it as much as we do. No.

At the university, for example, where I am, almost nobody tells jokes.
Yeah, but you're all studying of course, so I guess you don't get out much.
You probably have fewer chances than somebody who's not hitting the
book all the time.

In this respect, class differences are not the same as gender differences.
While a number of authors have claimed that separate male and female
cultures exist (e.g. Tannen 1994), this line of reasoning seems no very help-
ful. Men and women in the same class share their lives for a large part and,
concurrently, their culture. It is true that men and women have different
roles and positions within the same culture. In the case of telling jokes (and
more so, general humor) gender roles are more or less complementary: men
tell jokes and women listen. In this respect, perhaps not so much has
changed since Rose Coser (1960: 85) wrote: "In this culture women are
expected to be passive and receptive, rather than active and initiating. A
woman who has a good sense of humor is one who laughs (but not too
loudly!) when a man makes a witticism or tells a good joke. A man who
has a sense of humor is one who is witty in his remarks and tells good
jokes. The man provides; the woman receives." The fact that men "are
careful" about telling jokes when women are around indicates, though, that
to tell jokes is to fulfill a man's role, but it also belongs to man's domain:
the pub, the soccer canteen and the little circle of men that forms at parties.

Men's and women's domains seem more separate among the less educated than they are among the more highly educated and in a culture like
this there is presumably more space for men's activities such as the telling
of jokes. Many classic studies of working class culture produce an image of
separate men's and women's worlds in working-class environments
(Bourdieu 1984: 372-396; Gans 1962; Rubin 1976; Willis 1977; for the
Netherlands see Brands 1992; Brinkgreve and van Stolk 1997; Kapteyn
1985). Moreover, the influence of women's emancipation was felt earlier
and more pressingly in higher classes. This may also be one of the reasons
for the limited popularity of jokes in the upper middle class: the changed
relationship between men and women has led to do a decreasing distinction
between men's and women's roles and presumably also to a crumbling
away of men's domains. Thus, the possibility of and perhaps the preference
for telling jokes has probably crumbled too.

The gender and class differences sketched here are, of course, not absolute. What one sees are more general patterns within which exceptions very
possibly take place. Among the more highly educated, for instance, a difference in culture and lifestyle between the different age groups and social
sectors also exists (Ganzeboom et al. 1987; van Eijck 1999, 2001). This can

be seen in humor too. Jokes seem to be esteemed in the culture of the fraternities and in their extensions into, for instance, the financial and medical worlds (as in the doctor quoted above). This distinction between sectors runs more or less parallel to the distinction Bourdieu makes between cultural and economic capital; it can roughly be said that in sectors in which economic capital has prominence, jokes are more popular than in sectors were cultural capital is of prime importance. This is connected with standards of refinement, wittiness, authenticity and other "intellectual" and "artistic" demands that the joke will never be able to fulfill. People with a great deal of cultural capital usually assign more value to standards of this sort. In addition, I suspect a connection exists with the company culture of different sectors: as this becomes more competitive, more hierarchical and more masculine, more jokes will be told. As will soon become apparent, the telling of jokes is a rather competitive and status-oriented form of communication.

Joking and trading

In addition to the class and gender difference in evaluating jokes, there is an unmistakable connection with the nature of the work someone does. The connection between jokes and trade was one of the unexpected findings arising from the interviews with joke lovers: fifteen of those interviewed, which is almost half of the joke tellers (44%) had some sort of background in trade. Twelve turned out to work or have worked as retailers, wholesalers or representatives. Three others had a father who had been a tradesman. This relationship between humor and trade also plays a role in the popular image of tradesmen. Sales representatives in particular have a reputation in the area of humor: not only are they almost expected to tell a joke to every client but a substantial body of jokes *about* sales representatives also exists.

This relationship between humor and trade is founded on the ability of humor to quickly establish a connection. A joke "breaks the ice". As the owner of a hardware store, and of a wholesale business in medical equipment, respectively, said:

> In our work, you always have to make sure that you can come back, in every possible way. You have to be friendly, correct, and spontaneous. To fool around a bit, make a few jokes, that helps. Places I first visited thirty years ago – I'm still welcome there today – in those same factories. See what I mean? You've gotta be friends. (Gerben Stuijling, 59)

Naturally everyone wants to be liked, but we're also talking about the productive mood here. You've gotta look at it this way – someone comes into the showroom for the first time and we've never seen each other before. And that guy's got 10,000 guilders in his pocket. Now I'm pretty keen on transferring that money from his pocket to mine. But that doesn't happen just like that. You need a relationship for that. It's a question of trust. How can I win his trust? What I have to do is create an atmosphere that gives the other guy the feeling that his 10,000 is being well spent here. He's got to feel that he doesn't begrudge me that money. Everything is a question of getting him to think, "It's a lot of money but you're welcome to it". Calculations take place, additions, subtractions, but in the end he's got to think, "Yes, he's welcome to my 10,000". And who do you give that kind of money to? Somebody sympathetic, somebody with a good story and somebody who gives you the feeling that he's trustworthy. Humor can play a role in this. And then I'm not saying that I start firing off jokes, but humor in general. (Onno van der Meijden)

The telling of a joke is not only a quick and effective way to establish a friendly relationship; it is also a fairly impersonal and thus a "safe" way of doing it. Without overdoing the personal openness, an atmosphere of trust is created through which it is easier to sell something.

The telling of jokes is also one way of demonstrating a verbal virtuosity of great importance to tradesmen. People who want to sell something have to have the gift of the gab in order to tempt someone else into buying. Humor is an efficient means to this end. In his book about the wholesalers in flowers from the Dutch village of Rijnsburg, Strating (1997) points to the remarkable eloquence of this group he researched. And, indeed, my interviewed joke tellers were, without exception, very fluent verbally: they were not only good joke tellers but also generally very able speakers.

This relationship between jokes and trade alerted me to the joke as a communication style. Tradesmen like jokes because telling jokes is a form of communication that fits their daily activities well: telling jokes is for them primarily a manner of *speaking*. This is a different approach than that usually chosen in humor research, where the connection between the content of the joke and how it is valued is investigated. The fact alone that people exist who have made joke telling their specialty indicates that it is not a liking for specific jokes but the genre as a whole that concerns us here.

The joke is a humorous genre that links up with a certain communication style. This style seemed to run in families, just as being in trade did, in fact: three-quarters of the tradesmen had a father in trade too and this points to a direct handing down of this verbal competence so useful for tradesmen.

Even without the trade connection, joke telling was often a "family thing". Joke tellers often described either their father or grandfather as a "real joke teller", as a big example for them: they loved to emulate these funny fathers and grandfathers. Almost all joke tellers had learned to tell jokes at home. What is being passed on here is not only a "taste", a passive preference for a certain type of humor, but also a "style", a form of behavior. Telling jokes is a communication style characteristic of certain families and certain social groups.

Humorous communication styles

Telling jokes is an activity principally reserved for men with a low level of education. Within this group, tradesmen in particular seem to engage in joke telling, describing joke telling as a form of communication they use to forge a bond with others. Interestingly, also the objections to jokes, phrased mostly by women and college educated persons, seems to pertain mostly to joke telling as a social activity and a form of talk that is tiring, impersonal, predictable, forced, or loud.

This preference, as well as the aversion, can therefore not be elucidated based of the very variable content of jokes. The concept of communication style can, in my opinion, shed more light on gender and class differences in evaluating jokes and on the above-indicated connections between jokes and trade too. Different cultures and different groups within a culture, have different communication styles: different ways of speaking to each other and different standards for a speaking style appropriate to certain company or circumstances. These differences between communication styles are not only seen in basic facets of speech such as the speed with which people speak or the directness with which they formulate but they are also visible in matters having to do with relationships, such as the tendency to use speech to bring about closeness or, alternatively, to indicate hierarchies (Brown and Levinson 1983; Tannen 1984, 1994; Hymes 1974).

Many objections made by the highly educated and the female interviewees can be interpreted as objections against a form of communication. Very few objected to the content of jokes as long as this was not hurtful (racist or at someone's expense). What was objected to was that joke tellers attracted attention, forced other people to laugh or that they were loud and impersonal. In short, their problems were with the nature of the communication and not with the joke as such. This choice for other communication styles is also apparent from descriptions of the types of humor that were preferred: personal anecdotes, spontaneous jokes, and ironic or witty remarks. Most objections of joke haters had to do with joke *telling*. In addition to being confronted with a joke itself that you either like or dislike, as in the questionnaire, listening to a joke being told means being confronted with a specific social situation and social atmosphere.

Even joke lovers referred more to the form of communication than to the content of the joke itself. If I asked them why they loved jokes, they usually mentioned the exchange of jokes with others:

> When it starts to get interesting, then someone will begin and the others jump right in too and then you're into a half hour of fun. (Gerrit Helman)

> And then you're there, all together again, having a little drink, having a bit of fun together, downing the firewater, and then I strike while the wine is in, of course. (Albert Reiziger, 40, longshoreman)

> Yeah, that's the nicest about telling jokes. Say you're there with two or three other guys and they start telling them as well. That's the nicest. Then that guy's got a new one and then that guy over there. Then I start remembering a whole lot, you know? Somebody will say, oh yeah, I know one about that. That's when the real connection comes – through the jokes. (Joost Wiersema, 51, electrician)

What is central to these answers is joke telling as an activity, as a form of communication that counts as spontaneous, relaxed and sociable for joke tellers. I therefore have tried to find the background for differences in how jokes were appreciated in differences in humorous communication styles. In comparing telling jokes with other forms of humorous communication, I have stayed as close as possible to my respondents' words when they described and evaluated jokes and other forms of humor.

Telling a joke, or any attempt at humor, is what Erving Goffman (1959) has called "a presentation of self". By attempting to be humorous, a joke teller is giving a performance, which is intended to have some sort of effect on the way people perceive him (or, incidentally, her). However, this self-presentation is done for the benefit of an audience. Thus, telling a joke is also an "interaction ritual" (Goffman 1967, 1971) in which both the joke teller and his audience engage.

If we look at joke telling as an interaction ritual, it becomes obvious how much a joke interrupts the flow of the communication. The linguist Neil Norrick has described humor as a form of "interactional aggression in disrupting topical turn-by-turn talk" (1993: 134). Every joke, certainly if it is followed by laughter, disrupts the normal course of the conversation. A disruption of this sort has something unavoidably aggressive about it; the joke maker interferes with the course of the conversation and this can be interpreted as a takeover. This is even more so for jokes than for other forms of humor because the joke teller monopolizes the conversation for quite a time without interruption: in itself a symbol of conversational power. Corine Steen objected to this disruptive aspect of joke telling. She told about her neighbors, whom she could not always avoid at neighborhood parties:

> I always get the feeling that they can't do anything but tell jokes. Or that they use the jokes to lever themselves into the center of attention. I sometimes really hate it because it disrupts the conversation so badly. They hop from one joke to the next and you can't get a word in edgewise. I don't mean to say that these people on their own, if you could ever really talk to them, would be irritating. That's not necessarily true. [laughs]

The disruptive nature of joke telling makes it a risky activity. There are large profits to be won or lost in the area of status by telling jokes. To tell a joke successfully is to acquire status but if it misfires the teller can seriously lose face. If no one laughs or, even worse, if people start grumbling half way through that they "already know it" or that the joke "is really old" then the joke teller can stop right there. The risk is larger for a joke than it is for many other forms of humor, not only because the joke teller monopolizes the conversation for a period of time but also because he has made patently clear that he intends to be humorous; the framing (Bateson 1972; Goffman 1974) is unambiguous. To tell a joke, therefore, is always to take a risk. (cf. Lampert and Ervin-Tripp 2006)

This disruptive and status-seeking character of joke telling connects with something that can be viewed as distinctly masculine: joking is a rather competitive form of communication. This is particularly true when different people take turns telling jokes and thereby try to outdo each other. Each joker tries to be funnier then the one before:

> Not that you consciously say: "Now I'm just going to go on telling them until I've run out and I'm exhausted", but after the first, along comes the next. And then there's two left. And the minute you've finished, he starts up and then he's finished and you start up again. Not that you're aware of making a contest of it. But I guess unconsciously it could be... Not that we say to each other: "Hey, I know more than you do." No. But still, effortlessly and unconsciously. (Walter Adriaans, 39, garbage collector)

But what is the joke teller saying about himself? What type of "presentation of self" is joke telling? A joke is never created by the joke teller and often not even related to his own experience. In comparison with personal anecdotes, funny stories and spontaneously created witticisms, the joke is rather impersonal. This is dependent upon the context: a joke can be inserted in order to express a very personal conviction, thought or opinion. But even then it remains the case that the joke teller conceals himself behind the lack of seriousness of humor. Thus, even though a joke teller takes a great risk in terms of conversational bravado, in terms of content, the joke teller never fully reveals himself.

Joke lovers will counter this by saying that it's all in the "presentation". On balance, joke telling leans more heavily on presentation than on content. This is true of all oral genres: it is about performance, about the art of telling (Bauman 1977, 1986). And in the presentation, in taking the floor and attempting to make other laugh, the joke teller is, of course, implicitly saying something about himself: "Look at me. Laugh with me", which easily translates into: "Like me. Admire me." Other implied messages could be: "I'm amusing", "we're friends", and, by telling sexual jokes: "I'm not a prude, a scaredy-cat or a goody-goody." In short, the message of the joke teller is social: the *telling* is the message. In forms of humor other than the joke, the person telling a story can more easily convey a more personal or informative message in addition to the social message.

Joke lovers are ultimately interested in the "performance". The difference between the joke and other humorous communication is mainly a matter of style. Jokes are quite emphatically humorous. This has to do with the standardizing of the genre, which has made the joke always directly recognizable as an attempt at humor. Moreover, joke tellers do often quite emphatically "perform". The framing of the interaction as humorous is thus made very clear. This is why joke haters see jokes as becoming very quickly "predictable" (which mainly means that you know a punch line is coming), "exaggerated" and "emphatic". The joke teller puts pressure on his audience to laugh; the audience feels almost obligated to answer the humorous tone by smiling or laughing.

People also stay in the humorous frame for quite a time during the telling of a joke. As a consequence of this, the atmosphere becomes pointedly funny. The emphatic nature of the joke brings with it a certain effusiveness: joke telling implies a thorough and exuberant story style, the mimicking of voices, accents and all sorts of gestures. Joke tellers often love this part and say: "with gestures and actions, you can make it luscious. Then you can present almost any joke and make it amusing" (Gerrit Helman). "What I look for is jokes where you can use accents and movements and that sort of thing. You have to dare to do it of course. But it's brilliant." (Jasper Bentinck, 20, student at secondary vocational school) All these arm gestures and mock voices make the telling of jokes anything but modest. Other forms of humor are by no means as lavish in their presentation: irony and understatement are diametrically opposed to the joke in this respect.

The last aspect of performance in which jokes differ from other forms of humor is their lavishness. It takes a few minutes to tell a joke and this time element also contributes to the status-seeking element. Other forms of humor have less to do with storying and can be much briefer. This exuberance is both loved and hated too. "If you hear some people telling a joke, and then so effusively, with a separate voice for everyone, you can really get into it, you can see it right in front of your eyes", said Hanneke Meertens (38, planner). But: "it just goes on and on", sighed Ton Linge.

The joke differs from other humorous communication due to the factors mentioned: the telling of a joke has specific social effects (disruption, exuberance), the joke teller presents a certain image of himself (sociable, cheerful, competitive, masculine, daring), and the joke is performed in a recognizable, explicitly humorous way. A "profile" of this sort can be sketched for each humorous genre: irony, funny stories, personal anecdotes, teasing, practical jokes, witty remarks, sarcasm, playful insults, boasting or exaggeration all have characteristics that strongly influence the social effect, self-presentation and overall performance. How the idiosyncrasies of the genre are valued is then a question of communication style. Not everyone sees the same type of communication as funny, pleasant or inviting.

Gender and speech

A huge amount of literature exists about the differences in the use of speech between men and women (Crawford 1995; Kothoff 2006; Lakoff 1975; Tannen 1993, 1994). Very briefly, the findings amount to the following. Women use language primarily to establish contact with others. Men generally talk more (in contrast to the existing stereotype), are more decided and more aggressive than women and emphasize while speaking information transfer and the establishment of status differences. The image arising here sometimes sounds like a towering stack of clichés about masculinity and femininity (Crawford 1989), but many studies from the field of sociolinguistics and conversation analysis, confirm this general pattern. However, there is some debate about the role of humor in these linguistic sex roles. Most studies suggest that these gender differences do lead to different uses of humor by men and women, but the stereotype that women use less humor, engage less in humor, or initiate less humor, seems not to be confirmed (Holmes 2006; Kothoff 2006; Robinson and Smith-Lovin 2001).

A comparison of descriptions of women's communication styles with the characterization of joke telling above makes clear that telling jokes does not fit readily into the average woman's communication style. Jokes are relatively impersonal, uncooperative, disruptive and competitive, while women tend to be cooperative, personal, involved and not particularly focused on status, competition or establishing hierarchical relationships. Women, in speaking, focus more directly on the person spoken to; there is more turn-taking; more interruptions; more questions are asked, while a joke teller speaks for longer and thus takes control of the conversation.

This approach to men's and women's language has also been used for research into humor. Kothoff (1986), for example, has analyzed the conversations of German women, who may be closer in speech styles to the Dutch than the Americans portrayed in most sociolinguistic studies. She concluded that: "women joke about themselves and their experiences. For them, humor is a way to create solidarity and intimacy" (22). In contrast, men use humor as a "way to establish dominance" (19). Recent conversation analysis studies also show how men's and women's humor styles tend to vary between social contexts and social groups, and more generally, how people can use humor in various ways depending on their conversational goals. However, even though later studies nuanced this sharp distinction between status-seeking males and solidarity-creating women, men's humor general emerges from studies as less personal and more hierarchical, whereas women's humor tends to be more self-directed and supportive. Moreover, as Kothoff (2006) notes, women still encounter more barriers in their use of humor, especially more aggressive or transgressive humor.

These gender differences are also reflected in the objections of female respondents to jokes. As mentioned, women objected to the "predictability" of jokes, to the fact that the joke teller "wants all the attention" and to their impersonal nature. The objections to exaggeration and attention seeking are clearly connected to this competitive and status-seeking character of joke telling:

They find themselves much too funny. (Anna Pijlstra, 45, unemployed, general secondary education)

One joke is funny, but when they go on for ages? Repulsive! It *has to* be funny. You *have to* laugh. While I just want to *talk* about something some of the time. (Frouke Huizinga, 29, assistant to grade school teacher)

Added to this is the risky character of joke telling: women will be less quick to take risks like this. These gender differences in communication style also explain why women who like jokes still don't tell them: even if they have no objections to this male attention seeking, they will themselves be more careful and more cooperative in their humor. Part of this has to do with complementary gender roles.

The objections to the impersonal nature of jokes also cover hearing jokes from another. This is an objection mainly stated by more highly educated women:

I'm not any good at jokes. I can laugh at jokes but I like puns a lot better. And situations. The humor in what you have with someone, what you share. But, well, you're talking about jokes, aren't you? (Marga van Stolwijk, 48, psychiatric nurse)

OK. About jokes. Do you like jokes?
Sometimes I do, but actually more, um, spontaneous jokes. Funny happenings. Things that happen out of the blue, I get a real belly laugh out of things like that. Oh oh, I just thought of something. Shall I tell you a spontaneous joke, something that really happened? [She tells an anecdote about an embarrassing happening] Now that was a spontaneous joke. Yeah, joke, happening, something humorous, something that makes me think, well, if you'd wanted to make it up, you'd never've thought of it. (Marijke van der Moer, 34, high school teacher)

A number of times I asked my respondents, both men and women, what they imagined female humor to be. It is quite telling that they very often did not know how to answer, whereas everyone immediately could imagine what male humor was. Anke Vermeer did have an answer: she described the humor that she preferred to "old boys' humor":

Of course it's great if there's a sort of ping-pong and the atmosphere is just getting funnier and funnier. A couple of years ago I was at a book presentation, sitting with a woman friend on chairs while the director of an important publishing company [name] sat on the floor, because the place was really small. He was a bit fattish, older – at least, not all that much older than I was – but he certainly wasn't waiting breathlessly for his twenty-first birthday. The three of us started fantasizing about possible headings in the paper: "[name]'s Boss sawed loose from bookstore floor." "Publishing

house head man mowed down by kindergarten children at kids' book gala."
One thing led to the next and it just kept getting funnier. I like that more
than anything. There's a flow to it that builds and builds. At least it's not
some guy on his own acting funny [laughs], although I can really enjoy that
too. I mean, as long as I don't have to live with the guy. But anyway. I've
got no idea whether he liked it, but we were really going strong. I've got a
couple of women friends, yes, particularly women, and we do that sort of
thing in spades. You end up giggling yourself to death because the back and
forth just gets funnier and funnier. But jokes, no, I don't know about jokes.
(Anke Vermeer)

This is a sort of "shared humorous fantasy": a funny situation is commun-
ally thought up and then filled in further and further. This is also the sort of
humor described as women's humor by Kothoff (1986, 2006) and Lampert
and Ervin-Tripp (1998, 2006). This type of humor is less risky, individual,
disruptive and competitive than telling jokes. The same goes for short
funny remarks and witticisms but also for funny stories and anecdotes
where there is always room for interruption and that, moreover, can be told
cooperatively. "One's own nonsense", "spontaneous jokes" and "humor
about what you share" probably come as close possible to what could be
called female humor. All of these types of humor are completely different
sorts of social activity and they create a completely different sort of atmosphere than jokes.

Class and speech

In contrast with gender differences in communication styles, research results on communication styles of the highly and the less highly educated is
scarce indeed. Practically no research has been done into communication
styles of different classes – none in the Netherlands and very little outside.
If one reflects that language use is rather generally seen as one of the most
recognizable marks of class, this becomes even more surprising. There are
more than enough stereotypes about class differences and language use;
these include the bellowing and blustering, laughing laborer, who speaks a
juicy dialect and doesn't avoid obscenities, the bank director with a plum in
his mouth, being addressed jovially by one-time fraternity buddies as "old
man" and the academic, inserting his "ums" and extra, abstract verbiage
into his slow formulations.

    One of the best-known studies of class and speech is the work by Bern-
stein (1971). He described how the "linguistic codes" of different classes

play a role in social success: he contrasted the "restricted code" of the working classes with the "elaborate code" of the (upper) middle classes. However, his approach has been criticized for its portrayal of the speech of workers as deficient. Bourdieu also described "linguistic capital" as one of the social success factors (1977, 1991). Linguistic capital, the competence to speak a language in a socially valued way, along with cultural capital (knowledge, education, taste) and economic capital (money, property) make up a person's social capital. Bourdieu has also noted how different speech styles are valued in different social milieus (Bourdieu 1991: 66–89).

A comparison of the interviews with the highly and less highly educated does provide indications of their communication styles, partly because the objections against telling jokes are often objections against a manner of communicating. Naturally, standards for communication styles do not provide a complete image of the way in which people relate to each other.

People were often very explicit about the types of humorous communication they liked and even more explicit about what they *did not* like. People always find it easier to say why they dislike something than to say why they like it. As was apparent from already quoted opinions of joke lovers, they liked joke telling particularly because it was "sociable" (*gezellig*) and created "good atmosphere". What some of them added to this was that telling jokes resembled friendly "competition". A number of them connected this with the playfully insulting way of being together ("horsing around", "pestering") also mentioned in different (British) investigations as being typical of men from the working class (Collinson 1988; Paton and Filby 1998; Willis 1977). Gerrit Helman described an atmosphere as follows: "Yeah with men it's sort of – what I see when we're together is teasing and needling, a bit of larking around." And Martin van de Ven (30, truck driver) said: "Just having a bit of fun. Then I say to someone, 'hey you son-of-a-bitch', but I don't mean it. It's just goofing off. Then we both have a laugh."

While joke lovers in their arguments for jokes often didn't get much further than sociable, having a ball and maybe a bit of pestering, the more highly educated were very clear in their objections *against* jokes. Other than in the women's case, I will deal here only with their objections and not with the humor they prefer. This will be thoroughly dealt with in the following two chapters.

Corine Steen's objections to joke tellers have been quoted earlier ("you can't get a word in edgewise"). Highly educated people often call jokes forced, predictable and disruptive. Rob de Laat was the most damning: "I can enjoy a single joke now and then. But then up pops someone else with one and the first guy wants to outdo him and then you get into a chain reaction of some sort. And then everything just fizzles out. I think it destroys the atmosphere." Just as Corine Steen does, this respondent objects to the competitive aspects of joke telling. De Laat's objections also have to do with the emphatically humorous framing of jokes. An atmosphere clearly intended to be humorous is created and for De Laat this later just fizzles out. Steen added to this that she "doesn't get any energy at all" from joke telling; Ton Linge called the atmosphere "tiring"; Marijke van der Moer thought it was "just not funny".

Higher middle-class interviewees prefer less "emphatic" forms of humor: more restrained, shorter, witty remarks. The emphatic "presentation" of jokes is for this reason not very popular with the more highly educated either. This becomes quite clear when one looks at the more "intellectual" entertainers such as Freek de Jonge, who has often poked fun at really "dishing up" the jokes, sabotaging the "presentation" of the punch line.

Many of the highly educated also think that joke telling is loud or exaggerated. "I'm fond of a more restrained humor, more refined jokes," Ton Linge told me. This loudness of jokes is probably connected to the effusiveness that often plays an important role in their telling – the gestures, the raised voice, the imitation of accents. I would like to suggest that often the more highly educated in the Netherlands tend to prefer a certain reserve and tend not to be exuberant. The contrast between loudness and restraint is probably also the central contrast in more stereotyped images of class and language use: laborers roar with laughter while reserved intellectuals wring out a single ironic remark.

The more highly educated are also keener on personal ingenuity. This was very clear in their objections to jokes: they wanted humor that "meant something" and that was "spontaneously invented". This points to other priorities in judging humor: ready wit instead of pleasant atmospheres. Central importance was given by the highly educated to the possibility of rendering one's own experience in a humorous story:

> I don't live in a world where jokes are told. One of the reasons is that all the people around me are really verbal types who tend to transform their own work into something to be laughed at, at the very least into anecdotes. And they're really good at it too. So why would you need someone else's jokes? Not that the kinds of people I spend time with don't propound a heap of nonsense... it can be really irrelevant. But it's our own special brand of nonsense. (Anke Vermeer)

The objections of the more highly educated, and then the men as well, resemble the objections of women. Joke telling doesn't combine particularly well with their communication styles and some of the reasons for this are the same as those given when comparing jokes with women's communication styles: joke telling is too predictable and too impersonal. In general, the typing of the female communication style seems applicable to the upper middle class too (and within this, particularly to the sectors with a lot of cultural capital). The highly educated, just as many women do, tend to avoid competitive and disruptive communication. The upper middle class, at least in the Netherlands, is generally very sensitive to references to status differences and tries to emphasize these as little as possible.

Highly educated interviewees seemed inclined to communicate more "cooperatively": their speech included more questions and less decided statements; they took turns more often and they invited confirmation more often – all aspects deemed to characterize women's communication. Joke lovers and those with the least education were extremely decided in their speech, talked for longer, did not ask questions in return and often emphasized their own competence. In many ways, the manner of speaking of the highly educated (and their general behavior) can be characterized as "feminine", or at least less expressly masculine. I have already referred to a possible explanation for this, the fact that women's and men's domains are less separate in higher middle-class culture. The more cultivated behavior of the higher classes also has something womanly in the eyes of the lower classes. Bourdieu (1977, 1991: in particular 66–89) has written on this topic that laborers often see the speaking styles and the more cultivated or restrained behavior of the bourgeois French as effeminate:

> From the standpoint of the dominated classes, the values of culture and refinement appear as feminine, and identifying with the dominant class, in one's speech for example, entails accepting a way of using the body which is seen as effeminate ("putting on airs and graces", "la-di-da", "toffee-nosed", "stuck-up", "pansy", "mincing"), as a repudiation of masculine values. This – together with the special interest women have in symbolic production – is one of the factors separating men from women with respect to culture and taste: women can identify with the dominant culture without cutting themselves off from their class so radically as men. (Bourdieu: 1977 661)

Conversely, pronounced masculine behavior at higher levels is seen as raw and too little civilized. This all on its own could perhaps make telling jokes in the eyes of the upper middle class a perfect example of bad taste: it is so emphatically masculine.

On the contrary, this same emphatic masculinity within the working and the lower middle class is an important form of capital: a real man has to show that he is not affected, tarted up, conceited etc. A joke serves very well, not only because of the speaking style but also the word choice and the content. Even though a joke teller might not reach great heights in the taste hierarchy of Netherlands society, within his own group his specific competence can win him distinction and respect. Bourdieu writes in this vein about working class pubs where people go "to laugh and to make others laugh and everyone must do his best to contribute to the exchange of comments and jokes" and "to participate actively in a collective pastime capable of giving the participants a feeling of freedom from daily necessities, and of producing and atmosphere of social euphoria and economic freedom." In an environment like this "the possession of a talent for being 'the life and soul of the party', capable of incarnating, at the cost of a conscious and constant labour and accumulation, the ideal of the 'funny guy' which crowns an approved form of sociability, is a very precious form of capital" (Bourdieu 1991: 99).

Conclusion: Objections to jokes and criteria for good humor

Many objections to jokes, but also arguments in their favor, can be interpreted in terms of communication styles. Both joke lovers and joke haters speak about jokes as a manner of relating to others, as a form of self-presentation and as a performance appealing to others to a greater or lesser extent. The concept communication style provides insight into where class and gender differences in valuing humor – not just jokes – come from.

The fact that someone else possesses or prefers a different way of communicating leads not only to miscommunication and misunderstandings but also to discomfort, distaste or embarrassment: social emotions connected to a failed or wrongly placed performance. Naturally, individual jokes can also cause these feelings. The content of a joke and the humorous technique definitely play a role in its success. However, I think that the content of jokes is also partially a consequence of their diffusion. Jokes are produced and reproduced for certain groups. And even if people in those groups are not aware that they are taking part as a group or on behalf of a certain group, the jokes will nevertheless reflect the world image of those who tell them most.

However, the highly and the less highly educated, men and women, make different demands on the content of humor. The criteria for good humor discussed in the previous chapter – refinement, restraint and authenticity – can be recognized in places in the objections against joke telling. The criteria of refinement and restraint, as can be expected, primarily play a role for the more highly educated: they think jokes too effusive, too emphatic, too unrefined and too aggressive. Less educated women share these objections but they have a number of passive joke lovers among them. Refinement and restraint are criteria easily applied to communication styles. To tell a joke is indeed less restrained than producing a deadpan witticism: a witty comparison is easily more refined than a bawdy joke.

Authenticity is less easy to connect to communication style – I, at least, am not aware of an unequivocal criterion for the authenticity of an announcement, a joke or a speaking style. What is more, less agreement exists about what "real", "sincere" and "authentic" are. While both women and the highly educated often remarked that they saw it as a weakness that jokes were not individually created – and therefore not particularly personal, creative or authentic – this was not an objection acknowledged by joke tellers. Authenticity for joke tellers does not lie in the content of the joke but in its "presentation". And, in presenting a joke, naturally they see themselves as authentic: each joke teller thinks he has his own style, his own repertoire and his own way of "feeling" who will like which joke. Additionally, joke telling is experienced as spontaneous, companionable and thus: authentic. Jokes tellers think this activity much more real, more honest, friendlier, more direct and more spontaneous than the "affected behavior" of bosses, professors, directors and the lady researcher from the university. What is real and authentic plays an important role in judging not only humor but also persons, relationships and communication. But what real and authentic actually mean – on that point men and women, laborers, tradesmen and the university educated do not see eye to eye. For that reason, they cannot agree about jokes.

Chapter 4
The humor divide: Class, age, and humor styles

"Jokes, that's not humor," said Bart Winia, a 33-year-old graphic designer, when I interviewed him. "That's why I thought it was awful back then when your letter came saying you were doing research on humor, and based it on jokes." For him, and many like him, the telling of jokes has nothing to do with humor.

The joke tellers I spoke to all thought that telling jokes was almost identical with a good sense of humor. When I asked one of them, 25-year-old technical installer Richard Westbroek: "Do your friends have the same sense of humor as you?" he answered: "Yeah, you could say they tell the same types of jokes." And Christiaan van der Linden, a 35-year-old administrator described himself: "I think that I'm pretty down-to-earth but I have a good sense of humor. Actually I can really tell jokes well but can't laugh very hard at them. You've got people who can't tell jokes but laugh up a storm when they hear them." Note how van der Linden equates sense of humor with telling jokes (his own) and laughing at jokes (by others).

"Sense of humor" is a term that, just like "style", "taste" and "class", is used in both the descriptive and the appreciative sense. When someone is said to have a sense of humor, what is meant is: a good sense of humor – and what people mean by this will become clear in the following chapter. But people also speak of an unusual, special, nice, original, irritating, revolting, coarse, absurd or refined sense of humor. "Sense of humor" then indicates a certain style or taste in the area of humor. People have widely divergent ideas about what nice, good, funny or rather irritating, uninteresting, *un*funny humor is. They have different tastes as far as humor goes, different *humor styles*.

Some people have a humor style that includes a preference for jokes – for them a joke teller is someone with a sense of humor. But there are also tastes in the area of humor where jokes are completely excluded: in the preceding chapter, people were quoted who did not like jokes, but did like irony or humorous anecdotes about actual experiences. A shared humor style – a shared interpretation of a good sense of humor – is crucial to making a joke or telling a joke. If people differ too much from each other in this, a joke can almost not succeed.

In this chapter, I describe Dutch humor styles and their relationship to the joke. Like communication styles, these humor styles are connected with social and cultural distinctions. The thrust of this chapter, like the preceding, is style difference: a broader preference for a certain type of humor, a certain style or atmosphere that can be found in divergent jokes, performances, humorists and situations. I will begin my exploration of this style difference with standardized humor: comedians, writers, television programs.

Humor styles: High and low, old and young

The simplest way to track down humor styles is by looking at the patterns in the survey responses. I will take the results of the questionnaire as my starting point for my exploration of Dutch humor styles and their relationship to the joke. In the questionnaire I asked people not only to judge a list of jokes, I also asked how humorous they found certain television programs, comedians, comics and writers. Not all these persons and programs were exclusively humorous. I included, for example, Gerard Reve, who is primarily a writer. Ron Brandsteder too, the presenter of *Moppentoppers*, was added because he was emphatically put forward as the humorous face of the television station RTL4. All the names of persons and TV programs mentioned here are described in the glossary at the end of this book.

These judgments I analyzed with statistical techniques for tracking down correspondences in groups of data: if someone likes a certain comedian, which comedians or television programs does he like as well? Different analytical methods ultimately gave more or less the same – simple – answer: the analysis again and again turned up roughly the same four groups of humorists and television programs.

A graphical representation of these groups can be found in Figure 1. In this figure, three partially overlapping groups can be recognized. The first group that I call *veterans* is in the top left quadrant. This consists of older writers, comedians and comics. Many of them are deceased: Simon Carmiggelt, Toon Hermans, Wim Kan, Annie M. G. Schmidt, Wim Sonneveld and Max Tailleur. The people in this cluster who are still alive have been comedians for long time, and mostly have a rather tradition style: Paul van Vliet, Adèle Bloemendaal and Tineke Schouten. The appreciation for this cluster is connected with age: the older one was, the funnier one found them.

A second cluster, the *celebrities*, is not clear in Figure 1 but apparent from the factor analysis shown in Table 3. It was also connected with age but vice versa: the younger, the funnier. This cluster concerns the appreciation of three very well-known comedians, Freek de Jonge, Youp van 't Hek and Paul de Leeuw. This cluster was appreciated more by men than by women and is thus the only cluster to show a gender effect. Men and women appreciated de Leeuw equally. This is due to van 't Hek en de Jonge, who are considerably more popular with men. The appreciation of these humorists has little to do with jokes.

In addition to these two clusters connected with age, I found two groups connected with educational level. The first of these tastes includes André van Duin, Sylvia Millecam, Ron Brandsteder, Tineke Schouten, Max Tailleur and the TV programs *Banana Split, Flodder, Moppentoppers, Ook dat nog, Over de roooie* and *Oppassen!*. Thus, this cluster overlaps with the veteran cluster to some extent. These humorists and programs are found in the lower left of the figure. In this cluster: the lower their education, the funnier respondents find these humorists and television programs. The appreciation of this cluster is strongly connected with appreciating jokes. The humor in this cluster also often has to do with jokes: directly in the case of *Moppentoppers*, Brandsteder and Tailleur, indirectly with van Duin and Schouten who use jokes disguised as a sketch, or included in a monologue.

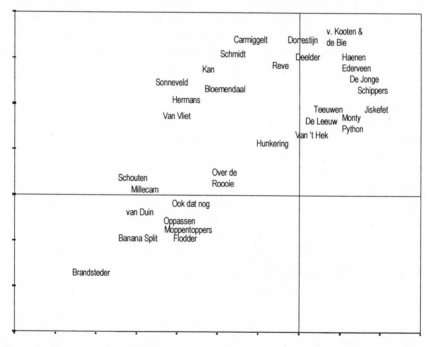

Figure 1. Humor styles: the appreciation of humorists and humorous TV programs (PRINCALS analysis)[10]

Table 3. Humor styles, social background, and joke appreciation[11]
Appreciation was judged on a 5-point scale. Knowledge of items in a taste
is represented as a scale from 0 (knows none) to 1 (knows all).

	Mean	SD	α		Relation with		
				Joke rating	Education	Age	Gender
Veterans							
Appreciation	3.27	.73	.81	.19**	-.04	.47**	n.s.
Knowledge	.94	.15		-.06	-.08	.37**	n.s.
Celebrities							
Appreciation	3.66	.93	.63	.11	.02	-.37**	M > F*
Knowledge	.99	.00		-.03	.07	.00	n.s.
Popular							
Appreciation	2.90	.75	.87	.45**	-.27**	.24**	n.s.
Knowledge	.87	.14		.12*	-.19**	-.24**	n.s.
Highbrow							
Appreciation	3.20	.70	.76	.01	.18**	-.13*	n.s.
Knowledge	.66	.23		-.10	.35**	-.11	n.s.

* p< .05
** p<.01

The final taste is connected more indirectly with educational level. This cluster, visible above on the right in the figure, contains six television programs of which five are (predominantly) screened by the VPRO broadcasting corporation: *Jiskefet, Haenen voor de nacht, van Kooten en de Bie, Monty Python* and *Absolutely Fabulous*. The last television program in this group is *De hunkering (The yearning)*, a rather unusual and not very empathetic dating show with Theo van Gogh that was aired only in 1997, the year I sent out the questionnaire. Additionally, this group includes the following cabaret artists/poets/writers (some are difficult to classify): Jules Deelder, Hans Dorrestijn, Arjen Ederveen, Wim T. Schippers, Freek de Jonge, Annie M. G. Schmidt and Gerard Reve. Hans Teeuwen, who currently is one of the most popular comedians, mostly among young people, but still relatively unknown when I did this research, belongs to this group as well. The appreciation of this group is to some extent, but not strongly, related to educational level. The influence of education lies here not so much in the appreciation as in the renown: the percentage of humorists and programs respondents said they knew, separate from what they thought of them, was clearly connected with education. Or: many of the more lowly educated simply did not know the items in this cluster and thus had no opinion about them. This connection exists too for the individual items: the appreciation of none of the humorists/television programs in this cluster correlated with educational level; but, with the exception of de Jonge (whom everyone knew) and *De Hunkering* (that almost no one knew), the respondents who did know the humorist or the program were significantly more highly educated than the respondents who did not know them.

These last two tastes can best be described as highbrow and popular or lowbrow humor. I am duly aware that these are not truly neutral designations. This problem of loaded terms is inherent in research into taste: taste difference is by definition not neutral, because it is almost always connected with social status differences. The associations – both positive and negative – called up by these terms are largely the same as those called up by the type of humor in these styles. And these are precisely the associations and distinctions that form the heart of this chapter, maybe even this whole book: distinctions having to do with taste and class differences.

The most problematic concepts are without doubt the terms having to do with low taste. While highbrow can sound quite elitist, this concept has social hierarchy on its side. Referring to tastes as lowbrow or popular quickly reeks of snobbism, and its Dutch equivalent, *volks*, is even more dubious. However, especially in the field of humor, people see these terms as positive: a *Moppentoppers* editor told me that they produced "really popular humor", for "the man in the street" – and he was clearly proud of this. Toon Hermans has always preferred to advertise himself as a "humorist for the common man". Shortly before he died, he proudly described himself as someone who was definitely not a *cabaretier*, but instead, he said: "My humor is meant for the common man and will always stay that way" (van Bilsen 1999).

Several interviewees stressed the positive affinity between humor and lower class, often using the Dutch word *volks* (popular, common, working class, of the people) to denote both themselves and their humor. Four of the joke tellers proudly said that they were "real boys of the common folk" (*volksjongens*). Others told stories filled with nostalgia about the "working-class neighborhood" (*volksbuurten*) they came from. In these stories featuring neighborhoods and common folk, humor played a large role: the word *volks* evokes "a good sense of humor".

As longshoreman Albert Reiziger said: "Crooswijk is Rotterdam's salt-of-the-earth neighborhood and that's where I come from. I think Crooswijk, being the working-class district it is, has more humor than the gentlemen's hangouts on the canals, don't you? A neighborhood like that, just like in Amsterdam, most humor comes from there, I think." Common neighborhoods, common men and working-class pubs – all these call up associations with jokes, laughing and a sociable atmosphere.

The feeling that humor is connected with common people was regularly expressed in the interviews. It was behind the words of Jaap van Noord, cited in the previous chapter, "that at the University a bit more laughter could be a good thing". It played a role too in the words of the 52-year-old shipwright at a wharf who talked about "a yearning at the top for diversion":

> We've all got nicknames, Tough Tony, Wild Woody, that sort of thing. Yeah, that's what we call each other. You probably don't do that at the university. I was on the works council for a while and got to talking to the director and well, I couldn't really avoid the nicknames, could I? He got curious and wanted to know all about it. He thought they were really funny and ended up asking me for a list. Well, I didn't mind, did I? Just goes to show you that there's a yearning at the top for diversion. (Harm Arends)

This sentiment was most clearly put into words by Bart Winia, one of the upwardly mobile, a graphic designer from, in his own words, "a working-class background":

> I noticed it at the art academy too, you know: people often see humor as something for the lower classes. I think I'd never have been able to finish university and then I'm only talking about the atmosphere there. Yeah, it's not a big thing if you feel good in a bit of a sterile – it seems sterile to me anyway – if you feel okay with that then there's no problem. But I'm glad to go off with some friends on my motorcycle now and then, that's a different atmosphere altogether. And I've trained in fitness centers and trained others too and that's another kettle of fish entirely, isn't it? And the guys behind the stalls on the market, they're a real laugh.
> But my question is, and maybe this is what your research is all about: what happens to the ones that go on studying, what's the psychology behind the fact that they treat humor the way they do? Listen, I'm not saying they've got to go around telling jokes all day long, but I think they're awfully inhibited when it comes to a good laugh. Because I've been to parties on account of my girlfriend [university graduate, GK] and, well, you'd be hard put to detect any humor going on at them. That's so strange to me because it's such an easy way to get to know each other. (Bart Winia)

Popular, lowbrow, and common are therefore, particularly where humor is concerned, not an exclusively condescending term. It calls up a mixture of positive and negative associations that penetrate to the essence of what I hope to discuss here

The judgment of humorists and television programs is connected with two social divisions: highly and less highly educated (meaning college education or higher and no college education), old and young. Gender differences played a surprisingly small role. As apparent from the figure, the contradictions run through one another: in a diminished way, the high-low educational level is seen again in the veteran cluster. The two mainstream *cabaretiers* Wim Sonneveld and Wim Kan occupy a central position in this cluster, between the highbrow writers Schmidt and Carmiggelt and the more popular performers Hermans, van Vliet, Tailleur and Schouten.

Preference for and aversion to veterans and celebrities are primarily connected with considerations about content. Many older people reject de Jonge, de Leeuw and van 't Hek because they are crude, while younger generations cannot appreciate the older humorists because they don't understand their references, or because they find them corny, slow or sanctimonious. Additionally, many young people don't even know these humorists because they are from "before their time". The boundary between style and content is, however, not very sharp: the coarseness so often complained of by those who are older is not only a question of differing pain thresholds, but also has to do with pursuing shock effects: a humorous style that became popular in the 1970s. However, questions of content weigh more heavily here than do those of style.

The high-low partition is more a question of style. It is difficult to connect with the theme of the humor or the extent of the coarseness. The unfamiliarity with the elite cluster is not as easy to explain as the unfamiliarity with older humorists, for whom some people are simply too young. The humorists and television programs in both clusters are available, in principle, to everyone; after all they all are shown on television. The difference between these two types of humor lies not in content but sooner in tone, approach, design, presentation and more generally, in the atmosphere it excludes: in style.

Not all humor allows itself be sociologized easily: approximately a quarter of comedians, comics and television programs on the list fell outside the four humor tastes. That is not to say that they were not valued, only that there is question of more individual taste variations that cannot be connected with a broader taste or social background. This is true, strikingly enough, of almost all non-Dutch television programs. Programs such as *Cheers, Friends, Laurel & Hardy, Married with Children* or *Tom & Jerry*, all of which have been very successful on Dutch TV, could not be connected in any way whatsoever with the appreciation of other programs or with social background. A number of Dutch humorists did not fit one single taste either: popular comics such as Harry Jekkers, Brigitte Kaandorp and Herman Finkers placed neither in the old-young nor the high-low category.

It is often said today that tastes are becoming more and more diffuse, that people have lots of space from which to choose their own style, that social background no longer has such an impact, and particularly: that classical contrasts between high and low culture are disappearing further and further (Crane 1992; van Eijck 1999; van Eijck and van Rees 2000; Katz-Gerro 2002; Lopez-Sintas and Katz-Gerro 2005). Marketing and promotional research switched some time ago to a much more intricate partitioning into lifestyle and 'orientation' that have very little to do with simple sociological background variables. In various corners of sociology, the death knell has been sounded for class as a useful theoretical concept (e.g. Pakulski and Waters 1996; Beck 2002). From this perspective, the (double) dichotomy I found was surprisingly simple: apparently, simply sociological background variables go a long way in explaining something as "personal" as sense of humor.

Style, status, and knowledge

The double taste dichotomy apparent from the questionnaire points to the existence of class cultures and age cultures, with accompanying taste and style differences. Class cultures, however, have to do with status too: the highly educated reject the taste of those without a college education, while their own style of humor remains inaccessible for those with a lower status. Even their *judgment* of humor styles of others is kept by the highly educated outside the others' reach. Lovers of popular humor are as little aware of the status of this humor in the eyes of those who love highbrow humor as they are of the fact that the joke is so little known in higher circles. This pattern of rejecting the other and making one's own inaccessible typifies elite taste; you see it also in classical music and literature. High taste is exclusive in the literal sense of the word; it excludes people (Bourdieu 1984; Gans 1999).

The less highly educated often didn't know the humorists and the television programs in the highbrow cluster. The relationship between knowledge and appreciation was asymmetrical here: the highly educated do not like the humor of the less highly educated; but the less highly educated don't even *know* the highbrow humor. For that matter, this works in the other direction in to a lesser extent: the highly educated are not always completely aware of lowbrow humor. How this works can be easily seen in

Figure 2, showing the appreciation of and the familiarity with highbrow humorists and television programs. Familiarity with highbrow humor is connected with education; within the group of the highly educated, part does and part doesn't appreciate it. You could say that a high educational level is a prerequisite for coming into contact with highbrow humor; and from that point on people can apparently decide whether they like it or not. A comparable figure for the popular shows a much less ambiguous relationship between educational level and appreciation. The "not knowing" is in any case much rarer; practically everyone knows the humorists and the programs in this cluster.

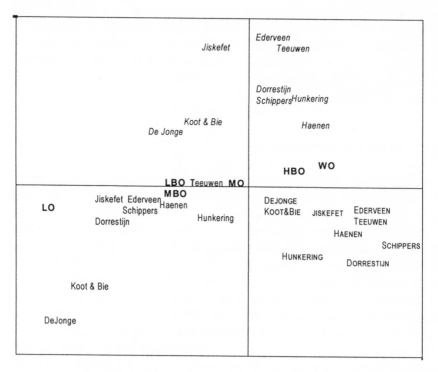

Figure 2.   Education and appreciation and knowledge of highbrow humor (PRINCALS-analysis). CAPITAL font = preference for (choice 4 or 5 on a five-point scale); *italics* = dislike of (choice 1, 2 or 3 on a five-point scale); ordinary font = no knowledge of it.
LO, LBO, MBO, MO, HBO, WO: Dutch educational levels ranked from lowest (LO) to highest (WO) level. For explanation of educational levels, see Table 2.

This may sound like a tangent – how do people move through the media? This is a broader question than just how people make choices from available television shows. It is about the way social position influences how people become aware of the existence of cultural phenomena, from *Moppentoppers* or Hans Teeuwen to the newest joke. In the case of jokes, the acquisition pattern can still be understood: knowledge of jokes is a direct result of social networks. If you are in the wrong environment, you seldom hear jokes. But for humorists and television programs, this is more difficult to imagine. Everyone in the Netherlands gets the same television programs beamed into their living rooms, but apparently people are only aware of a portion of what the television brings in.

Before I go further into the question of why people find something funny, the question of how certain types of humor enter a person's field of vision therefore must be asked. This is perhaps best seen by considering Arjan Ederveen. Shortly before my first interviews, he had caused a sensation in "my circles" with *Dertig Minuten* [Thirty Minutes], a series of slow, carefully acted, fake documentaries, for which he also won various awards. The most famous of the series is probably "born in the wrong body", about a farmer in Groningen who submits to a race-change operation: he is rebuilt as a Negro. Parody would hardly be adequate to cover this, for parody the tone of a documentary about a radical psychic process is too exactly maintained. Whether it was humor or in deadly earnest was actually no longer possible to say.

The questionnaire shows that only 51 percent knew Ederveen. Among the joke tellers almost no one knew him and the few who did were simply not interested: "Once, long ago, I saw the program", said Gerrit Helman, "after that I never watched it again. I don't really know it at all. It doesn't get to me." Comparable uninterested comments were made about other people and programs in this cluster, such as this one by Kees van Dokkum about Hans Dorrestijn: "It doesn't do anything for me. He stands there crooning on television and then I go yeah, could be, but it's simply not for me. Not even the character because I just don't care at all, but no, it doesn't do a thing for me. I don't have the antennae, I guess." This is how highbrow humor stays outside someone's field of vision: a program or a humorist leaves someone unamused, untouched but not irritated or angered either. There is not a single objection to content. Often it simply doesn't register; one doesn't even remember having seen it. It doesn't "do anything" for people – the humor doesn't and neither does the person, the story, the theme and the style.

Better known humorists and programs from the highbrow cluster were often rejected on similar grounds: not based on concrete objections but because they "didn't do anything" for people. The tone in this was often somewhat hesitant: "I don't know, maybe I don't like their faces or something ", said Claudia van Leer about the satirists van Kooten en de Bie, or even more vacillating, by Ton Linge: "van Kooten en de Bie. Yes. No, it could be that it was too highbrow for me, I don't know. Or they're too sharp or something. I didn't like them". People have hardly any arguments, in fact nary a word to explain what they don't like: they see it and nothing happens.

What they do see, if they happen to watch by accident, is often surprisingly different from what I have always thought I saw. On the topic of van Kooten en de Bie, 60-year-old sales representative Ivo Engelsman said: "If they're both dressed as women, well, someone else might like that but it doesn't say anything to me. It strikes me as a bit strange. But someone else could be lying on the floor, hahaha [fake laughter] really funny." He is talking here about van Kooten and de Bie's impersonation of two snooty ladies with pearl necklaces, in whom I had always seen very convincing personages. Engelsman sees a very cheap humorous trick: a man in women's clothes – a pretty banal form of humor, indeed.

A remarkable exclusion mechanism is at work here: people look at the same thing but see something completely different. Or, more accurately: they see *nothing* in it. Apparently there is something about the humor in the highbrow cluster that makes a great number of people, including a portion of the highly educated, lose interest acutely. This disinterest is a direct, irrational reaction, almost as direct as laughter or indignation. It is, indeed, as van Dokkum said, a question of "antennae", of what Bourdieu (1990) calls: habitus. Elsewhere, I have described these disinterested and puzzled reactions as "despondent readings" of humorists and TV programs (Kuipers 2006a).

To be able to appreciate highbrow humor, a habitus is required that not everyone has and that is connected with educational level. The appreciation of this highbrow humor calls for a certain distance comparable to the "esthetic disposition": the esthetic basic attitude also necessary to appreciating modern and abstract art. This esthetic disposition, just as the highbrow humor habitus, is connected with educational level, or more specifically: with cultural capital, with a way of looking, reasoning, reflecting and communicating that people learn at home but that for an important part is also acquired through education. This disposition is characterized by a distant way of viewing beauty and pleasure: not the directly accessible pleasure of something that is at the first glance attractive, beautiful or pleasant, but a pleasure at a greater remove, derived from things you "acquire a taste for". Literature, abstract art or contemporary classical music is not beautiful or pleasant on first acquaintance. Something similar applies to highbrow humor: at first sight it is not immediately funny, sometimes it can even be unpleasant at the beginning: Ederveen at first sight is slow, de Jonge seems in the first instance mainly busy and chaotic, and *Jiskefet*, *De Hunkering* or Hans Teeuwen are sometimes distinctly disturbing.

In practice, this habitus is exclusive but it does not arise purely from snobbism. Laughing at Ederveen is, for people with this habitus and humor style, just as much a reflex reaction as the disinterest of the joke tellers. For the producers of this humor too, this appreciation is automatic: highbrow comedians like Dorrestijn or Ederveen are not "being difficult" on purpose. They are so schooled in a certain idiom that it is no longer difficult for them. The lovers of highbrow humor have other ideas about good and bad humor; this is why they see in this humor something that others do not.

This also works vice versa: lovers of popular humor also see something that others do not see. The difference is that the others do not see *nothing* there, but something they reject: vulgarity, corniness, inanity, maybe they just think it's boring. However, it is not inaccessible in the same way; it can evoke rejection, boredom or annoyance but never this disinterest, born of lack of understanding and almost impossible to put into words. As Egbert van Kaam, one of the joke tellers, aptly remarked: "André van Duin, now that's someone everyone can listen to, one thinks it's corny, the next is laughing till his stomach hurts, but it's accessible to everyone". If the subject is André van Duin, everyone sees something about which he can have an opinion and about which he feels quite justified in having an opinion; for highbrow comedians this is much less the case. This is part of the profit of a higher education; it gives you more and more to reject and look down upon.

Highbrow and lowbrow humor styles

What ensures that humor "does something" for people? What do people see in the humor that they find humorous? The questionnaire describes this but doesn't provide an explanation. Interviews are needed to find this out. Thus, following the questionnaire, I talked extensively to 32 people who had filled the list in about what they think is funny, what they appreciate in their favorite humorists and what they saw when they watched humorous television programs. From this it became apparent that people have very different criteria for good and bad humor.

Three of the four humor styles from the questionnaire appeared possible to recognize in the interviews: the lowbrow style, the highbrow style and the veterans. The cluster with the celebrities, barely visible in the figure too, quickly fell apart during the interviews. Those who liked Freek de Jonge differed quite noticeably from those who liked Paul de Leeuw or Youp van 't Hek, both in their backgrounds and in their other preferences. My impression is that relationship between the appreciation for these three cabaret artists is the consequence of their being very well known: fame automatically leads to increased appreciation, but there is also an element of social desirability here. The veteran style did emerge from the questionnaire but this hardly occurred independently. Eleven interviewees had an above-average appreciation for and knowledge of the veterans, but this style always appeared in the interviews in combination with either a popular, or a highbrow style. During the interviews people often turned out to have a preference for either the more intellectual humorists in this cluster (Wim Kan, Annie Schmidt), or the more popular, like Toon Hermans and Max Tailleur.

The majority of the interviewees appeared well suited to either the highbrow of the popular style. Of the 32 interviewees in the sample, eight had a popular taste; twelve had a higher than average appreciation for and awareness of the highbrow humor style. There were hardly any "omnivores" (Peterson and Simkus 1992; Peterson and Kern 1996; van Eijck 2001) who liked both styles. Only four combined these two tastes, but these four, all men, had distinctly broad taste: they liked all types of humor equally well, thus including the forms of humor that did not fit in any of the styles, such as American comedies and British series. Eight of the interviewees fell outside every style. I will deal later on with these persons and their tastes, preferences and objections, but first I want to discuss the arguments of those who liked the highbrow and lowbrow styles. Why do they find humorists and television programs humorous?

Arguments for lowbrow humor

The lowbrow style was quite visible in the interviews: people who mentioned van Duin also liked Schouten, Millecam, *Moppentoppers, Banana Split, Flodder, Over de roooie* and *Ook dat nog*. Based on the filled-in questionnaire, eight of the interviewees from the sample (25%) fit in this cluster. These people were predominantly educated at primary or secondary level and they all had an above-average appreciation for the jokes. The majority of the joke tellers also had a lowbrow humor style: if I sort their interviews retroactively, 25 of the 34 have a lowbrow humor style. The remaining nine practically all preferred the older humorists, particularly Toon Hermans and Tom Manders (Dorus). André van Duin was the big favorite among the joke tellers, just as – not very surprisingly, since most of them I met during the selection for this show – *Moppentoppers*.

Lovers of lowbrow humor often formulated preference for and aversion to humorists in terms of the person: Tineke Schouten "comes across really hilariously"; Freek de Jonge is a "strange man"; Ron Brandsteder "makes a pleasant impression"; Silvia Millecam is a "wonderful person". The biggest complement that was given here was usually for André van Duin: "You only have to see his face to start laughing". This was also said of Silvia Millecam and Toon Hermans: "Just the way they look. You've just got to laugh" said 35-year-old army cook Patrick Kok. Only people with a popular humor style gave compliments practically equating person and humor. Objections too against people whom they didn't find funny were often directly aimed at the person: "Their faces just don't appeal to me". "Youp van 't Hek just doesn't come across agreeably." "Spontaneity" was highly appreciated in humorists and television programs: most of the comedians in this cluster were spoken highly of for their "spontaneous humor". This is also a characteristic of a person, not only of his humor.

> If I'm watching André van Duin, then it's just as if he's making up what's happening right on the spot, you know. He presents so all of a sudden as if it just occurred to him. I know for sure that that's not the way it is. It's rehearsed. But your feeling is: that comedian's spontaneous. He's not telling that in order to tell a joke but to make people feel sociable (Jan Jurriaans, 73, retired director of sports organization)

"Spontaneity" thus means not only artlessness, that someone comes across naturally. It is mentioned here in one breath with "sociability".

The need for sociability is connected with one more important consideration: that good humor is not hurtful. A funny joke, a good humorist and an amusing program may never "offend" or "insult". One more compliment for André van Duin by this man: "The way he tells something and the jokes too, he's never ever irritating. He doesn't make jokes at someone else's expense, you know." Hurtful humorists and programs are disapproved of. Often those involved were – for me – very unexpected persons. In this way,

Ivo Engelsman said of Wim Kan: "Doesn't appeal to me because he quite regularly offends people in politics and, well, I don't think that's very sociable. I really love pleasant humor without anybody getting hurt. I think that's nice."

"Hurtful" appears to be a slippery concept, that is highly dependent on context. This man objected to Wim Kan who used to offend politicians, while these politicians themselves often went to Kan's shows, sitting in the front row laughing heartily at the jokes at their expense. On the other hand, Engelsman, like many other people with a popular taste, liked ethnic and racist jokes as long as no one belonging to the targeted group was present. He didn't like Paul de Leeuw because he makes fools of people, Freek de Jonge because he goes too far, but he really liked candid camera shows, especially "if they take the mickey out of someone who thinks he knows everything so well and thinks nothing can get to him, and then they've got one more of that sort in their grip, I really like that." Being hurtful does not thus include all humor at the expense of other people. It's allowable as long as certain boundaries are respected. Engelsman formulated the golden rule here: it's not allowed if the victims are present – except when they deserve it.

More important than what exactly counts as hurtful – that will be dealt with later – is for the moment the general statement Engelsman makes about humor: he wants "pleasant humor": it has to remain sociable. Sociable, spontaneous, not hurtful, pleasant, "as soon as I see him I have to laugh" – here we have a description of a person as well as, an atmosphere. The image of good humor that emerges from these descriptions is the sociable evening: good company, pleasant atmosphere, nice people.

Other compliments have to do with the type of humor, apart from atmosphere or personal presentation. One big compliment was simplicity. Almost all lovers of lowbrow humor mentioned this: they liked "simple humor" "that you don't have to think about", that is "just plain funny". As Kees van Dokkum said of André van Duin, probably the most characteristic representative of the lowbrow humor style: "André van Duin is straight from the shoulder, you don't really have to think about it, it is just plain pleasant". A sitcom like *Flodder* shouldn't be too difficult either: "It has to be really relaxed. If I want to go to the kitchen then I can just go to the kitchen. And when I get back, I haven't missed anything [laughs]. It still just as funny". (Frouke Huizinga)

If people appreciate simplicity, "difficult" is naturally an objection. Intellectual humorists like a Freek de Jonge, but also Herman Finkers and

Youp van 't Hek are disapproved of for being too difficult; or because you "really have to pay attention".

> Freek de Jonge. I can't follow him at all. It goes too fast and then I haven't even heard half of it and then I don't even go to the trouble to keep on following it anymore, because by then it's not even interesting to me. If it starts costing too much to I think like: what's all that he's saying? Not that I really hate him or anything. (Claire van Kampen, 37, assistant accountant)

> I don't like Freek de Jonge. I think that humor should be easy. He makes a joke and then a half-hour later he comes back to it and I can't even keep track of that – at least I don't feel like bothering. Then I'm sitting there in the theater and I should be just relaxing, boom direct humor, not having to think back a half-hour, like "oh yeah!" It's not for me. (Gerrit Helman)

This reminds us of the earlier described lack of "antennae" for this humor: these people see it, don't know what to do with it and give quickly.

Almost all the people with the lowbrow style declared their love for impersonations; they found this sort "real humor", "lovely humor". Almost all the humor in this style is also (partially) based on types: van Duin, Schouten, Millecam, van Vliet, *Ook dat nog*, and *Flodder*, they all include highly stereotyped characterizations, complete with accents, costumes, and standardized phrases. Jewish joke teller Max Tailleur might not have used types, but one could say that he really did his best to turn himself into one type, complete with painstakingly emphasized external characteristics such as mustache, a heavy Amsterdam-Jewish accent, and, in the pictures on the covers of his joke books, even with a rather large nose. The other sitcom in this cluster, *Oppassen!* is somewhat less accentuated but does follow, as do all sitcoms, the pattern of the character humor: every personage is in essence a cliché. Types are often spoken highly of for representing craftsmanship and "professionality" – something surprisingly enough said particularly of women. Frouke Huizinga said of Millecam: "Well, she plays a lot of different types, but very, very expertly. I think she's extremely funny too. How she presents it."

"How he/she presents it" was a much-used phrase in these interviews. Just as for the jokes – that belong to this taste – presentation often wins it from content. This is a noticeable difference with the highbrow style, where preference for and aversion to are based on content, thematic material or form of the story. This also explains the marked preference for types (and sketches): this is the most emphatic form of humorous performance. This loving of the performance also determines expectations people have of humor: message or meaning, deeper or more extensive intentions are only mildly appreciated. People are not receptive to a moral – they tend to find it irritating, pedantic or even crude. As Claudia van Leer said: "Well, a comedian doesn't have to have a message as far as I'm concerned. They're there are to amuse you, they don't have to give you a message".

Arguments for highbrow humor

Lovers of highbrow humor use other arguments than lovers of lowbrow humor. In the sample, these accounted for twelve (37.5%) persons who looked differently at humor than the lovers of lowbrow humor. They were less focused on craftsmanship, presentation and "how they present it". Only once was a judgment about a humorist also a judgment about a person. Vincent Zwagerman, a 37-year-old man who quit university to become a carpenter, said of Paul Haenen: "He doesn't make himself anything more than he is. He stays very close to himself. He simply adopts a weak position. And I think that is also the foundation of humor, that you adopt a vulnerable position. At the moment that it's always about someone else, then it can in a way be less funny." While it is also being said here that good humor may not be hurtful, the tone is noticeably different from that of earlier quotes. The humorist is not regarded in the light of the "sociable atmosphere" but judged in terms of personal integrity. The jargon used is almost that of therapy or social work, of "good talks" about relationships and personal problems and not, as above, the language of the "relaxed" evening with "sociable" people.

The interviews with lovers of highbrow humor usually went more supplely than those with the lovers of lowbrow humor. Partially this is connected with educational level: the motivating and explaining of taste is a (in essence rather useless) skill mainly cultivated at colleges and universities. But I could also talk more easily with the less highly educated in this group. I only discovered this when I was working through the interviews in the light of the humor styles: the interviews that were the most supple, the interviews with people whom I experienced as noticeably reflective, the people thus with whom I could talk most easily and whose arguments for good humor I understood the best – were the interviews with people who loved highbrow humor. In this way my own reaction to the interviews unintentionally supports my thesis that a shared feeling for humor is the best foundation for a good conversation.

Arguments for highbrow humor were often formulated in the idiom of art and literary criticism and High Culture. In these talks, the word "artist" fell regularly and often people used an almost literary terminology: "He can formulate it stylistically in such a way that it is precisely that and not anything else. You can say something in a great number of ways and he makes a comparison at the right moment or uses a certain word combination, thus rendering the image with a fine precision. And that wins a laugh. A little while ago I read that thin booklet, containing short stories or short essays. Well, I was doubled up laughing" said Marijke van der Moer about Gerard Reve. Striking here is the mix of literary idiom ("stylistic", "image") with the really rather more vulgar humor vocabulary: "doubled up". Vincent Zwagerman called Paul Haenen an "artist in the area of communication"; Louis Baldé thought Ederveen to be an "original artist"; Roos Schuurman praised de Jonge for the "layered quality" of his stories. It is "more than humor" (Louis Baldé), "beautiful *and* funny" (Marijke van der Moer, Roos Schuurman). These people speak of humor in terms of style, esthetic appeal and originality. In their eyes, the esthetic appeal and humor must reinforce each other: "If it's embedded in a whole story then the jokes stay with me longer. You can recall them. So you can keep on enjoying them after the fact." (Marijke van der Moer)

The most important criterion for good humor in this group is "sharpness": humor has to cause a certain shock. This shock effect may not be "noncommittal" (Louis Baldé) or "superficial" (Bart Winia). In the following quote, Corine Steen is trying to explain the difference between the right and the wrong sort of coarseness:

> With Freek de Jonge at that time, then you had something like "arrggg, along came the yellow car. And at that precise moment grandma decided to cross the street in her wheelchair." Naturally, at that time there was no doubt about that being coarse humor too, but with that sort of thing [laughs] yeah, with that sort of thing I have a bit less of a problem. Yes, well, now why would that be less problematic? Of course, it's super crude. But for one reason or another it has been made so much part of the story that you think, wow, how did he ever manage it, how did he manage to return to the thread of the conversation or to the theme with that bit of humor, and then it turns out to be humorous in spite of everything. Whereas, if someone just goes on spurting filth, then that's not my sense of humor at all.

That is the shock effect as style technique, which not only de Jonge but also other humorists in this cluster employ. To illustrate the sort of shock effects common in Dutch cabaret, a quote from *Hard and zielig* [Hard and pathetic] the first show by Hans Teeuwen, a true master of this technique: "I went to the cinema recently and there I had seen this beautiful film and that was called Schindler's List. Yes that was so beautiful! That was a very beautiful important film, cause, see, the people always talk about the Jews and all, while er these Germans they weren't cuties either."

The *framing* in this technique is distinctly important, as is also apparent from the long quote above: just plain shocking is not good enough. "It has to be part of a story" (Louis Baldé), it must have a certain function. As Maria Romein, a 27-year-old architect said of Teeuwen: "He can be extremely coarse, but he does manage to hit *exactly* the point lying in a very sensitive spot".

In contrast with the lovers of popular humor, lovers of the highbrow style appreciate it if humor is more than just amusement. However, the old-fashioned "socially critical" humor is not much appreciated and people abhor "moralism". The humor has to "hold up a mirror" but the humorist should not too emphatically announce his opinion. The meaning and intention must instead lie in bringing about this shock effect: "I still think that one of the best characteristics a cabaret artist must have is that he can sometimes hold up a mirror to his audience. We can all make jokes but if you do it as your profession, you should be willing to hurt a bit" (Sybren Boonstra). Here it is not about humor that has to be sociable or pleasant. The humorists who belong to this style do not at all do their best to be liked; and the interviewees did not seem to find this question interesting in any way whatsoever. In highbrow humor, one is not involved in simply pleasing one's public.

The persons who appreciate this style often love absurdism, as is apparent from the presence of *Jiskefet* and *Monty Python* in this group. Precisely why this was appealing, they could not often put into words. This is not surprising, as science too is in the dark with regard to absurd humor. Roos Schuurman made an attempt:

> *Can you tell me why that absurdity appeals to you?*
> Yes, that is really difficult to say. Because there are also certain convoluted thoughts that are funny. What I really like about *Monty Python* is that an absolutely ordinary situation can get so carried away. And then you go and invert it. You don't think that a realistic situation is being acted out but it goes a step further: it's carried to such extreme lengths that you start thinking to yourself in certain realistic situations: what would happen if that were pushed to extreme lengths? And then it becomes funny. You get a sort of collision, people talking at cross-purposes and you often see that but then

in a less extreme form. I don't know exactly what it is, but I still find it really amusing.

Demands are made of absurdism. "I feel like that with someone like Bert Visscher. That's an absurdism that makes me think: yes [raspberry sound] search me. It's too easy or too close. Too simple, but then I'm also saying that humor should be complicated sometimes. It's just too easy. It's too obvious. Just like André van Duin."

Here Marijke van der Moer provides the last argument for highbrow humor: humor has to be complicated sometimes. This is a direct mirror image of the arguments for popular humor: there "simple" was a compliment and "difficult" an objection. van der Moer immediately uses it also as an argument against van Duin. It is the only argument that people were often fairly furtive about, because it implies the direct rejection of another type of humor and leads so quickly to making a high-low division. People were somewhat uneasy about this:

> Take Freek de Jonge, for instance, well I tend to think that it's usually reasonably well educated people who like him. With André van Duin, I guess I feel pretty sure that the people who like him are sort of not educated or only a little. I think that that could be said pretty clearly of a number of people, yes.
> *But do you also tend to make a high-low distinction in the humor?*
> [he snickers]
> *Sounds a bit like it...*
> Yes, yes, naturally. Yes. One humor for the happy few and one, er, sort of humor for... Yes, that amounts to making a value judgment, doesn't it? Let me say it like this: it is naturally awfully difficult to tell someone who's completely crazy about André van Duin why you don't like him. And vice versa: why is it now that I think Freek de Jonge is a really good artist? How would I ever be able to explain that to someone who doesn't see anything in his act and who doesn't get any further than "all he ever does is shock and it's just this and it's just that". That's pretty hard to do. And can you really go so far as to say: "Well, you're too stupid to understand this"? Yes, sometimes I do think that, of course, but it's not something you come right out and say to people very often, is it? But okay, it's just a fact of life that some expressions of humor require a fair amount of mental elasticity on the part of the receiver while other forms of humor can be consumed if people are sagging dead tired in their chairs on Friday evening and feeling something like, now I want to be amused. So, okay, yes, I do finally think that it's a bit like that. (Louis Baldé)

The awkwardness about making a distinction can be clearly felt. It is surely no coincidence that Baldé is more educated than his parents were. The upwardly mobile are not only appreciably aware of their own elitism; the comparison with other sorts of humor is more strongly present in them.

What surprised me the most about the arguments for highbrow humor is that the interviewees, in spite of their marked skill in formulating their arguments and objections, did not mention the most obvious characteristic of this humor, that which also connects all humor in this cluster. Corine Steen came the closest when she asked herself in the course of the interview with some surprise why she actually liked *Jiskefet*: "Yes, what can you say about that? Because naturally it's right in between everything I've just been saying. It's coarse. It's simple. And still it's enjoyable. Yes, I think it is the way it's presented. And the tone, how they put everything into a context."

What in my opinion typifies all the humor in this group is the ambiguity of the humor. In the highbrow humor, the boundary between humor and seriousness continuously remains unclear; there is always a certain irony in it; there are sudden transitions to other emotions. That is clearest in *Dertig Minuten*, where no one really knew anymore for sure if it was real humor. But with the others too, the framing is unclear: you keep on asking yourself to what extent Gerard Reve is really serious in his exalted praise of Catholicism; and whether the permanently depressed comic Dorrestijn is really so unhappy. This is the reason why you don't always know for sure why and about whom you are laughing: when watching Wim T. Schippers are you really laughing at farting and burping, or about a world in which people laugh at farting and burping? When Freek de Jonge tells jokes, are you then laughing at the jokes or at the fact that jokes are being told? Or were you not at all meant to think it was funny?

The contrast with the humor of van Duin, *Flodder*, *Banana Split*, sitcoms and joke tellers is here precisely the clearest: that humor is always emphatically *framed* as "funny". Just as for jokes: it is very unambiguous and emphatically meant as humor. The presentation is usually clearly either humor or something else – van Duin's face changes at once if he starts singing serious songs – and should there be any doubt, there are always taped laughter, moustaches, wigs and accents to indicate that we are dealing here with humor.

The best summary of the arguments for highbrow humor is perhaps found in the following phrase that often returned in the interviews: "more than just humor", "not just funny". People expect of humor that it means more and appeals to more emotions than only amusement. The agreement with Bourdieu's esthetic disposition, that describes how people do not much search for directly accessible pleasure in high art, but for "more than just the beautiful" is striking. The humor in this style is often mixed with other emotions; positive, such as esthetic appreciation or exhilaration, but often negative: shock, indignation, embarrassment, sadness, uneasiness, confusion. This can make the humor in this genre piercing or disquieting. Lovers of highbrow humor do not want just a sociable evening. They are looking not so much for an atmosphere as for an experience: an intellectual or emotional stimulus.

The figures show that different people find different things funny. The interviews add an element to this: behind these differences lies a very different image of what humor is, or should be. People don't just have differing ideas of what is funny, they have differing ideas about what is good and bad, amusing and irritating humor. This means that people, even if they laugh about the same things, are perhaps laughing for very different reasons.

That different people find the same thing funny, but consider it from a different style, with a different logic, can be easily seen in *Jiskefet*, a program that shortly before my research was very popular two seasons long but quickly thereafter forfeited the largest part of its audience at a rapid rate. At the highest point of its renown, during *Debiteuren Crediteuren* [Debtors Creditors], a series of sketches in an office, there were people watching the show who usually never watched VPRO, the intellectual broadcasting corporation that produced the program. These people appreciated *Jiskefet*, however, for often popular reasons. One of the interviewed joke tellers appreciated it, for example, for "how they present it": "It's just the way they do it, I really think that's fantastic. How they think it up. Every time an other type" (Jasper Bentinck). Another joke teller appreciated the simplicity: "Yeah, in *Debiteuren Crediteuren*. Yeah, I really liked that. Oh yes, the stupider the better. That's always the same. You sat there waiting till Miss Jannie [the depressed coffee lady in the office, GK] came in" (Joost Wiersema). Louis Baldé, on the other hand, approached it with highbrow logic: "*Jiskefet*, yes, I did watch it from time to time and then particularly *Debiteuren Crediteuren*. Still, I have to admit that after a time it became a bit limited. In the first instance, I thought it was a very original approach, a very original take on humor but at a certain point, after I'd seen it several times, the element of surprise was gone."

Additionally, many people appreciated *Debiteuren Crediteuren* because in it they recognized their own office. This sort of "realist" reading of the sketches is also closer to the popular than the highbrow logic:

I only saw a little bit of *Jiskefet* when they're in that office and then she comes along with the coffee, but that's because, I think, because I work in an office too. That was *Debiteuren Crediteuren*. But I really, really liked that. But then you saw really ordinary things happening that made me think, "Yeah, that sort of thing really does happen in an office". So I think that that was the reason I liked it. Otherwise, I never actually saw anything of theirs. (Claire van Kampen)

And then there were still people with their completely individual argumentations, difficult to capture in style, like Vincent Zwagerman:

Sometimes you sit watching and you're thinking, gosh, could it be that you're still sitting here watching? But when it's over, that's what I like about it, when it's over it is extremely funny [laughs]. Once there was a skit [loud voice] "Peter! Peter! Peter!" [This is a series of sketches in which three men in overalls, all called Peter, walk around in woods and supermarkets, continuously calling "Peter", GK]. And I still remember that I thought: now they're going too far! That doesn't make sense at all anymore! But meanwhile everybody is going around calling "Peter!" And then it happens again and I just double up laughing."[laughs] (Vincent Zwagerman)

The example of *Debtors Creditors* thus shows that this humor divide is not absolute: some forms of humor are open for different "readings" (Fiske 1989; Hall 1980), and thus can be appreciated for both popular and highbrow reasons. However, it is telling that the makers of *Jiskefet* were not particularly happy with the overnight mainstream success of their show, and they rather self-consciously tried to lose their mainstream by creating a series of sketches that was considerably less accessible.

Humor styles and taste variations

Not all humor is so easy to connect with age and class. There are (I hope that I have been able to demonstrate this) humor styles with an individual logic and individual criteria for good and bad humor, but not all humor can be judged using these criteria, and not all humor falls within these humor styles. Two of the most well known humorists of the Netherlands, de Leeuw and van 't Hek, for instance, do not. It was also so that not all the interviewees could be assigned to either the popular or the highbrow style; and even persons who do fall under a certain humor style do not always have the same judgment about any given humorist. Everyone has specific idiosyncrasies, preferences and objections. Added to this is the fact that other background variables than educational level also play a role. During the interviews, I encountered tastes linked with age and gender, with identification with a certain region (for instance, the comedian Herman Finkers is strongly associated with Twente, in the east of the Netherlands, and Bert Visscher is strongly associated with the province of Groningen in the north), sexual orientation (gays who were fans of gay comics Paul Haenen, Paul de Leeuw, or André van Duin) or political standpoints (satirist like de Jonge or van Kooten and de Bie were appreciated more by progressive intellectuals). Additionally, I encountered highly personal preferences for the "disgust humor" in American animation films such as *Rem & Stimpy*, slapstick, nonsense humor, wordplay or the humor of children.

Among the interviewees, there were different people who could not be fitted into the style lay-out: four people who thought everything was funny and thus fitted into all styles; four who found (almost) nothing funny and thus fitted into none of the styles; and four who found everything funny, but did not fit into any single style. The eight people who fell outside every style were, except for one, all women. The exception was a 38-year-old Surinamese doctor, Will Mungra, who thought Dutch humorists irritating and was, in any case, of the opinion that the Dutch have little humor. This seems to me to be a question of cultural difference lying somewhat outside the scope of this chapter.

Of the other seven, four had a sense of humor that did not fit any of the styles. It is tempting to search for the background of these individual tastes in gender: they are all women, all four of whom liked female comics like Brigitte Kaandorp and Adèle Bloemendaal. Outside of that though, there were few similarities. One of them was very close to the preference of many young people as far as taste went: she liked what she called the "hard, cynical humor" of van 't Hek, *Jiskefet* and *Over de roooie*. The second had a style very close to highbrow humor, but as a consequence of her age (she was 84), she did not know many of the humorists in this group.

Sofie Gooijer is the most interesting of these four because she showed more clearly in the foreground a pattern present as an undercurrent in many of the women I interviewed. The style can perhaps best be described as a mixture of recognizability, absurdism, and exaggeration. This can be seen readily in *Absolutely Fabulous* and Brigitte Kaandorp, this woman's favorite because of "those really silly things. The way she ridicules *Libelle* [women's magazine] with the anemone wall hanging, that's just great: nobody knows what you're supposed to do with a thing like that but you get an anemone wall hanging. And later on she tells how she has a baby, it's just really simple. That a baby like that has an entrance and an exit and it will become obvious all on its own what everything is for. Baby gets hungry, you start to react "pop!"; baby's still screaming, you fasten it to you and soon everything's quiet. I think that's really marvelous."

This is reminiscent of the "shared humorous fantasies" of Anke Vermeer in the previous chapter. Something that belongs here too is a preference for a homely sort of absurdism. Sofie Gooijer was one of the few who preferred the absurd sketches of *Jiskefet* to *Debiteuren Crediteuren*. Characteristic is what she remembers of the "*Heeren van de Bruyne Ster*" [Gentlemen of the Brown Star], *Jiskefet's* series of sketches on an East Indies Ship (the ship's name is a reference to homosexuality, which illustrates the use of shock effects and the marked disrespect for "political correctness" in highbrow humor). With these sketches, they forfeited all the audience they had built up with *Debiteuren Crediteuren*: "That the French were shooting at them with French bread. Now I think that's wonderful." Hers is an absurdism lacking hardness or shock effect – sooner nonsense than surrealism.

There were also three women, all three with low education, who did not fit the styles but who also did not have a recognizable individual style. These women thought very little was funny. They also made remarks about their own lack of humor: "Maybe I'm too stiff for that", "I don't think I find very much funny, I guess". Sometimes this was quite painful:

Do you think you have the same sort of humor as your parents or one of your parents?
My father didn't have any humor at all. My mother did, she could really laugh. She would even be laughing while she was reading a book. And then there she was laughing and then she started to read it out loud to us. We had to laugh too. My mother had much more humor that I do.
And your other sisters?
Well, my younger sister laughs all the time. She really goes through life laughing, likes everything, finds everything funny, and then my other sister now and then says: "She's got it so easy, she laughs about everything." Yeah, not everything of course but as a way of speaking. . . Yeah, my mother was laughing all the time.
And your father?
No, my father was somber. I think I might have got that from him. (Geertje Talma)

These interviews were awkward sometimes. The humorists and television programs that I asked about, elicited hardly any reaction: these women were hardly interested at all in what appears on the television in the way of humor. Two of them could not name any acquaintances who had a good sense of humor (a question I asked of everyone and that I will address in the next chapter). I suspect that these women had not only very few humorous acquaintances but also very few acquaintances altogether: they seemed to me to be people with a limited social network.

What the causal relationship with humor is here is difficult to say; it would seem peculiar to suggest that people start finding sitcoms more irritating because of a lack of social contacts. Perhaps there really are people who don't find anything funny. Perhaps a lack of interest in humor quickly leads to social isolation. I think, though, that the connection is the reverse: that people who have few bonds with other people gradually lose their "antennae" for humor. In any case, these interviews have convinced me how intensely humor is connected with social exchange.

The connection with gender is complicated. The cliché dictates that women have less humor; but these three women were very exceptional indeed. In such extreme cases, much more must be going on. One aspect seems important to me: the isolation of middle-aged housewives. These interviews made me conscious of how empty the lives of housewives can be, especially if the children are grown up. I had the impression that this had affected their zest for life. Because not only the connection between humor and social behavior but also the connection between humor and zest for life was never clearer to me than during these interviews. These three women, who saw very little humor in their lives and in the world around them, not only made an impression almost completely devoid of humor but the totality of their lives also seemed fairly cheerless to me.

In sharp contrast with this were the four respondents, all men, who thought everything was funny. They liked the humor belonging to all the styles: they liked both candid camera shows and intellectual fake documentaries like *Thirty Minutes*, they liked jokes and they also liked highbrow comic writers. Of course, sometimes there was something that they didn't like (coincidentally, or not, they all really disliked Ron Brandsteder), but their taste was very broad. The jargon they used was that of the "popular" humor; they were also less highly educated. These interviews actually went very supplely. And these people who thought everything was funny were all jovial people, quick to laugh and they made the impression that they had a flourishing social network in addition to their jobs. One of them was continuously waving at all the passing neighbors during the interview; the other had his whole family living around the corner. Three of them also worked in real men's worlds: the criminal investigation department, the army and the shipyard.

This is a mirror image of the women with a small network, no job, little humor. What we see in the latter are perhaps the extremes of a more general pattern, occurring among the more lowly educated: separate men's and women's worlds; women in the private domain, men in the public domain; men taking care of humor, women whispering jokes into their husband's ear so he can tell them. In these people we see this extremely magnified: the men are very social and very funny; and appreciate all sorts of humor. The women, with not much affinity for humor, very much focused on the inside world, in a world is completely separate from the men's world.

Perhaps of influence here is the classical division of roles Coser has already described: men make jokes; women laugh at those jokes that men make. In this respect, it is interesting that one of the women said that her father never laughed and her mother always. It is tempting to search for explanations in family dynamics – and I will hazard a speculation here about the psychogenesis of humor. The development of a good sense of humor is also an individual psychological process, in which in addition to social relationships, relationships within the family also play an important role. The descriptions of the joke tellers have already made it apparent that the humor in the family plays an important role in the development of a joke teller. There was often mention of mothers fond of laughing. The joke tellers, surprisingly often also mentioned joke telling grandfathers on their mother's side. Here a pattern is dimly visible through which mothers stimulate their sons to be funny; and fathers teach their daughters to laugh at their jokes.

Thus I have once more managed to sociologize the individual variations almost completely: that people didn't like anything, liked everything, liked something intractable, all seems to be linked with gender. There is, however, still another, much more important background category that still has to be discussed: age.

There is one thing on which older and young lovers of humor are hopelessly divided: the funniness of boundary transgressions and shock effects. The young often have a preference for "hard jokes", while those who are older object to the "coarsening" of the humor. The preference for "hard" humor runs through all the styles and layers: from the young woman architect who is a fan of Hans Teeuwen and the female Neerlandist who likes two other transgressive comics, Waardenberg and de Jong, to the sports teacher (and joke teller) who complained that his jokes about incest and people in wheelchairs were not accepted by *Moppentoppers*, and who liked Eddie Murphy: "There's a whole lot of cursing and swearing in it, but that's a matter of choice. You know ahead of time that he's got a foul mouth. The thing I really like the best is gross, dirty humor" (Jelmer de Moor, a 22 year-old gym instructor). Something similar was said by the logistics employee (also a joke teller) who liked Waardenberg and de Jong, because: "It's quite coarse. It happens instantly and is sometimes so coarse that I just have to laugh. They call a spade a fucking shovel. They don't mess around, it's just simply humor" (Gerrit Helman).

"Hard humor" [*harde humor*] is for people under sixty usually a positive qualification: a "hard joke" is a good joke. Those who are older often have difficulty with this. This doesn't only have to do with differences in pain thresholds, but also with pursuing shock effects as figure of speech, in which the elderly were simply not socialized. To shock was not the primary aim of the generation of the "great three" of the 1960s, Kan, Sonneveld and Hermans, no matter how diverse they may have been. Whether one only wanted to amuse or also to moralize, to satirize or to realize something artistic – to transgress boundaries through sensationalism was, in any case, not the aim. Instead, they tried to – and this is a word I have to use with the necessary reserve but it comes the closest – to keep things *civilized*. This goes for everyone from this period, from political comedian Kan to the lowbrow variety shows. This changed quickly after the late 1960s, when the country was shocked by a number of humor scandals involving jokes about religion, sex and nudity, the Royal Family.

Those who are older grew up expecting "civilized humor" and they see coarseness in a different light. My oldest informant, the 84-year-old law graduate Lotte van de Lans, who definitely did not seem easy to shock, was not so much indignant about the coarseness of Paul de Leeuw or van 't Hek, as somewhat surprised:

van 't Hek can be enjoyable too but I still think him too coarse now and then. Something like Paul de Leeuw. I have sometimes watched him and liked him. But the language they use. What does it add! But further away from the present day, you fall back on the oldies pretty quickly. Wim Sonneveld was a big favorite of mine. Wim Kan as well. But what's on offer today: Freek de Jonge, his tempo is frequently so fast. I frequently can't keep up with it. Maybe I'm too old for the mental leaps, too old I think to be able to follow it all so quickly. I do frequently think it's too difficult or something like that, but he is certainly witty.

She points here as well to another style difference between the generation from before 1970 and that afterwards: the tempo. In addition to becoming coarser, increased tempo is perhaps one of the most noticeable developments in cabaret of the last fifty years in the Netherlands. This becomes obvious if you see old recordings of Kan or Sonneveld: the tempo with which they speak and the number of jokes per given time period have increased significantly; the length of the sketches and monologues has been shortened. This is connected with a more general development in the areas of media, art and perhaps even the whole world. And meanwhile a counter-movement has arisen too: highbrow comics like Ederveen and *Jiskefet* are sometimes exasperatingly slow.

This intolerance for shock effects is more troublesome for people like van der Lans, who otherwise has a highbrow style, than for people with a more popular humor style. After all: popular humor is generally quite friendly and preferably not very shocking, while the highbrow style is dominated by this shock effect. Young people with a popular style often like de Leeuw or van 't Hek, who do both have this hardness. Highbrow humor, through its emphasis on hardness and pointedness, is difficult of access for the elderly. "Civilized" humor for the highly educated barely exists anymore in the Netherlands. Only very few comics, like Martine Bijl or Hans Liberg come close: stylish, sophisticated, well-cared-for, not aimed at shocking the audience and still not too easy. This seems to be an objective very few humorists have.

With this we arrive at a question that, until now, has remained underexposed: what do the more highly educated like when they do not like highbrow humor? In Figure 2 it could be seen that both preference for and objection to this humor is connected with educational level. This means that there are highly educated persons who know highbrow humor but don't appreciate it. Sociologists are used to searching for "progressive" and "conservative" elite tastes, connected with cultural or economical capital. Highbrow humor has some avant-garde features. The highly educated who love highbrow humor, according to the questionnaire, are, politically speaking, more left-wing and less religious than persons who know this humor but do not appreciate it, and they often live in one of the four large cities. They are, in other words, more likely to have more cultural than economic capital.

Among the interviewees with a highbrow style, a distinction can also be made between the hyper-intellectuals, who saw van 't Hek and even de Jonge as too "mainstream"; and a somewhat milder highbrow style. The litmus test for the distinction between the "highbrow" and the somewhat "looser" highly educated is their opinion of the celebrity comic Youp van 't Hek: highly cultured humor lovers think of him, in spite of his column in the Netherlands' most prestigious newspaper *NRC Handelsblad*, as somewhat coarse. van 't Hek marks the boundary between highbrow intellectuals and the more conservative highly educated. He is thus also judged using very changeable arguments: he is described as be both difficult and simple, both vulgar and deep. He was praised by interviewees for his "deep insight", cursed for his high tempo, appreciated for his simplicity and held in contempt for his "so-called morality".

But what do the more highly educated, who do not like the "avant-garde" intellectual highbrow humor, consider funny? The questionnaire shows that these people do not much tend towards a popular style but show a preference for non-popular humor that avoids shock effects: civilized humor. While they are on average not any older than the people who do love highbrow humor, they appreciate the veterans more. In addition, they tend to like English comedies like *Keeping up appearances*, *'Allo ' Allo* or *Mr Bean* more, and to prefer Brigitte Kaandorp and Herman Finkers, humorists who fell outside all the clusters and who tend more towards absurd humor. As their favorite humorist, they usually name Youp van 't Hek, but often Herman Finkers and even van Duin too. Highly educated lovers of highbrow humor also mention van 't Hek sometimes but they prefer de Jonge, and they seldom mentioned Finkers.

The clearest demarcation of the boundary between progressive and conservative highbrow humor is Herman Finkers. Of all the humorists, no one who escapes every classification to the extent he does. 15.9 percent of survey respondents mentioned him when asked to name their favorite comedian, second only to van 't Hek (23.8%) and before Freek de Jonge (12.6%) and André van Duin (11.2%). Just as for van 't Hek and *Debiteuren Crediteuren*, Finkers is someone who is appreciated for extremely varying reasons. He is amusing for people with a popular humor style, because his humor has no sharp edges, but also for people with a highbrow style on account of his curious, absurdist, convoluted thoughts. He manages to win over a lot of people with his accent and his references to his regional origin, but also with his linguistic jokes. Also, many people seems quite taken by his determined non-urbanity. However, Finkers definitely does not use shock effects, ambiguity, or any of the other characteristics typical of highbrow comics such as de Jonge. What Finkers represents is exactly the type of humor that humor theory had difficulty grasping: absurdism, plays-on-words based on linguistic play and not on boundary transgression. Absurd humor escapes the explanations of the humor theory, but also the logic of both the highbrow and the popular humor style.

Conclusion: Humor styles and standardized humor

From personal variations to class-linked distinctions, the different humor styles include more than preferences for and objections to the area of humor, or awarenesses or lack thereof of certain humorists and personages. Behind the styles, a complete, individual logic can be found: it is expected of humor that it be sociable or confrontational, hard or civilized, artistic or relaxed, that the tempo be high or, on the contrary, consciously low, that the content clearly be either central or "how people present it", that it be absurd or recognizable, exaggerated or non-committal, ambiguous or unequivocal, simple or complicated. And these expectations and ideas determine not only what people see as good or bad humor, but also what people "see" in a joke or a joke maker.

This chapter showed how people apply such logics to standardized humor: television shows, performances by comics, as well as jokes. This logic, however, should be just as clearly visible in the evaluation of everyday humor as it is in the evaluation of television programs and humorists. The question thus arises to what extent people with different humor styles also harbor different opinions about the role humor plays in daily life. How can the logic of these humor styles be seen in everyday humorous communication? Or: what is the relationship of humor styles to communication styles?

Chapter 5
The logic of humor styles

"Good humor" does not mean the same thing to everyone. In the previous chapter, it was shown that different *humor styles* underlie taste judgments about the standardized humor of professional humor producers such as comedians, comics and television makers. In this chapter I pose the question of what the scope of these humor styles is. Are the criteria of highbrow and lowbrow humor only applied to standardized humor? Do people have the same expectations of good humor in daily life as they do from the stage or television? And how can this be related to the genre that is central to the book: the joke?

Spontaneous humor in day-to-day situations is difficult for a researcher to grasp. Indirectly though, humor styles can be retrieved: by distilling them from the descriptions people give of good and bad humor. Just as communication styles can be typified using preferences for certain forms of communication and objections to others – as criteria for good and bad communication – humor styles must also be capable of description: as criteria for good and bad humor.

During the interviews, two terms kept returning when people expressed their preferences in the area of humor, "(good) sense of humor" and "coarse" humor. These terms were used both for standardized and spontaneous, everyday humor. People use these terms in order to distinguish between the humor – and the humorists – that they find attractive, funny, pleasant or, indeed, irritating, corny and unamusing. Some advanced their ability to tell jokes well as evidence for their sense of humor; others were of the opinion that telling jokes has nothing to do with sense of humor; and still others regarded jokes by definition as "coarse". "Sense of humor" and "coarse" are thus ascribed very different content by different people. In this chapter, I will use the meanings that people attach to these two expressions for judging humor, to uncover the logic underlying humor styles.

Distinguishing good humor from bad

Clearly, "sense of humor" and "coarse" are not the only terms used by people to pass judgments on humor. In the area of humor there exists a complete vocabulary: insipid, dull, dirty, coarse, piquant, vulgar, hard, sharp, dry. (It is striking how many of these descriptions refer to taste and tactility.) Most of these words are specific designations of one sort of humor. "Coarse" and "sense of humor" are relatively empty terms sooner indicating general judgment than describing content. "Good sense of humor" is first and foremost a description of a person: it indicates that one appreciates that person's humor without indicating what the nature of that humor is. "Coarse" (*plat* or *platvloers* in Dutch) indicates bad taste or lack of taste; a negative judgment unconnected with a specific objection to content, as is the case with words like rude, hurtful, superficial, difficult or forced.

In the second series of interviews I asked directly about the meaning people ascribed to these two terms. In the interviews with the joke tellers these terms already appeared regularly, but at that time I did not explicitly ask my informants what they meant when they used them. It did strike me, however, that the joke tellers gave these concepts different connotations than I would myself. Later on it became apparent that the use of these concepts corresponds with the preference for either lowbrow or highbrow humor.

Coarseness: Objections to bad humor

People who do not appreciate the genre often dispose of jokes as "coarse". One of the people who described jokes as coarse was English teacher Louis Baldé. In the interview, he also provided a sort of definition of "coarse": "I think insipid, childish is not in the least funny. I mean the van Duin-like genre. Coarse or zilch. Laugh or I'll shoot humor, that's hateful." Other interviewees who, like Baldé, preferred highbrow humor, also named popular comic André van Duin as representing "coarse" humor.

The description of jokes as "coarse" is in keeping with the meaning the more highly educated generally give the term. In essence, for lovers of highbrow humor coarse means "easy". All the objections they made to popular humor can be summarized in that one word, for instance in this already partially quoted fragment, in which Marijke van der Moer enumerates her objections against cabaret artist Bert Visscher:

> That's an absurdism that makes me think: yes, prrt [raspberry], search me. It's too easy or not deep enough. Too simple. But then I'm also saying that humor should be complicated sometimes. It's just too easy. It's too self-evident. Just like André van Duin. Sometimes I can laugh at it if indeed something just goes on and on, then you can't really escape getting caught

in the joke too. But very often – well, then it is simply too coarse, let's say. Too easy.

Van der Moer here specifically objects against Visscher here and, once again, van Duin. But in fact she gives a verdict applicable to all humor: for her, humor "should be complicated". It must challenge, stimulate or surprise.

"Coarse" for highbrow humor lovers does not only mean simple and predictable, but also corny, consciously naughty or "mischievous" in an imposed way. This also has to do with easiness: the boundaries that are transgressed in the joke are too self-evident. As Bart Winia says:

> You can score easily with coarseness but in a vulgar way. For instance in *'Allo 'Allo* they are continuously talking about "me sausage". Then I don't like it; they should make one show and use that stuff up and then shut up about it [fake French accent] "I stuffed the sausage down me pants". After a while, you've had enough of it. And then every time the canned laughter on top. So it does have a certain vulgarity, but then in a very easy way.

Examples of coarseness that interviewees gave were for instance: jokes about burping and farting, jokes based on suggestive remarks and "spicy" allusions, or exaggerated imitations or accents. The main objection to these jokes is that they are not *really* shocking and scandalous, because the transgression is too transparent for this. For this specific type of humor that is too simple, the Netherlands has the unsurpassed term *flauw* (corny, but in Dutch literally "unsalted", insipid, without spice).

In addition to these two meanings – simple and corny – there is also a third element in the highbrow meaning of coarse: easiness, exaggeration or "affectation".

> Sylvia Millecam. Oh yuck, yes. At the beginning I liked her a lot when they were sitting there, all four of them, in that program [*Ook dat nog*]. Yes, then I really liked her. But later on, that often happens with programs like that, they can't seem to leave well enough alone and then they go on and invent all sorts of new things and they start dressing up in costumes and things like that. I like it best if they just sit there and talk, but if it gets all complicated and they go and portray those exaggerated types, no. Then I don't like it anymore. Awful.
> *You find her exaggerated?*
> Yes! Horribly exaggerated. Yes, real affectation. (Lotte van der Lans)

The fixed phrase in the humor vocabulary is "they're laying it on thick" or, as van der Moer phrased it: "It *has* to be appealing. It is too contrived, too forced, too pretentious and it zeros in on a popular sort of humor." This too is a variation on "too easy": the joke maker is trying to be too emphatically funny. The objection to coarse humor refers thus to three sorts of "easiness": too easy from an intellectual viewpoint; too easy as far as boundary transgressions go; too easily recognizable as humor.

While I am primarily citing objections to coarse comedians here, all these same objections were mentioned to all sorts of forms of spontaneous humor. In daily interactions as well, people can make jokes that are not surprising enough, too corny or too emphatic. As became clear in Chapter 3, to a significant extent, people used the same terms to explain their objection against jokes: predictable, easy, forced and exaggerated.

An interesting example of jokes as a coarse genre, fitting for coarse situations was given by Marga van Stolwijk, a smart lady with a schooled and rather highbrow taste, who was brought up in a farmer's family, to my question of whether she knew a joke:

> I could tell you a joke, I've known it for years and it is very popular in certain settings, including rather coarse events like a village festival or something like that, you know. It doesn't amount to much, all it is is that someone throws pills into a chicken coop and the following day the chickens are going around clucking "piss poop, cha cha cha". Now that is a pretty strange joke and it's only really funny if you've already sunk below a certain level, that's what I think is special about that joke. For instance: there was once a village festival and then you had a float with a lot of others and then what you did then is you named the names of the local farmers. And that's what's fun about it. The joke is not much but then you go and say "then we went on over to farmer Kremer's and then... " Now, what happens is everybody gets into it, that's the good part. But I almost never tell a joke, because I usually start with the punch line.

Note that, in the end, she never told the joke. And in passing, she also says that she can't really tell a joke; just as so many women, she begins with the punch line.

What is also apparent from this quote is that, although coarseness is disapproved of, it can sometimes be fun. Two people quoted above expressed their objections against coarseness eloquently:

> Coarse humor is often fun if it crosses your path by chance. So you're just having a chat with someone and suddenly something emerges that has a double meaning. Not when you first hear it but when the other calls your at-

tention to it. And then you both have a laugh. That often has to do with coarse things. (Marijke van der Moer)

I think vulgarity is coarse, but not the way Youp [van 't Hek] uses it, something like him standing there with his hands in his pockets and then saying, "Indeed Madam, I am fondling my prick". That is incredibly coarse but in an amusing way. (Bart Winia)

People with the popular humor style, including all the joke tellers, gave an entirely different meaning to the same word. They did not in general object to simple humor, affectation or easy naughtiness. They tended to use coarse to mean the following:

Coarse, maybe I've got it wrong, but coarse, I'd put that in with the mean jokes actually. But you can interpret a coarse joke in another way. But that's the first thing I think of: a filthy joke or a dirty one. (Jaap van Noord)

Coarse is vulgar. Course is just plain vulgar. Look, at a certain moment you get these theater programs that use a whole lot of obscene language that plays a certain role within the framework of the performance. So you can't really always say that either. But I find coarse just plain vulgar. If it's too much about the people, people personally. And certainly about people who can't defend themselves. That's what I think coarse is all about. (Wouter Koeman, 51, police officer)

In this way of seeing it, coarse is not easy but vulgar or rude. Coarse humor is humor that transgresses a boundary. The first association people often had here was language use: smutty words and obscene language: "If they start carrying on swearing, I think that's so incredibly common. Vulgar is how I see it" (Claudia van Leer). Or: "Yeah coarse, then I think about coarse language. A bit, well like talking dirty. What you, say you're talking to someone that you don't know, you just wouldn't use words like that. I mean drunk people or people like that who'll just say anything" (Anna Pijlstra).

All needless hurtfulness or vulgarity counts as coarse for this group: coarse humor was defined as "common, ugly, mean", "nasty little jokes". Paul de Leeuw or Youp van 't Hek are often named as exemplifying coarseness: humorists who use rough language, consciously transgress boundaries and openly insult others. Coarse here is almost synonymous with "hurtful" (*kwetsend*). "Hurtful" is a word much more often used by those with lower education than those with higher; it was their standard objection to bad humor. Instead "coarse" for the highly educated is a somewhat more ordinary word – not really surprisingly, because it is a word consistently connected with attempts of higher classes to distinguish themselves.

Humor at the expense of others is not by definition hurtful or coarse. In the eyes of lovers of popular humor, jokes about others are not hurtful if certain boundaries are clearly respected. Television programs in which unprepared people are embarrassed, such as a candid camera show, or *Over de Roooie*, in which people were made to do unpleasant or degrading things for 1,000 guilders, were not found to be coarse either. After all, it has been indicated clearly here that boundaries exist: the victims have given their permission for transmission of the program. Often they are portrayed laughing: by doing this they make it obvious that they "can take a joke". Compare Ivo Engelsman from the previous chapter, who found Kan grosser than *Banana Split*: Kan made dignitaries look like fools, without their permission, and that was "affronting". In the candid camera show people are also made to look like fools but with their own approval. In the highbrow connotation, it is precisely the programs with the candid camera that are coarse, because the jokes quickly fall into the area of simple boundary transgressions. On this point, the two meanings given to the one word are diametrically opposed to each other. The meaning ascribed by people to "coarse" is closely connected with strict but contradictory rules governing making jokes about other people.

The definition of "coarse" as vulgar and hurtful obtained not only for lovers of the popular humor style, but also for the people who didn't fit either of the humor styles. Even more so than for the popular humor style, this meaning of the word "coarse" also pertains to a certain educational level: all respondents who had had neither university nor post-secondary vocational training, with the exception of one, used "coarse" to mean "vulgar". These are not only the people with a distinctly popular humor style but also everyone who does not have an highbrow humor style.

And the opposite: only people with higher education described "coarse" as "easy". This does not mean that the more highly educated do not have a problem with hurtful jokes or vulgar language use. They would use other words: vulgar, hurtful, shocking, banal, revolting, offensive. They don't have to like it, but they would not call it "coarse". Apart from that, educated people also denounce it less emphatically. A certain sharpness is indeed appreciated in highbrow humor. Give it a slight hint of refinement and a clear aim and humor is permitted to be vulgar, or full of obscene language and hurtful references.

The way in which the more highly educated defined "coarse" is easily connected with schooling: coarseness – bad taste – is placed opposite schooled, sophisticated, cultivated taste. For the more highly educated, usually people with a highbrow humor style, coarseness has to do with lack of intellect and refinement. For the less educated, with and without a popular humor style, coarseness means: lack of decency and courtesy. "Good taste" in the area of humor is not connected with intellect, but with sociability: it is the opposite of uncivilized, impolite and unsocial behavior.

"A good sense of humor": Criteria for good humor

The meaning people attach to "sense of humor" is closely connected also with humor style. I asked all 32 interviewees in the survey sample to describe someone they knew who had a good sense of humor. To this question three different types of answers were given, two of which were connected with the humor styles. The third type of answer occurred less often: it did not describe a type of humor but a relationship. Someone with a good sense of humor is someone with whom you share humor, with whom you are "on the same wavelength":

> We only need a couple of words to understand each other immediately. And with other you would think: what are they going on about? And he is also someone who thinks exactly the same way about that sort of joke. He doesn't even really have to tell a joke, but he knows right off, if he were to tell me a joke: no, she won't like that one or yes, she'll like that one. Or crazy things that happen to you and then you blow them up a little and then start telling them in a really strange way. So that other people think: I can't see what's funny about that. But then I do see what's funny about it. And so does he. (Josien Muller, 37, housewife, did not finish high school)

> She is a very intelligent woman, right? I don't think she would be described by everyone as humorous, because I think there would be occasions when she'd be called a dragon, but she and I put a whole lot into perspective by just laughing so hard that our backs hurt or we get sore stomachs. And we can talk seriously for hours and all of a sudden there will be a remark. We have a number of words, lacrimoso [not an existing word] for instance, thought up once upon a time during a game, the dictionary game. And we both know the meaning of the word that we once invented when we were playing the game. Then everything is put into perspective for me. For someone else that wouldn't be funny, but that you – the way she roars with laughter is something fantastic. The twinkling is fantastic, you know, and

then she'll say for instance, "oh don't go on about that, because that's just so lacrimoso." That's how it is. And you can have that with other people too. But not with men, now that I think about it. Men always find that confusing. (Marga van Stolwijk)

Here are two very different types of humor: Josien Muller likes jokes; Marga van Stolwijk prefers a sharp wit. "Sense of humor" says therefore very little about the *type* of humor that they appreciate, but quite a lot about the way in which these people deal with humor. Humor is for them an exchange, a part of a relationship. It is not coincidental that these people always name someone who is very close to them: their brother, husband or best friend.

This description of a good sense of humor primarily sheds light on the connection between humor and gender: with the exception of one person, people answering in this way were all women. In Chapter 3 it has already been described how women are more likely to use humor to express a personal connection. Here too it appears that women see humor sooner as an aspect of a relationship, while men tend to see it as a characteristic of a person.

In another way too the answers to this question about someone with a good sense of humor said a lot about humor and gender. Of the 32 interviewees, only two named a woman as the person with the best sense of humor. In an American research study by Crawford (1989), people also named men much more often when asked to describe someone with "sense of humor". Another conspicuous gender difference: of the 32 interviewees, four could not think of anyone whom they found to have a good sense of humor; all four were women. Two of these were the women described in chapter 4 who had such a dismal lack of humor. The answers to this question again produce the image of humor as a masculine characteristic – something more quickly associated with men – but also as a "masculine" strategy.

But perhaps the most revealing when discussing humor and gender is the fact that there were two people who found that they themselves had the best sense of humor: both were men. The one, in answering my question as to whether he knew anyone with a good sense of humor, first defined sense of humor; he then went on to describe himself:

With sense of humor what you're talking about is that you can appreciate the sunny side of life. Nice things, that you also see and notice them. . . I sometimes see these situations where the one begins to crack up and the other thinks, now what's going on this time? Now that's something I've got, I do see things happening. Some people don't see that at all. I see, I think more often the humor in things. And I can laugh about it, the one time really hard and the next maybe just a smile. (Kees van Dokkum)

The other was somewhat humbler. First he said that his female colleagues had a good sense of humor because "they understood his humor". "And," he continued, "because they can understand mine, you really get the feeling that they could be pretty humorous themselves too". Then I asked:

And do you know someone whom you often have to laugh at?
Well, I can laugh at anyone and everyone.
At one specific person...
Well, no, not at one person, eh? [to his wife] Do I sometimes feel like laughing at someone? Yes, often children, they can do such ridiculous things from time to time. But it's, um, men, no not men. Not women either, much.
Wife of the interviewee: *You simply think you're the funniest.*
Exactly. And that's just what I was trying not to say. Yeah, in company I often play the first fiddle. Yes, that could sometimes, now and then that could be negative, I guess. But okay, as long as people aren't prepared to say anything about it, I won't be able to change it, will I? (Jaap van Noord)

His wife didn't mean anything biting by this. It characterized the way they behaved during the interview: he monopolized the conversation; she filled in the blanks now and then with a few well-chosen remarks. Mrs. van Noord was also one of the women who fed jokes to her husband so he could tell them.

The two other types of descriptions of someone with a sense of humor were connected directly with humor style. These did not concern relationships, but a certain *type* of humor. People with a highbrow humor style described someone with a sense of humor approximately as follows:

We have a woman friend and she is often extremely sharp and knows how to describe things so concisely and succinctly in such a way that you can't do anything but laugh. She is in her nineties and can be extremely witty. Yes, witty. Every shot goes home. But that's pretty much what it's about, not so much in the sense of telling jokes, but simply the fact of making a telling retort and being able to say things in a way that you think, "Oh yes, exactly". Not really that you think, oh that's a real joker or anything like that. No, not that. (Cornelis Blom)

A good sense of humor. Yes, what I like about it is the surprise in it, the unexpected. What I also feel with cabaret artists. That cool type of humor, with an almost British tint. I'm always attracted to that in people. And, yes, that's something completely different from telling jokes, something more like a really deadpan grasp of situations. Well, look, you have to distinguish, of course, people aren't playing a role then. I mean it's no longer in the context of "Hoorah, now we're all going to spend a whole evening sociably telling jokes". No, what I find surprising is exactly the fact that it's completely built into the personality. And that at any random moment, if there's a conversation going on about almost anything at all, that just pops out completely unexpectedly. Because that is, of course, much much nicer than saying: well, now, why don't we just have a little session of joke telling. No, for me it's precisely the way that people express themselves about certain things, things they've experienced, and the way they weave it into the conversation, without it being deliberate. It just comes out.

But it is not deliberate. So these are not people who are very ad rem.

Well, that does play a role in it too. I do find being ad rem, having the ability to react immediately to situations, yes, that is part of it. People with that sort of sense of humor can often react ad rem to a remark right on the spot. A nice example of that, linked to the shocking jokes, that I experienced in a circle of friends, really did happen. Friends of friends of ours were about to go on holiday and everything was ready. In the car. And then you'll often see people going: now did I forget to do that, and that? That's really familiar. So at a certain moment the wife was still standing in the hallway, saying: "I think I haven't turned off the gas tap yet." To which he said: "Why are you Jews always the first ones to smell that?" I mean, they're married [laughs] so I guess you can assume that he's not an anti-Semite but I know him, I mean, that's the sort of thing he'd say. I mean if you were to go and write that down on paper, it would be shocking, but in the context and, of course, considering the timing. He isn't thinking about timing naturally because he didn't rehearse the thing, but splat bang, right on the spot. Yes, then you've got humor [laughs]. (Louis Baldé)

In this we hear the echo of the highbrow humor style: the same criteria are being used – sharpness, originality – but then applied to spontaneous humor. These criteria are the opposite of coarseness according to the highly educated: not simple, not too emphatically humorous, no easy boundary transgressions. In the following pithy summary it can be readily seen that good humor in the eyes of the highly educated reverses all objections against coarseness: according to Lotte van der Lans, someone with a sense of humor was "someone who thinks fast when it's a question of humor, who makes connections quickly and who is a bit original. And therefore not laughing about Laurel and Hardy or something; that's a bit childish and a bit naive".

For people with a highbrow humor style, someone with a good sense of humor is witty or nimble-minded: good with language, ad rem, quick with spontaneous witty or humorous remarks and has preferably an ironic, not too emphatic tone. Humor is connected in this perspective with creativity, observation and analysis – and thus absolutely not with jokes. It is "an ability to observe, to analyze, let's say, to make connections and to do something with them. The humor is what the person does right on the spot and then that's what makes it funny. And a joke, yes, with a joke if you've heard it twice it's not even funny anymore and then the humor has flown, hasn't it." (Corine Steen)

People who adhere to this view of good humor often also emphasize self-mockery and the capacity to put things into perspective. Vincent Zwagerman described his friend with a special sense of humor as a melancholy man with a huge ability to put things into perspective: "I have laughed a whole lot with Jan and that was more about the ludicrousness of life itself." Zwagerman's wife added to this: "He is actually very gloomy. He has a heavy, heavy weight around his neck." And Zwagerman: "Yes. And that's where the humor comes from." According to this definition, a sense of humor can then also be connected with less pleasant emotions or characteristics: sadness, bitterness, sharpness.

While "sense of humor" for my informants was a positive qualification, they did not always think the people they described were nice: witty, but not necessarily sympathetic. Maria Romein describes someone she admires for his humor, but someone who often makes people feel defensive:

> I had a colleague and I really thought he was very funny. He was terribly banal, not in a sexist way, he could just be extremely crude, but very precise in aiming at the sensitive points, you know what I mean? Which meant that people were often quite shocked and then later actually very glad that something like that had been said, you know. But still, he's someone who makes a lot of enemies too. He no longer works with us because he and his wife started their own architectural agency and it's going reasonably well and he wrote too – that's a very good example of his sort of humor [laughs]. We had phoned him to see if he had any documentation about his new agency. And he said he did and sent it to us. And he'd inserted a letter with it that really annoyed some people. Something like: okay, here is the agency documentation – a young architectural agency with one woman and one invalid, because one of his hands has only stubs of fingers on it. And on request we can also show ourselves as black, he wrote [laughs]. I really liked that [laughs]. I thought it was great. And it is actually really pretty vulgar or something. Lots of people couldn't appreciate it at all. There were really pretty angry about it.

Anke Vermeer found her nimble-witted acquaintance distinctly unsympathetic and intimidating:

> Yes, this one boy in my circle of acquaintances is actually fatally funny. And in an analytical, straightforward way. And I never know how to react. I can't react – yes, I can react to it, but it all falls flat on its face and then I am absolutely not funny or even nice. I think part of that is that he just doesn't hear you. But he can paralyze you with his wit. So much so that I just slump there limp in my chair. But it is, of course, more fun if there's an exchange of humor.

On the contrary, informants with a popular humor style always thought that their friends and acquaintances with a good sense of humor were nice. For them, a good sense of humor was not so much a question of wittiness or creativity as it was of sociability. Claudia van Leer, for instance, thought that her son had a good sense of humor. This is what she meant:

> He can immediately sense it, if it's fun. He also always knows how to present it. If he comes in somewhere and he feels that everybody's down, he knows how to turn that around right away. He can feel it so well and then he throws in a couple of small jokes. Really funny, things everyone can laugh about. And not insulting either and then the atmosphere brightens up. He does that very well.

Hanneke Meertens describes her brother-in-law's brother:

> My brother-in-law's brother is someone who has a real sense of humor, believe me. He's a joke teller, always up to something. You always end up thinking: how did he ever come up with that? There's always something. It's continuous, yeah, God, continuous laughter, non-stop craziness. He's always got jokes, and they're always ones you haven't heard before. And yeah, he's always got some trick up his sleeve. He makes complete idiots of everyone and of his parents, who don't realize it. And, you know, he's always at it, always the clown, keeping his end up. He doesn't bore you either, not really. He's someone who makes you think: yes, I could spend the whole day with him. That's fun, real fun. Sociable. Always cheerful and always, well...

These people "with a good sense of humor" are the real life of the party. Their humor is described as playful, pleasant, but never really hurtful: "small jokes everyone can laugh at". The descriptions make clear that these are often joke tellers as well. Additionally, their humor is often described as somewhat teasing. Many descriptions name the mutual exchange of humorous insults as an important element: a form of communication, as became apparent in Chapter 3, very popular with joke tellers, and always more popular with men. Sometimes it is very close to acting the clown:

> He's always going around needling, let's say, being a bit of a rabble-rouser. And also with a whole lot of practical jokes. He often makes the boss look like a twit and I really like that. And he doesn't do that in a secretive way but in a very open way, with everyone around. So the boss is also a bit of an idiot. Just a while ago he had to, they had to start finding wood for the dock. And then the boss said that wood has to be locked up otherwise someone's going to pinch it. And he made a big fat deal of it. Okay, so, the boss he's got a small office, so the guy had stacked up all that wood inside that little office and of course the boss couldn't get into his office anymore. See, that's what I really like. And so the boss started to screech about that. And the guy said: "well, that's easy as pie, just go get a saw and make a hole in it. (Harm Arends)

These descriptions are always about people who are sociable and in high spirits, "always cheerful": "An acquaintance of ours, Karel, an amazing sense of humor. Laughs a lot. Light-hearted man" (Jan Jurriaans). Just as for the arguments in favor of popular humorists, these are not only descriptions of likable humor, but also of a sociable, pleasant person.

Someone with a sense of humor is in this interpretation not only funny and sociable, he (in this group people only mentioned men as having a good sense of humor) is also able to take a joke that others make about him. The latter was often emphasized – again only by men: "He can also take a joke" (Jaap van Noord). "And he's someone who can also put up with humor, when it's aimed at him" (Harm Arends). It is striking that this proviso comes precisely from the people who equate coarseness and vulgarity. The question of jokes at someone else's expense is central here, both in the negative and the positive delimitation of humor. Humor here is inseparably connected with relationships and social situations: a good humorist is social, a bad humorist disturbs the good relationships.

Class culture and humor style

The highbrow and popular humor styles cannot solely be recalled in the judgments of professional humorists, but also in the expectations regarding people making jokes in one's own surroundings. Not only do the different meanings of coarseness and sense of humor correspond remarkably often with the humor styles from the previous chapter, it was also the women here who showed a somewhat anomalous pattern. The use of the concepts "sense of humor" and "coarse(ness)" offers insight into the logic upon which humor styles are based. This logic is not only the foundation of the judgments of standardized humor but of *all* humor. The question is now: what is the background of this connection between humor and social class?

Of the interviewees with a highbrow style, all but one, who dropped out of university to become a carpenter, have a college level education. Generally, they don't like jokes or are indifferent to the genre. Interviewees with a popular style usually have an education below college level, although this category is more mixed, and they tend to like jokes. Also, they rated the jokes in the survey significantly higher.

People with an highbrow humor style always equated coarseness with easy; they usually defined a good sense of humor as wittiness. These are complementary arguments: if a good joke is unexpected, creative and intellectually challenging, then a simple or predictable joke is bad. Objection and ideal are each other's opposites. The people who preferred sociable joke makers to witty humorists generally loved the popular humor style – and jokes. Here too we see that objection and ideal are connected: bad, coarse humor was vulgar and hurtful to them. And someone who is vulgar and hurtful is certainly not a sociable joke teller.

In the use of these terms, the arguments for highbrow and popular humor styles, as described in the previous chapter, can be recognized. The sociable joke makers are homey, playful, focused on creating a feeling of fellowship and preferably not hurtful. In this their humor resembles the sociable humor of popular humorists and television programs: it creates a pleasant, somewhat exuberant atmosphere. These sociable joke makers additionally, just as popular humorists, are sooner judged on their personalities and performance than on content.

For the witty humorists to whom highbrow humor lovers give their preference, content is more important than atmosphere, personality or performance. These people with a sense of humor are ad rem, intellectual, witty, sooner sharp than playful and once in a while unpleasant and not in the least sociable. Easy or corny they are not. The highbrow humor of *cabaretier* Freek de Jonge and the VPRO broadcasting corporation can be recognized in this description: quick-witted humorists offer, just as highbrow cabaret artists, an intellectual stimulus that does not have to be solely pleasant. The problematic nature of jokes at the expense of others was less often mentioned in interviews with highbrow humor lovers than those with popular humor lovers. The central theme for the highly educated was creativity and intellectual refinement. Humor, in this view, no matter how curious it sounds, is more of an individual affair than a social event: something that to be sure is shared with others, but in the first instance originates from the most highly individual creativity of the joke maker.

The place occupied by jokes in this dichotomy is not difficult to explain. It is clear that jokes are sooner sociable than they are creative; that it is easier to object to jokes because of their simplicity than because of their vulgarity. Someone who tells a joke is neither ad rem nor quick-witted – after all he did not think up the joke himself – but he is sociable. The telling of jokes can be disposed of as too easy – not self-created, too exaggerated – but not all jokes are vulgar. The logic of the intellectual humor style thus leads to rejecting the genre as a whole. The logic of the popular humor, on the other hand, leads to the appreciation or rejection of specific jokes: hurtful jokes.

I am now a step closer to answering the question at the center of this book: where do differences in the appreciation of jokes come from? People have different expectations with regard to good and bad humor; and the joke satisfies popular expectations of good humor better than it does highbrow. But what is the provenance of these humor styles? These humor styles, just as communication styles, are connected with differences in class culture. People who emphasize wittiness are more highly educated, while people who prefer sociable humor usually come from the working class or lower middle class. In the use of the terms the relationship with education is clearly visible: the highbrow interpretation of coarseness and sense of humor is founded upon an appreciation of intellect and intelligence. These are arguments for "schooled" humor. In the popular meanings, intellect barely plays a role. The emphasis lies on sociability: someone with a good sense of humor uses humor to be sociable and friendly. Someone who is coarse is unsocial, and hurts others and transgresses social boundaries without a single reason. The distinction between good and bad humor is seen here from a totally different perspective.

The distinctions between sociable and quick-witted humor agree broadly speaking with the prevailing distinctions between high or elite culture and low or popular culture. Comparable distinctions can be recognized in taste distinctions in the areas of art, literature, interior design and music: the contrast between simple and intellectually challenging; original versus accessible; innovative versus conventional; upsetting versus pleasant; ironically distant versus exuberant. While the appreciation of humor cannot be completely equated with the appreciation of beauty, the esthetic logic lying behind it seems comparable.

The highly educated with lots of cultural capital test humor, while it can hardly be included in the higher arts and certainly not in culture with a capital C, against standards obtaining for High Culture. They regard humor with a keen eye strongly resembling the esthetic disposition. That the highly educated have a similarly distant and cerebral attitude when watching jokes on a podium and on television was already clear from the previous chapter. Now it seems that jokes in daily life as well are judged using a similar intellectual method. Jokes subjected to this logic fail rather quickly: the pleasure of jokes is too direct, the provocation to laugh too unambiguously funny, too little challenging, too congenial. The joke is, in other words: too easy, too coarse.

One of the distinguishing characteristics of humor is that is always has a very strong affective as well as cognitive component: a joke, or any attempt at humor, is always based on the resolution of an incongruity (cf. Raskin 1985; Attardo 1991; Ruch 1998): a mental switch, or shift, from one frame of reference to another. In this sense, it is very easy to picture humor as a purely individual mental operation, a trick of the mind. However, this mental operation has a peculiarly affective and social effect: it leads to a direct and highly visible emotional response, which directly reflects and affects social relations. Moreover, whereas the exchange of humor usually has the effect of drawing people together, at the same time it often creates a certain distance vis-à-vis the topic or butt of the joke, by "not taking it seriously". The highbrow logic tends to stress the cognitive and distancing aspects of humor, whereas the lowbrow logic tends to downplay these aspects, focusing on the sociable and cohesive aspects.

Class logic à la Bourdieu can be recognized among the less educated too. They judge humor as they, in Bourdieu's eyes, also judge art, music, photography: less distantly, or more focused on the direct pleasant sensation that can be induced by something. Jokes are excellently suited to this: the joke is an effective way to create a pleasant, humorous atmosphere. In this sense, jokes are linked to what Bourdieu terms the "popular esthetic", which he defines in his characteristic style as: "the affirmation of the continuity between art and life, which implies the subordination of form to function, or, one might say, on a refusal of the refusal which is the starting point of the high esthetic, i.e., the clear-cut separation of ordinary dispositions from the specifically esthetic disposition" (Bourdieu 1984: 32).

In other words: high esthetic refuses to participate in the gratifications that the popular esthetic instead embraces: things directly connected with daily life that yield a direct, unambiguous pleasure. In the popular humor style, standardized humor and the humor of daily life follow naturally from each other. Professional humorists are described as person, not artiste. For highbrow humor lovers, the distance between the humor of daily life and standardized humor is much larger: cabaret artists are judged more as artist and less as person.

If criteria applied by those with low and middle education to good and bad humor are solely seen in terms of their contrast with the highbrow humor, an important aspect of this humor – and perhaps all humor – is disregarded. Lovers of popular humor do not at all see humor as a sign of intellect, beauty or esthetic. They place their stories about humor in a very different domain: the social, not the esthetic or the cultural. Both the ideal manifestation and the ultimate delimitation of humor are described in terms of their social effect. The idea of what good humor is is thus directly connected with the idea of what good communication is: communication style and humor style are closely linked.

These differences between popular and intellectual styles have a significantly larger scope than solely humor or even the appreciation of everything subject to taste. The definitions of good and bad humor are connected with more general ideas about creativity and sociability. And these themselves are again connected with a concept not once spontaneously named by any interviewee, but that was recognizable in almost all the interviews as an idea or, formulated in other terms, as an important theme: authenticity. In Western societies around the beginning of the twenty-first century, in which identities are not given but created and recreated all the time, authenticity, or "being yourself" has become a central theme and mission for everyone (Giddens 1991). You have to "express yourself", through style, taste, as well as everyday behavior. As became clear from the interviews, interviewees from all backgrounds tended to equate humor with such expressions of personal authenticity.

For all the interviewees, humor had to do with "being yourself" and "revealing yourself". This applies to the joke tellers: they saw telling jokes as something directly connected with their character – social, sociable, spontaneous, open – and saw the jokes as mirroring their personality. "You tell a joke because you like it yourself and you want to share it with everyone. I think that – yes: that you're born with it" (Alfred Kruger). "I think that in the first place you have to like the joke yourself. If you try to tell a story that you can't identify with then you won't tell it well." (Otto van de Meijden) Joke tellers too thus want to "reveal something of themselves": by telling the jokes *and* through the jokes themselves.

In the descriptions too of people with a sense of humor, the appreciation of the humor seems directly connected with the judgment of the humorist. Anke Vermeer's "paralyzingly witty" acquaintance is also "someone who doesn't hear you". The sharp sense of humor of Louis Baldé's acquaintance was "built into the personality". The humor of Zwagerman's acquaintance has to do with the fact that he is a very melancholy man. And lovers of popular humor couple humor to personality: Hanneke Meertens' and Jan Jurriaans' funny acquaintances are "always cheerful". Claudia van Leer's son always wants to "turn the atmosphere around if everybody's down". Evident from the quotes in the previous chapter is that humorists like van Duin are much appreciated for "how they are". Humor is seen as an important component of how someone *is*, as a part of someone's being.

While the idea of authenticity played a role in all the interviews, my respondents did not refer to it as such. They called people spontaneous, original, creative, sincere, direct, honest – all words that point to the idea of authenticity. These characterizations suggest that the person in question shows something of himself in his humor, an idea of equal importance for both popular and intellectual humorists, men and women. To once more refer to Erving Goffman and the notion of everyday communication as "interaction ritual": humor is always a presentation of self. People use humor to create, save or maintain an image of themselves. For that matter, humor can be used very adequately to falsify an image of yourself, to hide things from view, but this is often mentioned as a faulty use of humor: a good humorist, whether amateur or professional, projects through the means of his humor a "real" image of himself.

People, however, have very different ideas about where this authenticity lies. For lovers of intellectual humor, this authenticity lies in the originality of the joke maker: the joke maker reveals something of his quick, nimble-witted, sharp mind. The authenticity of the joke teller, the life of the party and of humorists like van Duin lies in their sociability. A popular humorist shows his individuality by being involved, friendly and sociable, by contributing to a good atmosphere. A word much used by joke lovers was "spontaneous". The good joke teller tells a joke "spontaneously" or has "spontaneous" humor, with which is meant: unaffected, social, not aimed at self-edification but at boosting the atmosphere. "Spontaneous" comes perhaps the closest to the popular meaning of authenticity.

The origin of the joke actually has nothing to do with this definition: what is involved is the underlying intention. The authenticity is apparent from the social message of the joke teller. Creativity does play a role in this definition, but this creativity lies in an aspect of humor not much appreciated by the highly educated – the art of "presenting" the joke. The personal creative contribution lies in the performance and not in thinking up the joke. The joke tellers always seriously prided themselves on their "own style" of telling jokes. In his narrative art, the joke teller reveals something of himself.

Thus different ideas of authenticity, spontaneity and "being yourself" belong to the popular and the highbrow humor style. To express authentic humor, those with low education use, among other things, an already existing repertoire, while the highly educated create their own repertoire – or at least, want to maintain this illusion. These are not gradual differences in meaning, but fundamentally different criteria. The fact that these gauges differ so much points once more to cultural difference between social layers: the highly and less highly educated are here employing a different cultural logic here.

These different ideas about authenticity are in my view connected with more general cultural differences between the highly and less highly educated. These ideas are related to the notions people have of social relationships and the place of the individual. My informants without a college education spoke of people in more relational terms. Self-images, self-awareness and presentation of self were primarily discussed in terms of groups, relationships and social networks. The more highly educated spoke of themselves and others primarily as individuals on their own, apart from social situations and relationships. The literature about differences in class cultures offers a number of clues for an interpretation of this nature. In general, the social structure of the working class is described as closely knit and more social, whereas the culture of the upper middle class is described as more individualistic (Collins 1977: 114-131, 1988: 214-219, 2004; Gans 1962). The relationship with different images of self and relationships is seldom explored here.

I am going to become speculative here – the lack of good literature about class cultures in the Netherlands constitutes a problem for me – but a distinction like this between more social and more individualistic self-images also seems visible in relationships and styles of friendship of the highly and less highly educated. For the highly educated, friendship and relationships have a lot to do with "psychobabble": the exchange of individual, confidential information about oneself. For the less highly educated, intimacy is sooner defined in terms of loyalty and shared activities. This is apparent from research by Straver et al. (1994) about marriages of the less highly educated. At any rate, it is also striking here once again to what extent the highly educated find themselves close to what is generally seen as "feminine".

Be that as it may, the different humor styles are connected with a different habitus that reaches further than solely the domain of the humor. Ideas that play a role in judging humor have a bearing on all social interaction. We are not just concerned with gradual differences: humor is placed in another framework. If the same standard is employed by different groups, but by one more strictly than the other, it means that this is the same standard that has later "trickled down". This is not the case here: the totally different meanings given to authenticity point out that it is not trickle down we are talking about here but different cultural logic. Good humor and good interaction lie in one line for joke lovers. The joke, as a form of communication regarding the relationship as more important than the content, better suits a world image where relationships are central. Criteria tailored to individual creativity imposed by the highly educated on jokes are of no value whatsoever to joke lovers. They are simply not what a joke is about.

Conclusion: Jokes, taste, and authenticity

"The joke is a placebo", said Freek de Jonge in his program *De Grens* [The Border] (1999). De Jonge, the favorite cabaret artist of lovers of highbrow humor, thus also objects to the lack of authenticity of the joke. He sees the genre as *unreal*: a substitute for real humor, humor without the active ingredient. "Placebo", elucidates de Jonge further, "means: I will please." For joke lovers and others with a preference for popular humor, humor must indeed be pleasant. For people with the highbrow humor style, humor does not have to please but challenge.

The objection that the joke is not creative and original, as already indicated in Chapter 2, was aimed at the joke much later than the other objections: lack of restraint and refinement. The criterion of personal, authentic, individual creativity is very much a late twentieth-century criterion (Giddens 1991). And yet this is the objection that has definitively discredited the joke for the highbrow. The emergence of the idea of authenticity as the most individual expression of personal creativity can be connected with a broader social shift that took effect primarily in the twentieth century: individualization.[8] This broader process includes constituent processes like the "emancipation of the emotions" (Wouters 1999), the psychologizing of the view of oneself and others – processes by which one's own interior world was explored further and further (Elias 1982; Wouters 1999, 2004).

It is, however, the question whether the divergent views on the meaning of authenticity are linked solely with further and further advances in individualization. After all, we are also concerned here with cultural meanings strongly connected with schooling, organization of work, and social networks and all sorts of other structural factors. Class culture is not only related to processes of cultural distinction and the related mechanisms of status decline and social trickle down, but also to the structural realities of work, school, and everyday life.

For instance, the sort of work done by college graduates generally requires more intellectual efforts, as well as more independence and individual responsibilities, leading to a higher degree of individualization and reflexivity (Giddens 1991). Working and lower middle class jobs often require more team work and cooperation as well as more, and more visible, hierarchy and less autonomy. Such structural differences are likely to lead to divergent perspectives on individuality and sociability. Moreover, as a result of structural differences, they same process of individualization may lead to quests for very different types of authenticity and individuality.

Class cultures within one society are certainly not separate from one another, but neither do they develop themselves purely in contrast with, or imitation of, one another. Different class cultures also have, to some extent, their own cultural logic. This leads to the same phenomena and processes acquiring different meanings in different groupings. This counts for a concept like authenticity, spontaneity and "being yourself": the same concept, presumably arising under the influence of the same process of individualization and differentiation of lifestyles, acquires totally different implications. The cultural logic of class cultures is not only connected with further and further advancing processes of social change, but also with tenacious, surviving, social structures.

The discovery of such a sharp distinction between Dutch class cultures is one of the more unexpected results of researching jokes. It is not so much the existence of the distinction that surprises as its scope: fairly fundamental differences in cultural logic apparently underlie these cultural differences. This is not to say that an absolute division into two class cultures exists in the Netherlands – two groups within one society with totally separate tastes and ideas about good, bad, funny, vulgar or corny humor. But there is, indeed, question of a social difference capable of having significant consequences: even small distinctions in sense of humor can have large effects on social relationships.

Part II. Taste and quality

Chapter 6
The repertoire: Dutch joke culture

Until now, the appreciation of jokes has been exclusively evaluated as part of a genre: the joke has been discussed as a form of humor, the telling of jokes as a form of communication. This approach has demonstrated that there are many ways of thinking about the joke. Some see the joke as "the pinnacle of humor" while others cannot see anything humorous about it. The type of joke has hardly been addressed at all, even though it really matters whether the subject is a sexual joke or a child's rhyme, something featuring mothers-in-law, Turks or pastors, a short riddle or a long story. Both joke lovers and joke haters like one joke considerably more than the next. In this second part of the book, I am going to focus on the evaluation of separate jokes: on differences in taste *within* the genre.

To be able to make any statement at all about how separate jokes and categories of jokes are evaluated, knowledge of the jokes themselves is required. That is why the first chapter of this part of the book includes an overview of Dutch jokes. Such a survey of joke culture inevitably becomes an overview of the sensibilities and preoccupations of Dutch society in the past decades: virtually all jokes have to do with taboos, painful topics, social fears and excluded groups. To make a topic fit for joking, it must have a strong cultural and social meaning. A hearer must be susceptible to what is being said to experience it as funny; the text has to closely approach a social or cultural boundary and then give it a little push.

This chapter is actually a short ethnography of Dutch joke culture. I am not going to address the context within which this culture flourishes, the place occupied by the joke in the midst of other humorous genres. For the moment, I will be dealing with the jokes here as an independent cultural phenomenon. The information in this chapter will therefore come closer than that in the previous one to mainstream sociological and anthropological research into humor, which primarily interprets humor as reflecting culture and social circumstances. In this chapter, I am going to temporarily adhere to the "barometer thesis" (Meder and Venbrux 2000), the thought that, in a certain way, humor reflects society as a whole.

While I will be looking primarily at the connection between Dutch jokes and the social boundaries and susceptibilities of "the" Dutch society, it has already been demonstrated that jokes are not equally valued in all layers of the society. This thus gives rise to the question of whether the content of jokes actually reflects Dutch society as a whole or is more likely to reflect the worldview of groups who tend to tell the most jokes: the less educated, and men. In the chapters to follow, I will try to establish connections between jokes and the way different factions in the Netherlands experience the world.

Jokes and social boundaries

Almost all the jokes that I have found touch on a certain social boundary, susceptibility or "threshold of embarrassment" (Elias 1978, 1982). The most popular joke categories deal with sensitive questions like sex, gender relationships, foreigners, aggression, religion, money, sicknesses, death, disasters and scandals. Much of the pleasure of humor lies in the short-lived, playful, lighthearted overstepping of a social boundary.

Not just in the social sciences but also in daily speech, jokes are usually categorized according to the boundary they touch upon. My interviewees regularly pointed to categories such as dirty jokes or sex jokes, jokes hostile to women, smutty jokes, jokes targeting foreigners, discriminating or racist jokes, sick jokes, disaster jokes and religious jokes (jokes about faith). I have also classified the jokes in my collection based on the boundary they overstep. This classification can be seen in Table 4 accompanied by a not very systematic but representative and rather exhaustive review of many of the themes or "humorous scripts" (Davies 1990; Raskin 1985) that occur within each category. The text will include examples of the different types of jokes.

Like every classification, this one must take into account exceptions and overlaps. The categories cannot exclude one another. For instance, jokes that stereotype often point to something unseemly: how dumb the Belgians are, how miserly the Netherlanders. The most important exception to this classification is the absurd joke: purely absurd jokes do not overstep social boundaries and thus fall outside the classification. Absurd jokes are based neither on the unseemly nor on violated social boundaries but on impossibilities, breaches of logic, language or the natural order of things. Absurd elements occur in practically every joke: jumpers from the Eiffel tower land on the ground in one piece, a genie grants wishes, dogs speak and Belgians cut corners with a knife.

Absurdity is always closely connected with humor. "Absurd humor" is perhaps more a question of degree than a category absolutely differentiated from other humor. Some jokes are founded in absurdity, however, like the

Table 4. Humorous scripts in jokes by transgressed boundary (The categories are roughly listed in order of their popularity)

Susceptibility	Scripts
1. **Sexuality and gender**	Ambiguity and innuendo; being over-sexed/ promiscuity; asexuality/ frigidity; celibacy; adultery; marriage (marriage as a mistake; authority relationships within marriage); sexual achievements & size; prostitution; (apparent) naivety; homosexuality; rape; incest; pedophilia; bestiality & sex with animals; ugly women & old maids; sex and aging; etc.
2. **Shortcomings** **and social deviance**	Jokes about uncivilized, unusual, maladjusted or incompetent behavior, such as: Stupidity; craziness; drunkenness; childishness; laziness; criminality; aggression; impoliteness; absent-mindedness; impaired speech; unusual appearance; filthiness; stench; naivety; cowardliness; gluttony; incomplete control of bodily functions; all sorts of lacking talent and incompetence
3. **Sickness, suffering and death**	Sickness; infirmities and handicaps; accidents & disasters; blood and mutilation; castration; famine; public scandals (e.g. Dutroux); horror stories; war (Second World War; holocaust jokes; Hitler jokes)
4. **Religion**	Blasphemy; Godly interference and punishment; hypocrisy; after-life; celibacy; clergymen; breaking religious commandments
5. **Money and wealth**	Poverty; richness; miserliness; covetousness; business acumen; prodigality; cunning ways of getting money
6. **Power and authority**	Role reversals: superior & inferior, civilian & law enforcer, child & adult; Jokes upwards: politicians, Royal House, celebrities; Jokes downwards: inferiors, servants, laborers
7. **Stereotypes and** **relations with Others** [usually combined with one of the categories listed above]	Stereotyping: see 2 Cultural rivalry and superiority; attitude jokes; insulting the audience; aggression and violence. Primarily ethnic, also, for instance, farmers, blondes, mothers-in-law, politicians etc.

following joke from the questionnaire. These contain nothing unseemly and even the punch line is based on an impossibility:

> A man goes to the doctor and says: "Doctor, I'm half deaf." "What do you mean, half deaf?" "Well," says the man, "I always hear exactly half of what anyone says." "That's new to me," says the doctor, "I'll just take a look then. Go on over to the corner of the room and stand there with your back to me. I'll be in the other corner. You repeat everything I say." So the man goes and stands in the corner, his back to the doctor. The doctor says: "Eighty-eight." The man: "Forty-four."

The humor in these jokes lies in the consistent use of a form of logic that does not fit the context. The second joke applies the rules of mathematics to the area of hearing. No social boundary is transgressed. Therefore this sort of joke was judged to be the least hurtful. (Chapter 7 will include ratings for offensiveness.)

With the exception of such exclusively absurd jokes, all jokes have to do in one way or another with overstepping a social or cultural boundary. These transgressions are not all of the same nature. The susceptibilities in Table 4 range from subjects, the simple mention of which can shock, to relatively innocent shortcomings like being dumb or absent-minded. The relationship between funniness and sensitivity thus differs for each joke category. Jokes about shocking events are funny, at least for those who like them, precisely because they shock. The other extreme is jokes about stupidity or drunkenness. These have to do with something unseemly but are seldom shocking. The boundary transgressions are not all of the same nature either: sexual jokes name something that must not be named whereas jokes about religion make light of something so solemn it must always be taken seriously. There is thus not only a huge diversity in the content of the jokes but also in the nature of the susceptibilities and the boundary transgressions involved.

As this chapter continues, I will deal with the different categories of jokes and shifts within them. However, I will not completely follow the classification in the table. Instead I have combined joke categories that touch on boundaries in a comparable way. I will begin with a category that I have called "jokes about shortcomings". This is not the largest category – the most widespread jokes are without a doubt jokes about sex and gender relationships – but by using this category I can most easily distinguish elements crucial to the understanding of all categories of jokes: the distinction between jokes *in which* a boundary is transgressed and jokes that *themselves* transgress a social boundary.

Innocuous jokes: Stupidity and other unseemly behavior

Jokes about shortcomings make up a relatively diffuse category that includes all sorts of jokes based on "incongruous" – impolite, unusual, unseemly or incompetent – behavior on the part of the protagonist in the joke. Often a type of behavior is linked to a certain section of the population. When this is the case, overlap takes place with jokes that stereotype. In many jokes, the person in question is neutral, or not further specified ("A woman goes to the doctor...").

Some jokes are based on specific idiosyncrasies and character faults such as laziness, filthiness or absent-mindedness. These bad characteristics often form the central focus of comedies and sitcoms, in which the personages are often types having *one* accentuated characteristic. I will now quote two examples of jokes of this sort, both about laziness. In the first, from 1969, the do-nothing is "a man" and in the second, more recent joke, as in many recent jokes, laziness is ascribed to Surinamese:

> A man who detested working lay dozing on his back in the shadow of a tree when all of a sudden his wife disturbed his peace and quiet. "There you are again lazing the day away, just as I thought! You're not capable of doing anything else!" The man opened one eye and said: "Still a lot better than doing nothing, isn't it?" (*Nieuwe Revu* 44 (1969), no. 15)

> A man from Surinam living in the Netherlands writes to his cousin saying he should come to visit. He also writes that money in the Netherlands grows on trees. So his cousin makes the trip. He walks down the ramp from the airplane, sees a 10-guilder bill lying near a tall potted plant and walks on. When he gets to the baggage area, he sees a 50-guilder bill lying under a row of planted indoor trees and keeps on going. Under the potted palm near the exit, he sees a 100-guilder bill; he opens the door and walks on. When he reaches his cousin, he tells him about the money and the cousin asks: "Why didn't you pick it up?" "Money grows on trees here, right? And tomorrow is another day." (Kuipers 1995)

The humorous technique of this sort of joke is always the same: exaggeration and enhancement of one single characteristic. Even though magazines and joke books may contain jokes of this type featuring neutral characters, as in the first example, most of the jokes of this type I encountered "in real life" target one specific group: dirty Turks, lazy Surinamese, sex-crazed nuns.

Tellers of jokes are keen on jokes about stupidity, drunkenness, craziness, coarseness and childishness – all deviant states offering a range of unseemly behavior broader than *one* exaggerated characteristic. Stupidity, especially, is an extremely popular "script" in jokes all around the world. Jokes about these generalized deviances are almost as widespread as sexual jokes, and also very popular: they were also very highly valued in the questionnaire. What the unseemly characteristics have in common, at least in the jokes, is their connection with a certain civilization lag: stupidity in jokes points to what is felt as retardation. Jokes about stupidity are always told about a group strongly resembling one's own, but finding itself to some extent on the periphery and having little political, cultural or economical influence: the "slightly backward" version of one's own group (Davies 1990). Stupidity and coarseness are often interchangeable in jokes – before the Belgians became the butt of these jokes during the 1970s, people in the Netherlands told the same jokes about dumb farmers and country people. Children too can be seen as having civilization arrears that will, of course, be rectified at a later date. Drunkards can be seen as experiencing a temporary regression in their level of civilization.

The socially unseemly behavior of children, crazy people, farmers, drunkards, Belgians and dumb blondes shows many similarities; all these groups are thought of as dumb, often somewhat naive, but certainly not unfriendly. More than that, what is alluded to is often a special, unrealistic sort of stupidity – a humorous logic (Ziv 1984). Dumb figures in jokes take figurative situations literally and apply the rules of one domain to another; they turn roles and power relationships upside-down and ignore natural laws. The stupidity often has a clearly absurd character.

Why does a Belgian take hay with him to bed? To feed the nightmares.

Two friends are both going out with dumb blondes. One says to the other: "I'll just show you how dumb my girlfriend is, okay?" He calls his girlfriend over and says: "Listen, here's five euros; can you go and get five crates of beer for me at the supermarket?" "Okay", says the dumb blonde and off she goes to the supermarket with the five euros. "That's nothing", says the other. "Shall I show you how dumb my girlfriend is?" So he calls his girlfriend and says: "Hey Anita, would you go to my place and have a look if I'm there too?" "Yeah okay", the blonde says and off she goes. A little while later the two girls run into each other. The one says: "My boyfriend is so incredibly dumb. He gave me five euros to buy five crates of beer for him while he knows I could never carry five crates all by myself!" "That's nothing", says the other. "My boyfriend just sent me to his place to see if he was there. He could just as easily have phoned!" (Jelmer de Moor)

A similar cracked logic is found in jokes about crazy people ("Doctor, my wife thinks she's a hen." And after she's been cured: "To tell you the truth, doctor, we miss the eggs"), about drunkards ringing a bell on a lamppost ("Yes, I know officer, but the light was still on") and about blondes losing their way jumping off a high-rise. Were it not that a population group is being stereotyped, these jokes would more probably be described as impossible or absurd than unseemly. Jokes about dumb groups are seldom painful, actually only when the group that is their butt occupies a vulnerable position in society, as in the scarce jokes about dumb blacks or, as some see it, the jokes about dumb blondes.

Children in jokes are presented not only as humorously dumb but also as shameless and particularly: as sexually naive – a type of uncivilized behavior permitting one to draw on the domain with the largest potential for humor:

> Johnny's class has been learning about animals with names ending in "or". The teacher asks the class: "Can anyone name one animal ending in "or"?" Bobby waves his arm in the air and says: "An alligator, miss." "Well done, Bobby, and what does it eat?" "People, miss." "Very good." Then it's Mary's turn: "A condor, miss." "Very good, Mary, and what does it eat?" "Sheep, miss." Then Johnny puts up his hand and says: "A vibrator, miss." The teacher starts to blush but doesn't want to discourage Johnny so she asks: "What does it eat, Johnny?" "I don't know for sure, miss, but my sister says it sure eats up the batteries" (Karel Vroon, 46, entrepreneur)

Here again, witness the connection between jokes about children and Belgians: Johnny does not only reason here in plays on words, Belgians are also portrayed as both sexually naïve, and often using logic dependent on wordplay (making these jokes exceptionally hard to translate).

These jokes about shortcomings, both when based on temporary lags in civilization and on exaggerations of one specific area, count as safe jokes. This is because these are jokes *in* which boundaries are transgressed, but the jokes themselves do not as a rule touch upon or transgress a boundary. Boundary transgression takes place *within* the joke but only once in a while *through* the joke. The figure in the joke isn't very civilized and there is an accompanying mitigating circumstance – he is crazy, drunk, still a child, a Belgian, a farmer or a professor – but the joke itself is usually not unseemly. Neither the joke teller nor the audience shares the shortcoming of the joke figure; both function as spectators while someone else does something unseemly.

There are jokes about shortcomings, however, that even when attributed to a joke person, are felt to transgress boundaries. They constitute a relatively small proportion of this joke category. Whether or not the joke touches a boundary or actually transgresses it depends partially on the audience – after all, not everyone has the same boundaries. But this also depends on the joke itself: some jokes anticipate a shocked or embarrassed reaction. Among other things, this has to do with the subject: aggressive or violent behavior often really transgresses boundaries, as do things referring to personal hygiene and bodily functions: toilet humor and jokes about spit, snot and vomit. The following scatological joke anticipates vicarious shame from the audience:

> A man has been crazy about white beans in tomato sauce all his life but he has the troublesome problem of flatulence when he eats them. When he got married, he promised himself he'd never eat white beans in tomato sauce again because he just couldn't inflict that on his wife. He keeps his promise for four years and then one day he passes a restaurant and smells white beans in tomato sauce. He can't resist the temptation so he goes in and eats not one, not two but three bowls overflowing with white beans in tomato sauce. And then it starts: ffffaaarrrt, ffffaaarrrt. The man walks home: ffffaaarrrt, ffffaaarrrt. Just before he rings the bell, he grunts out another huge one: ffffffffaaaaaarrrt. His wife says: "Darling, I've got a surprise for you. But I have to blindfold you first." His wife blindfolds the man and leads him to the dining room where he sits at his usual place. "No peeking now," says his wife as she goes into the kitchen. Quickly, the man farts one last time, loudly and extensively: ffffaaarrrrt! He flaps madly with his suit coat to wave away the smell. His wife returns and takes off his blindfold. And what do you know? Twelve of his friends are sitting around the dining table! (told at *Moppentoppers*)

Now a joke (quite friendly compared to jokes that I will quote later) that has to do with aggressive behavior:

> There's this guy sitting with his dog watching Ajax [Amsterdam soccer club] playing Feyenoord [Rotterdam soccer club] and every time Ajax scores a goal the dog jumps up and starts to bark. A guy sitting beside them says: "Wow, that dog's pretty crazy about Ajax, isn't he?" The first says: "Yeah! Right out of his mind." The other asks: "But what happens if Feyenoord scores a goal?" The guy with the dog says: "Then he jumps up into the air, makes a pirouette and lands on his feet." "Boy", the other says, "that's pretty amazing. Now, when he's up in the air, does he turn right or left?" The first says: "Yeah, that depends where I whack him first." (Huibert Busser)

These are jokes that touch upon a taboo. They don't just describe something unseemly, they *are* a bit unseemly. The laugh that follows a joke of this kind, something I have dubbed the "oooh" laugh, is a laugh containing shock and indignation. The person laughing often covers his mouth with his hand and this is one indication that the joke transgresses a boundary.

This distinction between jokes that themselves transgress a boundary and jokes in which a boundary is transgressed, applies to most joke categories. It is impossible to delimit this precisely: whether or not a sore spot is touched depends on each individual and each group and is furthermore dependent on the company and context. It is possible, however, to point to a difference in content between jokes that anticipate a boundary transgression and those more focused on reporting someone else's unseemly behavior. A joke like the following, for instance, anticipates audience sensitivity to certain references:

> What do you get when you cross a Turk with a black man? Someone too lazy to steal. (Kuipers 1995)

Here references are made to two shortcomings, laziness and thieving, but they are not explained. The fact that they are named (and ascribed to two ethnic groups) is apparently funny enough all on its own. In jokes purely based on transgressing a boundary, it is enough to do something that is not allowed – to say a dirty word, to insult a social group. In jokes based on describing a shortcoming, exaggeration is often used: to achieve the humorous effect, a certain shortcoming is isolated and highly magnified. The basic technique here is not violating a taboo but drawing a caricature. Thus, these jokes are generally longer and more elaborate.

The audience's position, that of the laughers, differs too. The audience is a spectator in jokes about a Belgian's or a child's shortcoming: the person who doesn't know how to behave is someone else. But the laugher stops being a spectator and becomes an accomplice in a small conspiracy when the joke itself transgresses a boundary. Jokes that do not themselves transgress a boundary are also referred to as jokes "for under the Christmas tree", implying that they are safe jokes. But they also run a greater risk of ending up insipid or corny. They don't shock but they don't give that special charge from doing something forbidden either. Jokes that themselves transgress a boundary often make people laugh harder but they also run up against resistance more quickly.

Sexual jokes: From allusion to transgression

This difference between boundary transgression *in* and *through* the joke can easily be seen in the development of the most popular Dutch joke category, the sexual joke. As a consequence of a significantly changed sensitivity in the sexual area, the sexual joke has developed from a category primarily based on boundary transgression through the joke – simply naming the unmentionable was painful enough and therefore funny – to a category in which the humor lies in the unseemly or inordinate behavior of the joke personage. I will deal quite thoroughly with the shifts in the sexual joke, not only because this development can provide insight into the relationship between jokes and social boundaries, but also because the most popular Dutch joke genre deserves thorough treatment.

Sex is the favorite subject for jokes. As far as that goes, there was a unique agreement among the sources: most jokes that humorists told me had to do with sex; most published jokes had to do with sex and Internet jokes have to do almost exclusively with sex. A great number of jokes, as far as I can tell, also had to do with sex fifty or a hundred years ago. But, at the same time, Dutch morals in this area have changed significantly: sex has changed from something shameful that could hardly be mentioned into a subject that is indeed still sensitive, but can be talked about nevertheless (Wouters 1990; 2004). In other words, the sensitivity now is of quite a different sort than fifty years ago. Sex is, however, still funny.

Until the 1960s, people distinguished sharply between "dirty" and "clean" jokes; older interviewees still did this. Even the most polite jokes about sex were loaded, as is apparent from this story told by a one of the joke tellers I interviewed, a 76-year-old owner of a furniture company:

> Then I told something and later the chairman [of the countrywoman's organization] came up to me and says: "You told a joke about that rooster; it was in bad taste." I say: "Bad taste?" "Yes, you know, what that rooster did." I say: "Then you understood it wrongly."
> *And what sort of joke was that?*
> "That was a very simple little story. I go to a farm with my son and when we get there a rooster's doing his business with a hen. My son asks: "What's happening to that hen, daddy?" I say: "Oh, the rooster's putting stamps on the eggs." That's all. Back then people thought that that was going too far. Nobody liked it. It was in bad taste. That's nothing, right? These days that's less than nothing." (Gijs Kronenberg)

Another one of the joke tellers, who worked as a professional entertainer, got into problems at the beginning of the 1960s with a joke that wasn't even about sex, only about a "young lady in the bath":

> I remember to this day that I was still in the dressing room when the pastor blustered in. He goes: "I certainly hope that the level's not going to sink any

further." I go: "What do you mean, level, I don't get it? I go: "What did I say then?" I'd told a very silly little story about a young lady who was so thin that she'd finish her bath and then make sure she go out of the tub before pulling the plug or else she'd disappear down the drain. Believe it or not, that pastor thought that was a dirty story. It was bad taste to talk about a young lady in a bathtub. That's just one example of how it was back then. (Fred Crooswijk)

Sexual jokes like that had the same clandestine status as ethnic jokes do now: they were only told in closed, (male) company: "Those jokes were told, but in the pub or at a party at home perhaps. They existed of course, but they weren't told on the stage or in public" (Fred Crooswijk). The sharp distinction between "clean" and "dirty" jokes is a problem in my research: huge numbers of the jokes that were once told can no longer be traced. The secrecy surrounding these did not diminish their amusement value; their "naughtiness" made them more appealing. The realization of doing something forbidden plays a large role in all jokes about taboos: something forbidden is always fun. The social aspect is also important here: one shares a forbidden pleasure.

Wim Kan, who for years did a New Year's Eve comic monologue, first on the radio, then on TV, told a variation on the daring Gijs Kronenberg joke in his 1976 monologue: "That one dog has sand in his eyes and the other one is pushing him back home". These days, the same joke barely merits a smile. Unimaginably well-behaved jokes deemed publishable in the 1960s, in something like *De Lach, a* magazine seen as very daring in those days, are not even funny anymore and some are not even understandable. In addition to jokes, *De Lach* featured photographs of women in bathing suits (that grew smaller and smaller as the years passed). The composition of this magazine shows clearly how the joke has always been connected with the male world and especially: with sex.

De Lach's standing was so low that all the magazine archives in the Netherlands taken together have saved as few as five examples. This is the sort of joke published in *De Lach:*

Friend, to just-married, young woman: "Oh, how nice, where did you go for your honeymoon?" The newly married woman turns red and looks at her husband, saying: "Gosh Hank, that's true too. Where were we anyway?" (*De Lach* 3-11-1950)

Characteristic of this joke and of all published sexual jokes from the same period is that it cannot be said with certainty that the joke has to do with sex.

But the suspicion is aroused. The technique of this joke doesn't differ much from that of the "stamps on the egg", even though the reference is somewhat less explicit. The intention is to call up thoughts of the unspeakable subject of sex without once mentioning an improper word. The teller of the joke can always hide behind the fact that he has said nothing indelicate. As another of the interviewed joke tellers explained:

> They kept saying: "Yeah, you always tell jokes that're a bit shady." And I'd say back: "Repeat one bad word then." "Well, you don't really use any, do you?" And when I did tell a joke, I often announced: "Ladies and gentlemen, before we begin, I just want to say one thing; if my words send your thoughts in certain directions just remember, it's your own brains doing the dirty work." (Evert van Roden)

Here lies the pleasure of ambiguity and innuendo: words send thoughts "in certain directions" but the taboo is not violated.

Due to the diminishing sensitivity for sexual references, much of the pleasure of ambiguous references has been lost. After all, a certain susceptibility has to be addressed: the less painful something is, the further one has to go to be funny. Jokes that are still told, purely based on sexual allusion, count as rather harmless. They are conspicuous in often having to do with children and they are significantly more explicit than "stamps on the eggs":

> The teacher asks the children to make up rhymes like: "Bobby walks through the lobby." Different children try different rhymes and then Johnny puts up his hand: "Aunt Ruth's in the pool doing a stunt and the water comes up to her knees." "But that doesn't even rhyme," says the teacher. "I can't help it if she's in the shallow end, now can I?" says Johnny.

Nowadays jokes that once elicited punishment from the pastor and the chairman of the countrywoman's organization don't amount to much. In the 1993/1994 season, the following joke was told in *Moppentoppers* on prime time television:

> Sam is lying on the roof, completely naked in the sun, reading his newspaper when he falls asleep. He probably dreams of a nice little piece of tail because he gets a huge hard-on. Moos comes up onto the roof and thinks, oh oh. Moos picks up the newspaper, rolls it up and covers the projection with it. He goes back downstairs, runs into Sarah and says: "Saar, you ought to go up on the roof, Sam's got something for you in the newspaper" (Brandsteder 1994: 44)

That was a pretty average joke from the program *Moppentoppers* that was generally rather rigorously censored (about which all the joke tellers I contacted at this show complained at length). Sexual jokes are now noticeably less clandestine and much more explicit.

Not only have the permissibility and the degree of explicitness of jokes about sex changed: their whole nature and import has shifted. Where older sexual jokes were based on a reference to a subject that could not be named – a boundary transgression *through* the joke – many recent sexual jokes are about unseemly sexual behavior of the joke personage himself. As apparent from the rather bizarre summing up of the scripts of sexual jokes in Table 4, the present-day repertoire is a display card of unseemly or excessive sexual behavior. These jokes are primarily based on the description of personages who cannot or will not behave in a restrained and civilized way in the sexual area. One example from one of the joke tellers:

> Along come three dogs and they all sit down in a waiting room and after awhile one of the dogs says to the other two "hey, what're you doing here?" "Well", says one, "I have to be put down." "Why's that?" "Oh, the usual. There I am sitting in the kitchen last week, my master's cutting up a delicious beef heart, he's preparing it beautifully for me, a splash of water, a sprinkling of aniseed, really delicious as usual and I'm thinking, oh glorious food. Well, what happens next? In comes Miranda the cat and gobbles up my whole bowlful. So I think, aha this is the second time already. You've just had your last chance, Miranda. So I liquidate her. And now I'm sitting here." "And you, Pluto, why are you here?" "Well, last week, there I am walking with my master through the park, just trotting along peacefully, minding my own business, and along comes one of those really tiny terriers, you know, and he begins to mount my leg, right there and then. What do you suppose that faggot of a dog was thinking of? He was going nowhere fast, must've thought I had a hole way down in my leg or something. So I took a nip to the left and a couple to the right, right on goal, and that was curtains for one horny terrier." "But you, Fido, what are you doing here?" "Well, last week I go upstairs and I smell something like spring flowers and I ask myself, what's that? So I wander through the bathroom following the smell and there's my mistress kneeling enticingly over the edge of the bath, wearing only her miniskirt and no panties, scrubbing the enamel. So, well, I think this is my big chance, isn't it? So I jump on her and give her a good going over, wow, that was really something, sparks all around." "So you're being put down too?" "No, no," he says, "I gotta get my nails clipped." (Jelmer de Moor)

This is not about naming a taboo subject; that is done rather unceremoniously. What it is about is the control and regulation of sexuality: about unseemly sexual behavior (that also gets rewarded). Increased openness has been accompanied by an augmented necessity to regulate sexuality in daily life both precisely and flexibly (de Swaan 1990; Wouters 1999, 2004). The world presented in sexual jokes is a world in which this sort of regulation does not take place.

The import of many recent sexual jokes can be summarized succinctly as: everyone wants sex all the time. These jokes sketch a completely sexualized universe, a world in which everyone is preoccupied with sex. This becomes clear not only in jokes like the above but also in joke books with titles like *Nudge, nudge* or *Darling, I'll be working late tonight*, illustrated with pictures of blonde women in short skirts, lustful men and witchy wives. Sexual jokes call up a world in which the regulation of sex is no longer an obligation, in which women are always available, in which marriage only exists as an obstacle and in which lascivious men (even if they are dogs) are always rewarded in the end (Legman 1982; Mulkay 1988).

At present a sexual joke can also easily be a clean joke. The boundary between unseemly and "clean" jokes runs through the genre and is not distinguished by language use or degree of explicitness. In shocking or unseemly sexual jokes, there is often question of combinations with other more painful boundary transgressions, as in the following:

A man visits a whorehouse and says: "I've heard that you have something very special here, a whore who can sing while she does a blow job." "That's right", says the madame, "there's only one condition – she won't do it unless it's completely dark in the room." The man agrees; he goes into the room. He can't see anything at all but it is as rumored, she begins to give him a blow job and she sings at the same time. When it's done, he's still very curious about how she managed to do it. So he goes back one more time and takes a penlight with him. He goes into the room and she begins her blow job and her singing and when she's really busy, he very carefully clicks on his penlight. And what does he see there on the bedside table? A glass eye in the water glass.

This joke, that was not always understood, was included in the questionnaire and went too far for many participants. This had to do with the explicit language, but particularly with the rather gruesome character of the sexual act and the deformation of the woman in question. This joke deals with other types of boundary transgressions than the purely sexual. To begin with, this joke teeters between amusement and disgust – a form of "sick" or "morbid" humor. What's more, the reference to the glass eye makes it sick humor in the more literal sense of the word: amusement about sickness. To laugh at handicaps is an unseemly boundary transgression, irreverence about what should be taken "seriously".

Irreverent jokes: Religion, power, and suffering

Taboo is defined not only as that which cannot be discussed but also that which must be approached solely with appropriate seriousness. To make jokes about such "serious" subjects counts as unseemly and transgressive. It is precisely this obligation of reverence that, at the same time, makes these events excellently suited as subjects for more or less clandestine jokes. The majority of the tabled categories are not subjects that may not be spoken of at all but subjects that must be approached with the necessary respect and seriousness: religion, money, those in power, death, sickness, suffering, disasters and to a certain extent, ethnic difference. These are definitely not subjects that cannot be mentioned or that are shameful. Much is said about them; often much *must* be said about them. The taboo does not lie in naming these subjects but in handling them frivolously.

Irreverent jokes of this sort are, for instance, the very popular jokes about religion. To laugh about God was taboo for a very long time in the Netherlands. The largest Netherlands postwar "humor scandal" had to do with religion: the infamous "icon worship" in the Dutch version of a British satirical show *That was the week that was,* caused a wave of indignation and popular fury in 1964. The television was addressed as a godhead: "give us this day our daily program, be with us, oh Image, because we know not what we would do without You".[12] Jokes about religion were, if possible, even more loaded than jokes about sexuality: in magazines and joke books, I have found not a single reference to indicate that people told jokes about religion, God, godly intervention or servants of God before 1960. Jokes tellers have told me that jokes of this sort did exist. They remembered jokes about celibacy or, a very common genre, jokes about the vicar, the rabbi and the pastor, told only behind closed doors.

These days religion, just like sex, is a suitable subject for a safe joke. At least, that is the opinion of the large majority of the Dutch. There still are a number of strict Christians, mostly Protestants, who disagree, but their power is waning. On the other hand, in the growing Muslim community, people also do not look kindly upon the mocking of (their) religion. However, in the public domain, the tolerance for religious jokes is very high, illustrating the high level of secularization of the Netherlands.

In the questionnaire, jokes about religion were very popular. The favorite joke was about religion:

> There's this man with a bible store and he's looking for someone to sell bibles door-to-door. So he sticks a sign in his store window: WANTED – door-to-door bible salesman. A man comes in and says: "IIIII would llllllike to ssssssell bbbbbbibles." The storekeeper: "But Sir, with your speech defect, do you think you'd have any luck?" "IIIII'd rrrrrreally llllike to be gggggiven a cccchance." "Well then," says the storekeeper, "I like to give everyone a chance, so I guess I'd better give you a chance too. Come back Monday at 9 o'clock." The stutterer returns Monday morning and gets a huge stack of bibles. At 12:00 he returns to the store empty-handed. He's sold all the bibles and goes off again with a new stack. At 4:00 he comes back again. His second load of bibles has been sold and he asks for more. "Okay by me", says the shopkeeper, "but I'd sure like to hear how you're managing it. You've sold a formidable number of bibles!" The man says: "Ttttthat's easy. IIIIII rrrring the bbbbbell. Ssssssomeone ccccomes to the ddddoor. Ttthen I aaaask: "Wwwwould you llllike to bbbbuy a bbbible? Or ssshall I rrrread it ttttto you?"

In jokes about religion, the sacred is mixed with the profane. Often two specific profane domains are plumbed for the mixture: money and sex. The joke above uses money and in this case sales: bibles are sold by threatening a long exposure to stuttering. Other jokes mix religion and sex, as does the following popular (seventh of the 35) joke from the questionnaire:

> A mother superior goes to the doctor and blushes while she whispers to him: "Doctor, I don't know what it is, but I have a blue spot between my legs and I have no idea where it came from." "Then I'll have to have a look", says the doctor. After a short inspection, the doctor says: "No need to worry, Mother Superior. It's only the sticker from a Chiquita banana." (Evert van Roden)

This irreverent blending of the divine with the banal makes these jokes funny and also loaded. Religion in itself is not taboo but to laugh about it was once taboo and is still daring.

This shows the complex interplay between humor and sensibilities: things that become less tabooed do not necessarily become less humorous. The fact that jokes about religion and sexual jokes presently cause less pain has led to their increased acceptation but not to a decrease in their popularity: there are still many jokes about religion (especially if you count all the jokes being played out at the heavenly gates). They were also very highly valued in the questionnaire.

There is a domain in which the diminished painfulness of the subject has led to the practical disappearance of the genre; jokes about authorities and hierarchical relationships practically died out after the 1960s or '70s (it is very difficult to accurately date a joke). These were primarily jokes in which someone with a low status acted shamelessly with regard to a superior, reversing the hierarchy of power:

> Clerk (in the dark to someone bumping into him): stupid idiot! (and then noticing that it was the chief)... that I am! (*De Lach* 8-4-1927)

> Judge: "It is incumbent upon me to order you to spend a week in prison for giving offense to a civil servant in function, by insulting him with following words: drop dead!" The accused: "Do you consider that offensive? You could just as easily drop dead!" (*Katholieke Illustratie*, 8-5-1941)

> In agitation
> "You don't have to look down your nose at me like that," said the maid, "you were in service yourself once." "Yes, but for much more distinguished people than you," the lady snapped back. (*Katholieke Illustratie* 11-9-1941)

These are jokes in which the main person in the joke behaves in an unseemly fashion – boundary transgressions within but not through the joke. These jokes were freely published, indicating that they were socially acceptable, "clean" jokes. They were also much published: a large number of the jokes in Dutch magazines until the 1960s concern power relationships.

Just like the older sexual jokes, these hardly elicit a smile anymore. Even the cast is dated: office boys and head clerks, servants and maids (often called Mina) and ladies of the house. There were also more clandestine variations on this theme of role reversal in which one attacked the existing hierarchy in a small way. Political jokes were one example. This genre, at least according to my respondents, still had the luster of the forbidden.

In the Netherlands, political jokes seem to have waned after the 1970s. The only exception to this are jokes about politicians with highly exceptional personal characteristics. In these jokes, power position is clearly less humorous than obese figures (incidentally, only for women politicians) or odd hairdos. Also, there were some jokes about the flamboyant, openly gay, anti-immigrant politician Pim Fortuyn, but mostly after his assassination in 2002, making these jokes more like disaster jokes.

The decreasing amusement value of politics lies, in my opinion, less in the much regretted decrease in citizen involvement than in the fact that a joke about the prime minister is no longer felt as an amusing/shocking instance of irreverence. Hierarchical relationships weigh less heavily now than they did in the 1960s, a shift that Abram de Swaan (1990) has termed a "transition from management by command towards management by negotiation". This has made reversing roles in power relationships or poking fun at the powerful less amusing. Of course, people still always make jokes about their own boss, but these are jokes about a personal relationship, not about authority in its own right. Power relationships as a separate subject are no longer a very sensitive topic and therefore no longer very funny.

There is only one exception to this: the members of the Royal House are undiminished in their popularity as a goal for humor. Other than cabinet ministers, head clerks or judges, the members of the Royal House possess an unassailable position of power, with all its accompanying privileges, restrictions and imperatives. The joke in the questionnaire about the Royal Family was very much appreciated (fifth of 35). This joke is about Prince Bernard, the late husband of former Queen Juliana, who has been involved in a number of scandals, including one about bribes:

There's this man who parks his bike near Soestdijk Palace [the residence of Juliana and Bernhard]. Along comes a member of the Royal Constabulary and says: "Sir, don't you know you're not allowed to park your bike there? Not only that, but his Royal Highness Prince Bernhard is about to arrive." To which the man answers: "Oh that doesn't matter, I've already locked it" (Karel Vroon)

Jokes about the Royal House kept on being really shocking much longer than other jokes about those in power – in 2003, the minister of justice has called upon comedians not to make fun of the Royal Family – and they have remained funny for longer. Except for this category, jokes "upwards" or jokes in which power relationships are dealt with irreverently have practically disappeared.

Only in children's jokes do power relationships continue to play an important role: a large proportion deals with confrontations between children, often the little boy Johnny, and teachers, fathers and mothers. A very popular child's joke is the following about Johnny, based on role reversal in power relationships:

Johnny went with his grandmother to do the shopping. He saw a 10-guilder bill lying on the street. He wanted to pick it up when his grandmother said: "Don't do that. Everything that's on the ground is dirty." Then, a little bit later he saw a 100-guilder bill in the gutter. He was just about to grab it when his grandmother said: "Don't do that. Everything that's on the ground is dirty." Then his grandmother tripped and fell so that she was lying on the ground and she looked up at Johnny and said: "Johnny, please help me to my feet." Then Johnny said: "No, I can't, everything that's on the ground is dirty." (heard from a boy about 10 years old; see also Meder 2001)

Children are confronted with outspoken power inequalities much more often than adults. They live, more than adults do, in a household based on orders.

As thresholds of embarrassment have shifted, a new genre has flourished: the sick joke. Sick jokes are also based on an irreverent treatment of serious affairs: sickness, death, social disasters and scandals, in short, someone else's suffering. As far as I can tell, these jokes blew over from the United States around 1970. The fact that they are new gives rise to the suspicion that they were to some extent created to fill the need for new clandestine jokes following the demise of the old taboos. Jokes about death, sickness and misery existed before this time – as becomes clear from older joke collections, morbid humor is timeless (e.g. Dekker 1999) – but jokes like the following were rare:

> The poor man from the Gooi [a region in the Netherlands that was very poor around 1900]
> "You say that you live from the steam-powered streetcar in the Gooi. Have you got shares?"
> "No, but I'm a funeral director."
> (*De ware Jacob*, 10-10-1903)

Since 1970, sick jokes have reached unprecedented heights (Davies 1999; Dundes and Hauschild 1987; Oring 1992: 29-40) and presently every disaster is immediately followed by morbid jokes: the famines in Biafra, Ethiopia and Somalia, the airplane crashes in Surinam, Amsterdam, and Lockerbie, the arrest of the Belgian child molester Marc Dutroux, Lady Diana's accident, as well as the attacks on the World Trade Center in 2001 (Kuipers 2002, 2005). Often these jokes are recycled: jokes about the exploded Space Challenger in1986 were told again when Space Shuttle Columbia exploded in 2003. Also, some of these space shuttle jokes reemerged as jokes about the attacks on the World Trade Center.

Other events are longer lasting and more constant subjects of such morbid joke cycles: the persecution of the Jews in World War II, handicaps (blindness, deafness, deformities) and deadly sicknesses like AIDS or cancer. Two examples:

"Can Johnny come out and play baseball?" Johnny's mother: "But children, Johnny doesn't have any arms or legs." "Oh that's okay, we'll use him as a base!"

Dutroux walks into huge, scary, dark woods, holding a little girl's hand. All of a sudden the little girl says: "I'm really scared in here, Mister. Dutroux says: "What about me? I've got to go back alone." (Internet, March 1997)

These jokes cause one to feel aversion, shock and – with luck – amusement. This is also where the power in these "hard" jokes lies: in bringing about mixed feelings.

The large attraction of sick jokes, but also the large resistance they encounter, can best be seen in what is without doubt the most controversial joke category: holocaust jokes like the following:

Why does a showerhead have eleven holes?
Because a Jew only has ten fingers.

Holocaust jokes are unanimously condemned but are at the same time quite pervasively known. It is precisely the enormous bluntness of these jokes makes them funny under certain circumstances: they are jokes that simply must not be told. Holocaust jokes violate the ultimate taboo: they are irreverent about the most serious subject known in the Netherlands, the persecution of the Jews. Jokes about the persecution of the Jews are more blasphemous in the Netherlands than jokes about God. It is thus not surprising that the major humor scandals of the 1990s (several of which involved Theo van Gogh), and also the first scandal of the 21st century centered on this same subject: television presenter Rob Muntz was fired when in his television program he menaced Jews in Vienna with a gas cylinder. Comics and satirists, when looking for the most painful spot, invariably end up ridiculing the Holocaust, and so do joke tellers in everyday life (cf. Kuipers 2000).

The rise of sick jokes is connected with a broader cultural development: the significantly increased importance of empathy and identification with others, or increasing "psychologization" (Elias 1982). Sick jokes emphatically refrain from taking into account others' sensitivities. This is a serious transgression of boundaries: by laughing at someone else's misery, people temporarily ignore the extremely important standard dictating that people must empathize with others and respect the feelings of others (Elias 1982; de Swaan 1995). These jokes as such can be described best as a form of "dis-identification" (de Swaan 1997). Admittedly in the form of a joke and only temporarily but nevertheless: the switching off of identification with others.

And moreover: pitiable and suffering others. It will strike no one as surprising that in the questionnaire these jokes were judged to be the most offensive. They transgress the most important boundary that has been established, particularly by joke lovers, at present in the Netherlands. Not only are they shocking but they are also hurtful and offensive – people often feel personally attacked by them.

Hurtful jokes: Jokes at the expense of others

A last category in my classification of susceptibilities are jokes at someone else's expense: offensive and stereotyping jokes. By my interviewees, this category was often summarized as "hurtful jokes". This is a distinction that runs through the categories. Each category can include jokes at another's cost. Sexual jokes often stereotype women and homosexuals. Additionally, certain jokes about religion can be experienced as a very personal attack. Even it is clearly not feasible, on the basis of empirical evidence, to interpret jokes as expressions of aggression, or correlates of conflict – after all, there is no such thing as a conflict between the Dutch and the Belgian, despite the many Belgian jokes I collected, while jokes about some groups that clearly pose a threat to Dutch society, such as formerly the Russians – jokes often do have a rather aggressive bent.

There are four ways in which jokes can be made at someone else's expense. One of these is the stereotyping joke in which a characteristic is ascribed to a whole group (for instance, Turks are filthy, blacks are lazy, Jews are miserly or Belgians are dumb). A positive stereotype can also be ascribed to one's own group; then care is taken to include in the action a group that is less successful. Thus the rise of jokes about "a Dutchman, a German and Belgian..." and in the multiethnic society of today also: "a Dutchman, a Turk and a Moroccan..." (Meder 2001)

Sick jokes can sometimes also be hurtful or offensive for a certain group: a reference to a specific "out-group" makes clear that the joke is about the suffering of others, not oneself. In sick, ethnic jokes, for instance, a reference to ethnicity is combined with a morbid reference: Jews and gas, Africans and famine.

There are also jokes that offend in a much more direct way. These I call attitude jokes (Kuipers 2000). These jokes refer not so much to a specific group characteristic as to an attitude held about the group: "there are too many", "they should be done away with":

A bus carrying five Turks has gone off the road and into the water. A farmer stands crying along the edge of the canal and someone comes up and asks him: "Why're you crying? Don't you think it's a good thing that some Turks have drowned?" "Yes," says the farmer, "but a lot more would have fit in that bus." (many varieties in interviews, never in joke books)

What's the difference between a pregnant Turkish woman and a trampoline? If you jump on a trampoline, you take your shoes off first. (Kuipers 1995)

That last joke is perhaps the nastiest that I encountered during my research. Attitude jokes of this sort do not contain references to unseemly behavior or bad characteristics; the boundary transgression lies in direct offense. The very explicit aggression in many attitude jokes is not only offensive but also shocking. References to aggression shock quite quickly. Explicit violence is a very sensitive subject – a boundary transgression *through* a joke. Combining it with an ethnic reference containing just as serious a boundary transgression, the explicit mention of ethnicity, means that these jokes often occasion more resistance than they do amusement.

A fourth possibility for using a joke to offend can be seen particularly in jokes about religion and in sick jokes. The jokes about the pedophile Marc Dutroux, for example, were often also called offensive with regard to children, but more particularly with regard to people "whose child had been subjected to something like that". People can be hurt when others ignore the meaning that something has for them. The offensiveness is more indirect here than with the other types; no one is directly attacked. Jokes like these make it possible to observe how the situation influences the "offensiveness". Jokes about religion are very quickly shocking but they become offensive only when someone in the neighborhood feels offended. The diffidence that many joke tellers, particularly the older ones, felt in telling sexual jokes in the presence of women has to do with the fear of offending women.

At present, the largest and most important category of jokes-at-the-expense-of-others is the ethnic joke: jokes about ethnic minorities. Other groups targeted by jokes, such as women, mothers-in-law, blondes, the elderly, farmers or gays are not nearly as often the butt of jokes. Contemporary ethnic jokes originated around 1970, in my estimate at approximately the same time as sick jokes. The rise of the ethnic joke is related to the arrival of ethnic minorities. New out-groups came into existence and could be laughed at. The presence of ethnic minorities quickly came to be seen as a social problem, as a "difficult issue" – and this made them an even more appropriate focus for humor (Kuipers 2000).

The rise of the ethnic joke is also connected with a broadening Netherlands horizon. The dumb Belgian, as well, only came into being in the 1960s. Until that time, even jokes about stupidity, the most widespread ethnic humor, were not told about an ethnic group but about farmers. It is true that in the 19th century, jokes circulated about dumb German migrant workers, the poops (from the German "Bube" or boy, but it sounds as offensive in Dutch as it sounds in English), but these disappeared probably around 1900 (Meder 2000). Only about the Netherlands' oldest ethnic minority, the Jews, have jokes been circulating for centuries. These began to change strongly in character around 1970s: the "classical" Jewish jokes about business acumen, miserliness and Sam and Moos (traditional Jewish names) began to disappear slowly. The youth of today does not think of Sam-and-Moos when it hears the words Jewish joke. With the exception of Jewish jokes, ethnic difference in the 1950s and '60s hardly played a role in the joke culture of the Netherlands.

Some scripts now used for ethnic groups did exist: even though there were no dumb foreigners, there were dumb farmers. Jokes about laziness were told about neutral joke personages but also about domestic servants. Not only the targets but also some of the scripts appear new to me. Jokes about filthiness, for instance, probably made their entrance into the Netherlands with the Turkish joke (probably once again imported from the United States). No jokes about filthy Jews existed in the Netherlands as opposed to Germany. Attitude jokes too, as far as I can tell, are new. Some mother-in-law jokes fall into this area:

> Young women friends talking among themselves.
> "Pretty awful isn't it, that my mother-in-law can't be buried?"
> "You're not kidding! Why is that anyway?"
> "Because she's not dead yet" (*De Moppentrommel*, volume unknown but probably between 1945 and 1955)

At the most, jokes of this sort weakly reflect the vicious attitude jokes about ethnic minorities. Only the National Socialist jokes, very little known, but of which many were circulated, show certain similarities to attitude jokes. It was not only new to tell ethnic jokes, many of their scripts were also new to Dutch joke culture.

The rise of the ethnic joke cannot only be explained by the increased ethnic diversity in the Netherlands (and the resistance to this), but must, in my opinion, be understood in the light of two more general mentality changes: the changed meaning of relationships of authority and the tabooing taboo of ethnic difference. References to ethnic difference produce to a certain degree an effect similar to that produced forty years ago by using sexually loaded terms. Herman Vuijsje has called this circumspection the "ethnic taboo" (1997). While this taboo seems to be losing some of its power (it is slowly becoming practically a must for cabaret performers to make a joke about blacks), ethnic difference, at least in certain circles, is still rather unmentionable, making it a clandestine but extremely thankful subject for jokes. Just as with the old sexual jokes, we see that very simple references to ethnicity or race are deemed enough for a joke:

> What do you call a black man rolling off a mountain? Rolo [chocolate candy]

> What do you call a Turk in the sea? Salt licorice.

As was the case for sick jokes, the need for new clandestine jokes makes itself felt as old taboos disappear.

The amusement value of ethnic jokes also has to do with power relationships. Ethnic jokes are always jokes downwards; migrant groups in the Netherlands have lower status than autochthonous Netherlanders. Jokes downwards meet with more sensitivity in the Netherlands than jokes upwards. In practice, "offensive" jokes target groups or persons with a lower social status. Bosses and superiors can be insulted but not so easily hurt. It is easiest to hurt someone either very close to you or inferior to you.

People in the Netherlands often refrain from emphasizing superiority. The shift in meaning of authoritative relationships has made superiority and differing power levels more painful: one does not wish to reveal that one feels oneself better than others. As Goudsblom remarked: "To be inferior was always painful; now it is also painful to be superior" (Goudsblom 1998: 108). Jokes downwards have thus become more dangerous. Jokes about maids – pre-eminent inferiors – published at the drop of a hat in the 1940s now seem tasteless and sometimes even offensive.

> Mrs. Smith: Good grief, Marie! What are you thinking of, giving birdseed to the cat? I've told you again and again that that's for the canary. Maid: Yes ma'am, but that's where the canary is at the moment! (*De Lach*, 3-8-1927)

> Drastic evidence
> Were you lying in bed reading again last night, Mina?
> Of course not, ma'am!
> Don't deny it! How did this flea get into this book otherwise? (*De Lach*, 23-12-1932)

Jokes about persons with lower status belong perhaps to the only Dutch joke category that has become more painful since the 1960s. Jokes of this nature are presently seen as outstanding examples of the offensive joke.

In ethnic jokes, differences in status play an important role. Attitude jokes target again and again the ethnic group with the lowest social status: first it was the Surinamers, then the Turks and now, to an increasing degree, the Moroccans. Jokes about filthiness also – from time immemorial the objection against the "lower class", "the great unwashed" – are still told about the group with the lowest status. Dirtiness has always been a stereotype connected to differences in social status: Cas Wouters (1990) described the fear of the higher classes for the working class as "social hosophobia" (also see Kuipers 2000). In this connection, it is interesting that jokes about Turks also directly combine poverty and filthiness:

> Why aren't the lights turned on at the garbage dump at night?
> If they were, the Turks would think it's late-night shopping. (Kuipers 1995)

A good ethnic joke is sure to break three commandments at once: it is at the expense of another – it offends –, it refers to an unmentionable subject – it shocks –, and, in the egalitarian Netherlands a very serious boundary transgression indeed – it targets a low-status group. It is no wonder that many of these jokes rely on such a simple joke technique: with so many boundary transgressions, a refined punch line is not necessary. The humor of jokes of this sort lies solely in causing a shock effect: an "ooh" laugh. As one of the joke tellers aptly put it:

> Racist jokes, yeah, if you just tell 'em straight, they already pack a huge punch, you know what I mean – you don't even have to present them (laughs). Most are really short, all in one go, ratatattat. I think the longer they are, the less they come across. The shorter you make 'em, the more punch they pack, yeah, the harder they are, that's for sure. (Gerrit Helman)

Jokes at the expense of another do not by definition break boundaries. In other words, not every joke directed at a person or a group is offensive. For example, jokes about Belgians and Germans – national groups with the same status as the Netherlanders – are permissible, even jokes about Surinamers, as their status is increasing, are tolerated to an increasing degree. Of course, these jokes are also meant to insult (jokes about Germans can be very venomous) but they are not seen as "hurtful". This has to do with status differences: Belgians, Germans and Surinamers are strong enough to fight back:

they can take it. Jokes upwards are naturally permissible as well, but as we saw earlier, unless they deal with royalty, they tend to fall flat.

Here standards for humor conflict with the character of humor. People usually find it more fun and easier to make jokes about people to whom they already feel superior. It is no wonder that the oldest theory about humor is a superiority theory stating that all humor is an expression of feelings of superiority (see Morreall 1987). Jokes "downwards" are more attractive than jokes upwards or about an equal. And, whether we like it or not, the arrival of the ethnic minorities has introduced into the Netherlands large, clearly recognizable, easy to stereotype, social categories possessing a low social status. And moreover, the presence of this immigrants made it possible to adapt ethnic jokes from the large international reservoir of jokes, that until 1970 couldn't as easily be imported because there were no natural targets. Therefore, jokes about migrant groups flourish, but only behind closed doors.

Conclusion: The hardening of the humor

This circuit of Dutch jokes concurrently traced the history of these jokes. En passant, the most important shifts in the second half of the twentieth century have passed in revue. One trend is clearly seen here: the hardening or coarsening of the humor. While the harder jokes told earlier on can no longer be traced, jokes that did get published and informants' stories make it safe to state that jokes told in the 1990s were clearly harder, coarser, more explicit, more shocking and more aggressive than jokes told in the middle of the twentieth century. Things now openly appearing on television merited a reprimand from the pastor in earlier days. Jokes that are now clandestine were unthinkable in the 1960s: the language use, the explicit references, the omnipresent sex, the coarseness, the insults and the aggression in recent jokes transgress all the boundaries then operational.

Themes have, of course, been added as time went on – in 1965 one did not tend to laugh so hard at Turks or famished Ethiopians – and themes have dropped away – in a society where no one employs maids, jokes about maids tend to fall flat. But the tone of jokes has changed as well. An important part of this has to do with shifting thresholds of embarrassment in Dutch society. In many areas, rules and standards have become more relaxed and consequently humor has to go further to be funny. Because much more is tolerated, jokes have to push harder to transgress boundaries.

It is also true that in areas where sensitivity has not diminished, humor has nevertheless hardened. People have become more rather than less sensitive (Wouters 1999) to aggression and violence, stereotyping of ethnic groups, to emphasizing of superiority, and to pain, misery, disasters, sicknesses and death. Notwithstanding, jokes about these subjects have flourished. The development already described, the advance of the shock effect as a style technique, has also penetrated into the area of the joke.

This means that humor does not only follow and reflect the shifting standards: the process of the hardening of humor is asynchronous with the shifting of the boundaries being transgressed. There is a larger tolerance or even appreciation for "hard" or "coarse" humor. This development can be seen in all forms of humor. A comparison between the "big three" of the 1960s, Kan, Hermans and Sonneveld and the "new" big three, de Jonge, van 't Hek and de Leeuw, indicates a growing appreciation of hard humor. A classic trickle down is evident between these two groups of three: hard, sick, aggressive and shocking jokes began to be told in the progressive, intellectual, avant-garde cabaret and in the just as elite television programs of Wim T. Schippers and van Kooten and de Bie. At present, the "hard joke" is generally accepted and then to such an extent that currently, the avant garde cabaret artists of the 1970s complain, like Freek de Jonge, occasionally feel the need to object to the hardness of their colleagues' jokes. The hardening of the humor seem to have gotten a momentum that even its initiators do not always appreciate.

This does not seem to me to be an autonomous development within humor. Is not difficult to find examples of an increased desire for shock effects in the rest of society. In art, in entertainment, in films and in vacation spending, to name a few divergent areas, a desire can be observed for increasingly extreme, shocking, aggressive, upsetting or sexually explicit stimuli. This development gives rise to both concern and dissension. While the symptoms are more or less clear, the diagnosis is difficult: scholars, and media commentators attribute it to modernization, individualization, equalization, postmodernism, the disappearance of God and family, the falling away of standards, the lack of taboos, the spirit of the '60s, the lack of authority and social cohesion – all the great social and cultural developments of the previous century are said to be responsible for this increasing sensation seeking.

Instead of adding one more to the series of existing interpretations of this trend, I will confine myself to stating that humor and jokes are influenced by this development too: developments in the joke are connected to a general change in mentality. The effect of this shift on humor is particularly visible in the changed meaning of boundaries, boundary transgressions and shock effects. Not only have boundaries shifted but a change too has taken place in *how* boundary transgressing itself is valued.

In Chapter 4, reference was made to the fact that youth appreciates "hard" humor more than those who are older. This agrees with the development to which I want to draw attention here: those who are older were socialized in a different sort of humor that transgressed other boundaries but in which even the boundary transgressions themselves were seen differently. The youth of today has grown up with jokes about filthy Turks and dumb Belgians, with the pinnacle of sadism (give a blind person thumbtacks and tell him they're contact lenses), with the idea that sex is a safe subject for jokes and that to say "hard" about a joke is to recommend it positively. People born before, say, 1950, grew up with jokes about Sam and Moos, judges and mothers-in-law, with jocular references to "stamps on eggs"; they grew up thinking that there were clean and dirty jokes and that ladies existed who simply couldn't stomach the latter genre. Their magazines published the jokes described in Chapter 2: "little jokes that would bring a fine but especially pleasurable laugh to the faces of their readers". In short, they grew up with the idea that humor, in the first place, had to remain civilized.

Chapter 7
Temptation and transgression

"Well, I think jokes in general, it hardly matters what kind of joke we're talking about, I think they're all equally funny", Huibert Busser, a personnel worker I had met at *Moppentoppers* told me. "But I've given it a bit of thought. What is a really good joke? What's required for it to be good? That's – at least this is what I think, but that's only me – it has to hold the attention of the person listening from beginning to end. And there has to be an unexpected twist in it somewhere. The best jokes are like that. If you could find a joke like that that doesn't offend any group and that, on top of that, isn't sexist, then you'd have a world-class joke. Those are the cleverest of all. Clean jokes that catch the attention and don't let go from A to Z, and you can tell them in an interesting way too."

The question Busser is asking himself here – what is needed for a good joke – is the main theme of this chapter: what is a good and what is a bad joke? Do people have the same criteria for this or are there differences in taste among joke lovers? What we are talking about here, in other words, are taste differences *within* the genre.

In passing, factors have already been addressed in this book that play a role in the appreciation of not only genres and styles but also individual jokes. One important factor is the extent to which a joke impacts on a boundary. In general, a joke is seen as funny if it touches upon a social boundary; but the minute this goes too far, appreciation for the joke quickly fades.[13] Opinions as to what goes too far or, indeed, not far enough to be funny, differ markedly. Added to this is the fact that, as we saw in Chapters 4 and 5, transgressing a boundary is not appreciated by everyone in the same way: "hard", "coarse", and "hurtful" jokes have different places in different humor styles.

Important too in appreciating jokes is the extent to which people identify with the content or the intent of the joke. In humor that clearly reflects a worldview, such as satire or political humor, identification is of prime importance, but it also significantly affects the appreciation of other forms of humor.[14] For instance, while a good ethnic joke has the potential to amuse anyone, they are more fun for people who – secretly or openly – agree with their intent. A lack of points to identify with works against a joke: an anecdote you do not agree with, or in which you do not recognize your own situation or standpoint, quickly becomes unfunny. The outspoken masculine perspective of sexual jokes, for instance, ensures that women quite quickly like the genre less.[15]

Identification and transgressiveness are related to the content of a joke. In addition to these factors of content, there is another aspect in which jokes differ from each other: their form. Even within the rather uniform and strongly standardized genre of the joke, variations exist in the structure of the joke and the "joke technique", the build-up to the punch line. As we consider these questions of form, it is not immediately clear how differences in how they are appreciated could be connected to social background. Psychologists, most notably Ruch and Hehl (1998), have studied the relationship between personality and the appreciation of humorous form, but generally they have used a wider variety of humorous genres (as I have in the American study reported later in this book). Within the genre of the joke, it is easy to predict the direction in which boundary transgressions and possibilities for identification will influence appreciation. But it is harder to think of an instrument or classificatory scheme with which to dissect joke technique.[16] I will attempt to connect variations in the form of jokes with differences in their appreciation.

The question of differences in the joke's form is directly connected with the question of quality differences among jokes. Quality, in all cultural genres, from high to low, is sooner sought in form – technique, delivery, style – than in content. In addition to the way good storytellers deliver a joke, joke tellers sing the praises of the "real find" and the "masterful build-up". Busser, too, concludes that the form of the joke determines its quality. The best jokes "hold the attention from beginning to end" thanks to the delivery or to an unexpected twist. Ask the question "how do differences in the appreciation of separate jokes arise" and the question of what a *good* joke is, is not far behind.

The balance between funny and offensive

If, during the interviews with joke tellers, I asked for the determinants of a good joke, they usually hastened to tell me what was *not* good: hurtful or coarse jokes.

> *And what sort of jokes do you like?*
> You know, dry humor. Humor that's not coarse. Not discriminating. Not hurtful. And not too racy. But funny. You want to know what I really hate? Humor and jokes about illness. Or about Belgium and Dutch people. And I

don't tell racist or discriminating jokes either, or about certain diseases. (Matthieu Cnoops)

Getting back to jokes, what kind of jokes do you like?
Me? Well, that's hard to say. I don't like dirty jokes. And coarse jokes. (Jacob Hitters)

So I always tend to tell ordinary jokes, just plain funny ones.
And what do you mean when you say, just plain funny?
Well, what I... I really think people're stupid, you know, if they make fun of the disabled or people who're really seriously ill or something like that. I don't like that much. That's not my thing. Take for instance the case, you know Dutroux, that's going on right now. Now that's something really serious, I think it's really terrible what he was up to. If I were in charge, if people'd ask me, Mrs. Wijntuin, now what would you do with that man? I'd make cuts all over his body and then I'd get the children to pour vinegar into all the openings. Really. What he did to those children! So I think those are really stupid jokes, totally beside the point. And yeah. Jokes I like are jokes that are a bit appetizing, you know. About Sam and Moos and well, little delicious things that just link up. (Chantal Wijntuin)

On this question of the transgressive and hurtful jokes, joke tellers were most voluble: which jokes can be told and which go too far? Even the way they formulated their answers was very similar. The boundaries one established and the rules one employed as well as the argumentations, protestations, escape routes and ways of stating exceptions to the rules were often put into words in remarkably similar ways. What compilers of joke books and editors of *Moppentoppers* said was close to what the joke tellers told me. A discourse about jokes and boundaries exists, shared by everyone involved in Dutch joke culture. Within this discourse, the same statement is reiterated again and again about the connection between humor and boundary transgressions: a joke that is hurtful or offensive goes too far, and is no longer funny.

A fine balance has to be established between being funny and transgressing boundaries in order to produce a good joke. To explore the relationship between appreciation and offensive, I will turn again to the ratings of the jokes discussed earlier in Chapter 3. The questionnaire results clearly show the negative effect of (strong) boundary transgression on joke appreciation. Respondents were asked not only to indicate how funny each separate joke was but also how offensive or coarse they thought each to be.[17] The correlation between (aggregated) funniness and offensiveness turned out to be -.44 (p < .01). Overall, the coarser the joke was thought to be, the less it was appreciated.

Also, for many of the individual jokes, there was a negative correlation between funniness and offensiveness. Table 5 shows the factor loadings for the factor analysis of joke appreciation that was also discussed in Chapter 3. The first factor I interpreted as a general factor for "joke appreciation", correlating both with gender and class background. The second factor has to do with innocuousness (positive loadings) versus offensiveness (negative loadings). The jokes with negative loadings generally also have a negative correlation between funniness and offensiveness. Moreover, they tend to be at the bottom of the ranking: they were not very well liked.

As Table 5 shows, the connection between funniness and offensiveness is most pronounced in extreme cases: jokes seen as so offensive that they can hardly be appreciated at all. These jokes go too far for almost everyone; they are explicit ethnic jokes like the following two:

What's the difference between a Jew and a stew?
A stew doesn't scream when it's put in the oven.

I'm walking with a friend around the red-light district in Amsterdam and all of a sudden he shoots three black men dead. I say: "What're you doing?" He says: "I've got an MHL, a migrant hunting license." So I buy one too. A week later, we're walking in a notorious neighborhood in The Hague and I shoot five niggers. Along comes a police officer and says: "What do you think you're doing?" "I've got an MHL." The police officer says: "Yeah but that covers the cities, not the reservations."

These jokes were appreciated very little indeed: they were placed last and third from last in the order of appreciation. In these, the dosage of the boundary transgression was too high: the transgression is then so large that almost no one finds the joke funny. At least: in a questionnaire. Of course there are circumstances under which a joke of this nature is shown to better advantage, and then the balance between funniness and coarseness could tip to favor the joke. However, jokes that were not offensive at all were necessarily rated very highly. Even though one of the least offensive jokes ranked second, the other jokes that were generally regarded as very inoffensive – mostly absurd jokes or wordplay – received mediocre ratings overall.

The jokes that were liked best were those seen as medium transgressive: they were neither the most offensive nor the least offensive. These were jokes that touch on a boundary but do not go too far. The balance between funny and coarse was then (for the average respondent) just right. One joke that satisfied this demand for medium coarseness has already been cited ("Wwwwould you llllike to bbbbuy a bbbible? Or ssshall I rrrread it ttttto you?"). On average, this joke was appreciated the most and was placed precisely in the middle of the scale of offensiveness (18th). The joke that placed one step further on the scale of offensiveness (19th), is also an example of a well proportioned joke.

> A primary school teacher promises a surprise to the one who solves the riddle. Her first riddle is: it walks around on a farm, it's spotted and it gives milk. Johnny puts up his hand and says: "A cow." The teacher says: "That's good, but I meant a goat."
> Her next riddle is: "It walks around on a farm, it's got feathers and it lays eggs." Johnny tries again, saying: "A chicken." The teacher says: "That's good, but I meant a goose."
> Johnny's pretty sick of this by now and he says he's got a riddle for his teacher. He says: "It's hard and dry when you put it in your mouth and it comes back out all soft and damp." The teacher turns red and Johnny says: "That's good, but I meant chewing gum."

Even though Table 5 first of all illustrates the negative effects of extreme transgression, it also shows a general positive effect of milder boundary transgression. This seems to depend somewhat on the nature of the jokes. Especially jokes about religion (Trevor's nails, Mother Superior) can be deemed offensive and still liked, which seems to be less likely for ethnic or sick jokes. However, a light or medium boundary transgression usually enhances the amusement value of a joke.

The positive effect of transgression is most obvious from the one joke on the questionnaire that achieved a positive connection between coarseness and funniness:

> Madonna doesn't have one; the pope has one but doesn't use it. Bush has a short one and Wolfowitch a long one. What is it? A last name.

This jocular reference to something that perhaps still counts as a taboo subject for some, is extremely mild by contemporary criteria. Generally, it wasn't thought either funny or offensive. However, the positive correlation here suggests that people who saw a boundary transgression in this joke and so liked it better than people for whom this joke did not even approach a boundary.

Table 5. Appreciation and offensiveness of the jokes in the questionnaire Factor loadings[18] (Factor 1 = joke appreciation. Factor 2 = Innocuousnessversus offensiveness), average appreciation, rank order for average offensiveness, and correlation between funniness and offensiveness

	Factor 1	Factor 2	Mean	Rank Offensive	Relation Funny-Offensive
11. Bible salesman	.48	.22	3.93	17	-.20
30. Vacuum cleaner	.54	.34	3.87	34	-
7. Johnny & teacher	.61	-.01	3.87	18	-.17
5. Flood	.49	.15	3.76	21	-.22
27. Prince Bernhard	.56	.27	3.56	22	-.11
16. Football	.44	.14	3.55	26	-.13
29. Mother superior	.54	-.21	3.54	14	-.30
14. Belgian jeweller	.60	.12	3.49	23	-.12
1. Trevor's nails	.39	-.33	3.46	8	-.37
24. Child on phone	.47	.39	3.43	30	-
34. Drunk	.54	.07	3.37	24	-..21
18. Mose skiing	.42	.37	3.33	7	-.40
19. Drink with both	.54	-.41	3.33	19	-.19
28. Two blondes	.60	.06	3.33	25	-
17. Black baby	.55	-.20	3.18	11	-.30
8. A bit hoarse	.31	.42	3.15	35	-.14
20. Half deaf	.39	.46	3.10	31	-
12. Millionaire	.59	.30	3.07	28	-
21. At heaven's gate	.52	.03	3.07	13	-
26. Mother in law	.64	.10	3.00	16	-.12
35. Plane crash	.55	.11	2.89	20	-.17
31. Blonde brain cells	.52	-.29	2.79	15	-.22
6. Skeletons	.44	.29	2.77	29	-
4. German & Jew	.55	-.11	2.73	10	-.11
23. Man & dog	.54	.37	2.71	32	-
2. Mose in restaurant	.40	.53	2.70	12	-.20
33. Fairy godfather	.39	.00	2.70	33	-
32. Truck driver	.59	-.45	2.69	3	-.47
3. Last names	.45	.34	2.62	27	.12
13. Diana	.43	-.43	2.53	6	-.28
15. Whore who can..	.51	-.31	2.35	9	-.19
9. Migrant Hunting	.60	-.44	2.34	2	-.43
25. Turkish woman	.51	-.52	2.32	4	-.39
10. Johnny as base	.58	-.25	2.26	5	-.34
22. Jew & stew	.53	-.48	1.84	1	-.39

Varying viewpoints on offensiveness

There was a broad statistical spread in judgments of offensiveness: some jokes were not found to be offensive at all while others were seen as extremely coarse. However, there were also large differences between respondents: even more difference of opinion existed about how offensive jokes than about how funny they were. The statistical spread was, as one might expect, the least for the most offensive jokes. The coarser a joke, the more people agree that it is coarse.

Generally, older people were more easily offended by jokes than younger people, as is apparent from the .42 correlation between the "innocuousness" factor and age (p < .01), as well as the fact that age correlated .185 (p < .01) with average rating of offensiveness. In the previous chapter, I have described the hardening of the humor in the past decades, which implies that people of different age groups have grown up with different standards of offensiveness. There also is a slight gender difference here: women tended to rate the jokes as more offensive then men (p < .05). However, the innocuousness factor showed no gender relation.

Table 6. Correlation between average appreciation and offensiveness for separate social background variables

	Correlation Funny-offensive	Number of Respondents
Men	-.29*	200
Women	-.40*	117
Education up to secondary level	-.46*	187
Education college level and up	-.39*	147
Age below 31	.00	81
Age 31-60	-.48*	208
Age 61 and up	-.77*	48
All respondents	-.44*	340

* p < .01

I also investigated connections between funniness and offensiveness for separate groups. It is possible that, even though groups do not differ in their judgments of what is coarse, they do have different views on how transgressiveness contributes to a joke's funniness. As Table 6 shows, correlations between ratings for offensiveness and funniness were quite similar for men and women, and even more so for people of different educational backgrounds. Even though, as we have seen, these background factors affect appreciation, and, as we will see, they sometimes affect the judgment of offensiveness, *relations* between these judgments do not differ much.

Once I had broken the respondents down into age, however, I did find big differences: respondents under thirty did not connect funniness and offensiveness; respondents between thirty and sixty connected them approximately as strongly as the whole population and those over sixty made the connection very markedly. We are not concerned here with the extent to which something is seen as coarse, but with the effect of the judged coarseness on the appreciation of the joke. In other words: we are concerned with what boundary transgressions mean in appreciating humor. This proves that older people are not only more sensitive to the transgression of certain pain thresholds, but also that they do not consider "hardness" as something agreeable. Young people see the offensiveness of a joke as a completely separate issue from how funny it is.

The results were produced by averaging the joke scores; there are *no* jokes in circulation that do not sound the right tone for some people or in some circumstances. Of all the jokes in the questionnaire, there was not one that was not deemed the best possible at least once and the worst possible at least once. And for offensiveness, the spread in evaluations was even wider.

Even racist jokes, condemned on all sides, received the highest imaginable score from some people. Often, these high scores were given by respondents who had voted for extreme right wing parties. This is evidence not only for differences in pain thresholds, it also shows how the effect of agreeing with a joke, in other words, of *identification*. Presumable, these respondents not only saw these jokes as less hurtful, they also agreed with their intent. This is one of the few places where the role of identification can be distilled from the questionnaire. In the case of the people with anti-migrant views, the identification is positive, but the opposite happens too: believers appreciate jokes about religion significantly less than others do. Regional identifications may intensify pain thresholds as well: people from Rotterdam appreciated a joke about their local soccer team significantly less than others did:

> Willem van Hanegem approaches Van Gaal and says: "I've heard that football's connected to intelligence. Have you ever heard that?" "Yes," says coach Van Gaal, "football has a lot to do with intelligence. Watch while I demonstrate." So he calls Kluivert over and asks: "It's your father's son but not your brother. Who is it?" "Dead easy," says Kluivert, "it's me." "See what I mean about intelligence?" says Van Gaal to Van Hanegem. So Van Hanegem tries it out for himself. He calls Ed de Goey over and says: "It's

your father's son but not your brother. Who is it?" De Goey, who has to have a good think about that, walks around the field a bit. On his way, he asks Taument the same question and he says: "Yeah, of course! That's me." So Ed de Goey returns to Van Hanegem and says: "I know who it is. It's Taument!" No, it's not," says Van Hanegem, "it's Patrick Kluivert."[19]

These results show that whether someone is offended by a joke may be mitigated or intensified by identification: the extents to which people take a joke personally, or agree with the purport. The role of identification in the appreciation of jokes, and in the mitigation or intensification of offensiveness will be discussed in the next chapter. In the interviews, the question of boundaries imposed on a joke occupied a much more central position than identification. This probably has to do with the fact that people always find it easier to discuss why something is not funny. Distaste is always more easily put into words than preference.

Tempting the laugh

The question now is: what does this negative connection between offensevenss and funniness mean? Do people like jokes less because they go too far? Or is the opposite true: do people think a joke is more offensive because they don't like it? In daily affairs, one seems to assume the former: coarseness negatively influences appreciation.

In practice, people can like a joke and think it goes too far *coincidently*. A serious boundary transgression, incorporated into a good joke, can tempt people to laugh at something they actually disagree with. An audience can be carried away by a good storyteller or a good joke with a clever, original or unexpected punch line, and all the while disagree with its content.

> Those Marc Dutroux jokes. I never tell them. I don't like them and I've got children too. They don't make me laugh either, I don't think they're a nice form of humor. Although, if I have to be completely honest, someone told me one last week and I burst out laughing in spite of the fact that I... Well, when I'm listening, yeah, I do think it's funny but it's not good at all what happened. Someone said: "There's a new Citroen on the market with three hidden children's seats. Called the Citroen Dutroux." Yeah, I had to laugh. (Huibert Busser)

> Well, now and then you get these racist... Yeah, sometimes you find yourself laughing. I catch myself at that sometimes. About Turks, it's a lousy sort of humor. No, I don't like that kind of thing. But, in spite of all that,

sometimes there's a real find in one of those lousy jokes and then you end up laughing whether you like it or not. (Joost Wiersema)

This means that people are laughing against their better judgment: amusement beats moral condemnation. Someone I spoke to in the context of my degree research into ethnic jokes said: "I don't like it myself, but my sense of humor does" (Kuipers 1995). While it may not be entirely legitimate to hide behind the bloody-mindedness of your sense of humor, this statement more than adequately shows how amusement can be a reflex reaction. Particularly the "harder" jokes produce "mixed feelings": shocked, but amused nevertheless.

The moral judgment about the joke is often no match for the qualitative judgment about the "real find", as Wiersema calls it. The way a joke is put together is more important than how hurtful it is or even: what it's about. For jokes "on the edge", the joke's quality balloons in importance. As it becomes more hurtful, more must be done to tempt a listener to keep on seeing it as a joke. The joke technique has to be better, the storytelling style pertinent.

This means that the truth is more complex: a joke that goes too far is no longer funny, but: a joke that is not funny, goes too far more quickly. To an audience, a funny joke about a sensitive topic can tempt them to laugh, but an unfunny joke about a sensitive subject is nothing but an insult, a coarse remark or a dirty word.

So how does this temptation to laughter work? Providing a general formula for this quality is not easy. What can be done is to illustrate the difference between a very good and a decidedly less good joke. The two jokes which follow share a subject:

> A racist in Amsterdam always gets into his car in the evenings and goes and runs down Turks. One evening he gets into his car and drives away. There goes a Turk. He puts his foot to the floor, looks in his rearview mirror, and bingo, one down. He does this another couple of times. Then he sees a minister trying to hitch a ride so he picks him up. The driver sees another Turk but thinks: "I won't run him down, I'll just drive right up next to him." He's already passed the guy when he looks in his rearview mirror by habit and sees the Turk lying there dead anyway. The minister says: "Good thing I opened my door, or you would have missed that one."
> What's the difference between a rabbit and a Turk that have been hit by a car? There are no skid marks for the Turk.

While the subject of these jokes is approximately the same – running down Turks for racist ends – one is much funnier than the other. The first joke was on the questionnaire and was found to be almost as offensive as the joke about the migrant hunting license, but significantly funnier. Its punch line is more unexpected. To ethnic aggression, a second impropriety has been added, one that at the same time grants it some legitimacy: the minister condones the action. The second joke is much less sophisticated; it is thus much less successful in convincing the audience to see it as funny instead of offensive.

In a less insolent way, two jokes with comparable themes, cited earlier, demonstrate a similar quality difference. The joke about Johnny and his teacher ("That's good, but I meant chewing gum") has almost the same punch line as the joke about the last names of Madonna, the Pope, Wolfowitch and Bush: the listener is supposed to think of a penis, but the punch line comes up with something much more innocent (chewing gum and last names). The joke about Johnny, however, is more extensively constructed and events are thrice repeated. The insinuation is colored in by letting the teacher blush. And, with the insinuation, an extra sensitivity is evoked: the balance of power is reversed. The joke about the last names also evokes more sensitivities than just sexual ones: the Pope, Wolfowitch and Bush are persons in positions of power. All the unseemly references in this joke, and certainly those in the punch line, are tamer than in the joke about Johnny. But the most important difference here lies in the build-up: if the punch line about the last names had been incorporated into a real story, it would have been much funnier.

World-class jokes: The joke tellers on joke technique

The joke tellers too, as we have seen, began answering the question of what they thought was a good joke by saying that the joke should not be too offensive, coarse, racy or hard. First they indicated the margins of hurtfulness within which the joke could be good. The question remains what they then expected of a good joke. After all: if a group exists that is qualified to say what a good joke is, this must be the group of real joke tellers. Do they differ in their opinions about joke technique or do they use the same criteria of quality for jokes?

When I asked joke tellers to explain what a good joke was their answers usually had very little to do with the joke's content. Their answers had to do with form. Because joke tellers tend firstly to classify jokes according to the content, this question often created some confusion. Hans Wagenaar gave this answer to my question of what he thought were funny jokes:

Oh alright. Jokes about bar people and and... [silence] I don't really have an enormous preference for what I like. I like a joke that's just told normally, one that's reasonably up-to-date, well, that's not always possible, is it? Actually, if the joke is just really well put together, then I usually have to laugh. So you can't really say I like one type best. I'm not going to tell you: it's hard to recover from Belgian jokes because I'm rolling on the floor, or jokes about Turks or people from Surinam or any of that. Discriminating or what have you, none of it matters to me. If it turns out funny and it's just a good story, I laugh.

Every joke teller has a joke he sees as his "best" joke. If I asked what made this joke so good, the answer never referred to the subject or the import of the joke. We would suddenly be discussing the build-up, the punch line and the form. What Huibert Busser said at the beginning of this chapter was very characteristic. For a joke to be good: the joke had to hold the attention of the listener from beginning to end; there be an unexpected twist in it somewhere. Other joke tellers said, for example:

What do you think are the best jokes?
Long jokes. With a really dry punch line. Something that sends you barking up the wrong tree. I think that's the best work. For example [he tells a long joke indeed about a confusion of tongues between a farmer from Groningen and a Frenchman in a Parisian hotel]. You have to make a long story of it, that way it' s most effective. That's the sort of joke I'm really crazy about. (Joost Wiersema)

There are sexual jokes that are so good, so cleverly worked out in their build-up their story their atmosphere, but you can't tell them because the point is obscene, but to my mind they're really so perfect. [He tells a medium off-color but rather distasteful joke.] So that's not possible, is it? While really, as far as jokes go, it's a world-class joke. Because it turns out so surprisingly. That's the way a joke should be. It has to be surprising. You shouldn't get the feeling "I know where this is going." (Eelco van Doorn, 48, professional entertainer)

To me the real power of a joke is: you tell some stupid story and when no one is expecting it anymore: boom! The coin falls! (He tells a joke about a man who won a goose in a lottery and then kept it in the belt to his trousers). Now that's a real joke, all the way through the joke not one thing happens, just some really silly story, and then who would be expecting such an ending? Look, and that's what I think telling a joke is. You get everybody's attention, everybody knows what's going on, everybody's had something like that happen to them sometime or other, you know what I mean. And everybody's paying attention and wondering when it's going to happen, but not one of them knows when it's going to happen, and then along it comes and everybody collapses. (Albert Reiziger)

Is there are a certain kind of joke you like really well, or do you not have favorites?
No, I couldn't say that. The joke is what matters. Yeah, the joke is what matters. What matters is the joke. The punch line is what matters. That's what it's all about. A good joke with a story and then a punch line you didn't expect. And then it doesn't matter if it's about Turks or... (Frederik Doeks, 64, retired sales representative)

Many joke tellers told me their "best joke" to support their argument. I did not include these jokes in the quotes but they are without exception long, spun-out jokes with lots of carefully constructed suspense.

The joke tellers emphasized the fact that the joke turns out best if it has a story so that you can get "into" it. They were quite scornful about riddles and brainteasers: if they told one at all, then preferably in between the longer jokes. For the joke tellers, the fact that the joke has to have a "story" is just as important as good delivery. A joke that tells a story creates more opportunity for a real performance: within a long story most space is found for the art of storytelling.

The way joke lovers talk about the characteristics of the good joke fits well into the division into humorous styles set up by the literary scholar Walter Nash (1985). He arrives at a simple, but usable division into two basic humorous styles: *compression* and *expansion*. These style resources can be found in all forms of humor: the short, pointed humor of wit versus the continuously expanding hilarity of humorous stories, events and performances.

The joke, in this division, clearly is an expansive genre. The genre is most suited to long digressions, and an expansive storytelling style is the strategy chosen by almost all joke tellers. Compression, on the other hand, is humor appreciated instead by many joke haters: ironic, witty remarks, jokes with hardly any framing; humor that is not built-up but just whisks past and then disappears into thin air. Nash's division does not, however, coincide with the division into highbrow and lowbrow humor. In jokes there is clearly a tendency to expansion, but the distinction between compression and expansion runs through all humor styles. Herman Finkers, popular among joke tellers, is a master of condensed, pointed jokes. And comic monologues by Freek de Jonge or the absurd humor of *Monty Py-*

thon and *Jiskefet* have all the characteristics of highbrow humor, and are not based on condensed humor, but on a continuously stepped-up, humorous effect.

While all joke tellers described a good joke in the same way – long build-up, good punch line – not everyone agreed about the precise dosage of this build-up. Some people liked really long, spun-out jokes, others lost patience with these more quickly. Spinning something out is a technique with a clear risk, something all joke tellers mentioned in warning, and something many joke haters objected to: predictability. This does not necessarily mean that someone *really* can figure out the punch line ahead of time, "predictability" instead means that the listener, around the time the punch line makes its appearance, has long since lost interest. The risk of expansion is boredom and with it: the disappearance of the surprise effect crucial for humor.

There were but a few dissidents among the joke lovers: people who preferred short, quick or sharp jokes; or who used both forms alongside each other. Joke tellers who chose for a less exuberant, emphatically humorous storytelling style often preferred somewhat shorter jokes. One joke teller from Groningen, in the north, based his preference for shorter, "dry" jokes on his regional background: "So I really don't like very long jokes. You can see the punch line on the horizon miles ahead of time. What I like most is a short joke, but loaded." (Alfred Kruger). In saying this, he pointed to comedian Herman Finkers, whose regional upbringing he also connected with his pithiness. Short, quick jokes, however, are often associated with "dryness": humor presented as not too emphatically funny. And it is humor of the sort that people in the east and north tend to champion. In the west and south of the Netherlands people instead describe their own humor (and their accent) as "juicy" – it can't be entirely coincidence that the metaphors are almost each others' opposites.

An important reason to choose condensation as a joke technique is to enhance a shock effect. Those who like harder jokes, such as Gerrit Helman and Richard Westbroek, both in their twenties, told short, quick jokes much more often. Their ideal joke was without a doubt different: a joke that had to be short for its intense shock effect. As Helman said about racist jokes: "I think the longer they are, the less punchy they are. The shorter, the fiercer. So then they're harder too, of course." They often reacted to the longer jokes with some irritation: "*Moppentoppers* with a whole bunch of gestures and a kind of precious theatre acting; really not my thing" Westbroek said. Racist jokes, explicitly dirty jokes and sick jokes are often not much longer than a couple of lines.

There is one more domain in joke culture where the short, compressed jokes flourish: the children's joke culture. My youngest interviewee, a girl of fifteen, told many shorter jokes and riddles. The second youngest, twenty, alternated; he told short riddles, but also longer, primarily dirty jokes. He was still at school and was probably still sitting on the fence between the children's joke culture and the man's culture of dirty jokes and a masculine tone. The fact that children in general tell shorter jokes and riddles has doubtlessly to do with the degree of difficulty of the genre. The telling of jokes is a skill that children learn relatively late (McGhee 1979, 1983). And it perhaps has to do with the fact that learning is such a central event in children's culture. Riddles strongly resemble a test. And dumbness, the main theme of the Belgian jokes extremely popular with children, will appeal more as a theme to groups whose cognitive skills are constantly being tested.

The children's joke culture is almost completely separate from the joke culture of adults. The repertoire, that otherwise hardly changes as time passes, differs enormously in theme and form from the jokes of adult joke tellers. The jokes are not only shorter but also much more absurd. In places where the themes coincide, like in jokes about sex, the approach to the subject differs strongly from that of the adult joke tellers. In the children's joke culture, there exist other criteria for a good joke (Opie and Opie 1967; see also Meder 2001).

Outside these two domains – the hard jokes and the children's jokes – it appears that there is very little variation in the criteria applied to a good joke: all joke tellers, and, in fact, all respondents to the questionnaire, seem to have approximately the same idea about what the structure of a good joke is. A split like this in technique does justice to the joke too. In the previous chapter, we dealt with content, and I arrived at a much broader classification. This also suits the genre well: the joke is rather varied as to content but much less so as to form. The strong standardization of the genre contributes to its uniformity: an oral genre profits from a clear form, within which content can be extensively varied.

The importance of joke-work

The importance of expansion as the basis for jokes was confirmed in a most unexpected way during the analysis of the questionnaire. There appears to be a very simple factor that has a huge effect on appreciation: the *length* of the joke. The longer the joke, the funnier.

This is one of the most unexpected discoveries of this research: a correlation of .55 (p < .01) was found between the average appreciation of the joke in the questionnaire and the number of words in the joke. The length of a joke is thus an indication of its potential to amuse: its quality. The statistical connection between appreciation and number of words was even stronger than between funniness and offensiveness: the number of words in the joke is thus more strongly connected with its score than how the transgression is apportioned! Moreover, this correlation remained intact when it was split up into gender, age and educational level. Few differences thus exist between social categories in judging a joke's form. For all social groups, the same obtained: the longer the joke, the funnier it was.

In fact, analysis shows that even groups having different judgments about the joke as genre still ranked the jokes in a way very similar to groups who did like jokes. As a result of the very different views on transgressiveness, rankings of different age groups differed. But people with different educational levels and humor styles, men and women, did indeed produce different average values, but the *relative* judgments by these groups agree strongly. In other words: the different groups do not appreciate jokes equally but they employ approximately the same criteria to determine what a good or a bad joke is. For age difference, this is to a large extent reversed: no difference was found in average appreciation of the jokes as a genre, but scores ascribed to the jokes themselves show a wide spread, leading to a different rank order for different age groups. This suggests that, within the (flexible) margins of pain thresholds, people often agree about what a good or a less good joke is. And along with more ephemeral indicators of quality, length of the joke seems to be one of the main factors determining this judgment of a joke's quality.

But what does this connection between the length of a joke and its appreciation mean? I would say that it points to the importance of good build-up. The longer joke gives the joke teller more time to approach the punch line in well-chosen steps, adding more context, and working towards an expectation which can be reversed more effectively in the denouement. The jokes that were most popular, such as the joke with the stuttering Bible salesman, or Johnny and his teacher, were long mostly because they follow threefold pattern characteristic of jokes. In this way, enough context is provided to set the stage for a good punch line. The more context the listener has, the easier it is for the incongruous punch line to be soluble or understandable, or, as Elliott Oring (1992) called it: an appropriate incongruity.

Moreover, a long build up gives the audience more time to get into a mood allowing it to be carried off into the light atmosphere surrounding humor. The "humorous mode" as Mulkay (1988) calls this, is the playful, non-serious mood in which one does not take things literally, and this makes things which usually cannot be done or said acceptable: "In the humorous domain the rules of logic, the expectations of common sense, the laws of science and the demands of propriety are all potentially in abeyance. Consequently, when recipients are faced with a joke, they do not apply the information-processing procedures appropriate to serious discourse" (Mulkay 1988: 37). Humor is a form of thinking and communicating that has its own rules: the criteria for successful humorous communication are not "true" or "untrue". The only thing that counts is "funny" or "not funny" (Raskin 1998). The power of this mood is also evident from comedy performances and other public forms of humor, in which the more the audience laughs, the funnier everything seems to be. This probably applies to the length of jokes too: the longer they are, the more time there is to get "into" the joke.

Form – quality, joke technique, delivery – is but one of the ways to bring about the transition to the humorous mode. The setting and the storyteller both play an important role in creating a humorous atmosphere. Everyone has experienced a situation in which everything seemed funny, no matter how bad the joke was; or a joke teller was so naturally funny that everything he said was hilarious. The opposite happens too: sometimes the situation can be so serious or the mood so dejected that even the best joke doesn't come across.

To achieve any humorous effect at all, it is essential that the correct mood be created. It seems that the form of the joke plays a large role here: this is evident from what the joke tellers have said and from the discovered effect of the number of words. Whether or not the joke can tempt someone to laugh is, in the first instance, a question of humorous technique or "jokework" or *Witzarbeit* (Freud [1905] 1976) and not of subject or import. And these formal aspects of humor lie not only in issues difficult to access like joke quality or the performance but also in simple questions of form, like joke length.

This discovery of the importance of joke length is diametrically opposed to many assumptions originally guiding this research, as well as most research of humor appreciation. Usually, it is assumed that content is the main factor in appreciating humor (e.g. Derks et al. 1998; Martin 1998). At least beyond a basic level of comprehension and complexity of humor, social scientists tend to explain differences mostly from factors such as understanding, offensiveness, or identification. Even linguists, generally-more attuned to matters of form, tend to look for "semantic" factors in understanding varieties between jokes (Attardo 1994, 2001).

A main exception is in the work of psychologist Willibald Ruch, who developed a three-factor model of humor appreciation, with one factor based on content (sexual references) and two on form: jokes with and without full resolution of incongruity (Ruch and Hehl 1998). Ruch and Hehl relate the appreciation of these two types of humorous form to personality characteristics, such as intelligence and temperament as well as other aesthetic preferences. Generally, humor with complete resolution of incongruity, such as most of the jokes in the questionnaire, are liked less by people with preference for complexity and abstraction. Preference for humor in which incongruity is not fully resolved, such as absurd jokes and cartoons, is correlated with a liking of complexity, abstraction, and chaotic patterns. Even though this is phrased differently, and framed in terms of personality rather than habitus, these findings are remarkably reminiscent of the esthetic disposition: humor here is placed in a wider preference for more or less complexity and ambiguity. Ruch and Hehl conclude that "the attempt to identify the *major* sources of variance (setting aside the minor ones) surprisingly did not yield content-related factors" (Ruch and Hehl 1998: 139). This study points in the same direction: humorous form is a more important factor in determining humor appreciation, as well as differences in appreciation between groups.

Rather to my surprise, the discovery of how important the length of a joke is confirms the argument – but not necessarily the entire theory – of Sigmund Freud. He began his book *Jokes and Their Relation to the Unconscious* (1976) with an extensive, often ignored, exposition of the "joke-work": the build-up of jokes in language and text. These humorous techniques were important to Freud because they made possible the expression of unconscious longings and urges: by camouflaging them as a joke, sexual or aggressive thoughts could be smuggled past the censor or superego. Freud took the form of the joke as the starting point for his analysis. He compared it to the dream in its ability to "unlock" the unconscious.

Although I don't necessarily agree with Freud that there is a "censor" that has to be misled, there are always barriers to overcome, both internal and external, before people are able to lose themselves in the humorous mode. These restrictions could be social regulations and taboos (Douglas 1967), as well as internal inhibitions. Moreover, in order to laugh, people also need to overcome some of the more mundane conventions governing everyday life, such as the fact that most communications are serious. Thus, as we also saw in Chapter 3, any attempt at humor entails the crossing over into another mood and frame. This is the quality of a good joke: it is capable of tempting people into crossing such boundaries, into laughter.

"Humor is humor": The incompatibility of humor and morals

To tempt someone into laughter: see there the power of good humor. If people are amused, they consider only the quality of the joke. The humorous mode blocks other emotions: this non-serious mood combines badly with sympathy or feelings of tenderness, anger, embarrassment or indignation. This is why inappropriate humor often evokes strong feelings of outrage: a good joke temporarily switches off moral considerations. In the humorous mode, ethics don't count for a brief space of time. In this respect, humor is not unlike play, art, entertainment, or ritual: it is framed as "non-serious" and separated from the "real world". Often, such "non-serious" forms of communication imply some form of transgression, for instance into (mock) violence, exuberant emotion, irregular or licentious behavior.[20]

This means that *if* a joke does tempt someone into laughing, all rules, including the rules of humor – that to offend is bad, that certain words may not be used, that ladies and the elderly must be respected – become temporarily inoperative. Sometimes one loses sight of these rules altogether, but often an ambiguous mood comes into existence in which one is angry, embarrassed or touched *and* amused all at once. Many humorists of the highbrow style try to bring about this ambiguity. Lovers of popular humor are less keen on ambivalence.

This power of humor to switch off moral considerations is the backdrop of many discussions, prohibitions, scandals and much censure surrounding humor. Hurtful, revolting or offensive jokes can use the non-serious nature of humor to go further than hurtful, revolting or offensive statements can; this often evokes strong reactions, particularly because jokes of this nature continually threaten to escape moral judgments. Ethnic jokes – to name the most contentious genre – exist not just because they express thoughts people do not dare express in a serious mode. My experience, enhanced by my interviews, is: if people want to say racist, sexist or other incorrect things, they will do so. The jokes are upsetting because certain ideas are capable of adopting humor as a vehicle, to such an extent that they become *attractive* into the bargain. And that is how they can occasionally tempt people, who would never express these ideas seriously, into laughter. Humor is most threatening – and therefore quite quickly very attractive – if it breaks through moral or emotional boundaries people cherish.

The amoral character of humor forms the background of my informants' protracted discussion of what went too far and what was permitted. They talked about it so much because there is no unequivocal solution to the dilemma. The joke tellers themselves often contradicted their own forceful statements on impermissible jokes. The discourse about humor and boundaries reveals a certain degree of internal contradiction. Many joke tellers began by resolutely dismissing jokes about foreigners, illnesses, incest or religion. But at a *Moppentoppers* selection, I heard one man who said he did not consider jokes about incest permissible under any circumstances tell an incest joke, admittedly sotto voce. The woman who made such bellicose statements earlier in this chapter about Dutroux, had told a whole series of these jokes at an earlier meeting. The man who assured me that he did not wish to hear a single joke about illnesses, had shortly before told me a joke he found highly amusing about a boy with water on the brain. He followed it up, apologetically, with: "Well, for me humor is humor".

At first I thought these contradictions were connected with my presence: that the interviewees were assuming I would have a problem with offensive jokes. I also thought it perhaps was due to the situation-dependent nature of hurting and shocking: if no one is present who can be hurt, perhaps it doesn't count as hurtful. Both things are partially true, but neither clarifies the enormous contradictions I encountered in many interviews. Joke tellers like Gerrit Helman were aware of this too: "Things I think you shouldn't tell? Jokes about illnesses or things like that. Like, your parents have died of cancer, and you start thinking about it, you know? But I tell them anyway!" As is apparent from his decision, he was aware of his inconsistency; this was true of many (perhaps all) of the joke tellers I spoke to.

At the heart of the expostulation on determining the dosage of funniness and coarseness, two conflicting ideas reign: the standard that jokes may not go "too far" is set against the – quite pertinent – observation that "humor is humor". I heard the statement quite often and it forms an integral part of the discourse on joke culture. For instance, Egbert van Kaam used it: "Humor is humor. If I'm watching a film, I'm aware that none of it really happened and that applies to jokes too. A joke is a joke." Fred Crooswijk used the same phrase: "Yeah, humor is humor and as far as I'm concerned anything's possible."

At the same time there were jokes that, in spite of their humor, were found to be offensive or unsuitable. Where humor is concerned, internal contradictions would seem to be the order of the day. Humor ducks away from moral judgment, and provokes it over and over at the same time. This

is what makes discussions about jokes that go too far, that I have been involved in over the years and to which I have been witness even more often,
so hopeless (e.g. Oring 1991; Davies 1991a; Lewis 1997).

The way usually chosen in the Netherlands of escaping from this discussion is to use self-censure. Risky jokes are only told in closed company:
"You have to keep it separate. I'd never tell that in public, if you could hurt
people head on like that. But among friends, a few guys in the living room,
sure, no problem. They have to be friends, you know, safe." (Egbert van
Kaam) This solution works as long as a consensus exists about what goes
"too far". In the Netherlands, this is easier to realize than, for instance, in
the United States. In the Netherlands, quite reasonable agreement exists
about the impermissibility of jokes connected to ethnic difference, illnesses, disabilities and the Second World War. Jokes like this were seldom
submitted to *Moppentoppers*, to joke pages are even to sites on the Internet:
self-censure makes active censuring almost superfluous (Kuipers 2006b).

Discussions about the boundaries of the joke come up primarily in the
Netherlands in areas where private and public overlap: at work, at parties
and also on the Internet. In truly public situations, offensive humor is approached first from a moral – and thus not a humorous – point of view. As
a consequence, ethnic, sick and other offensive humor is practically invisi-
ble in the public domain. Where it does unexpectedly show itself, wholesale condemnation rather than discussion is the reaction.

Conclusion: Form and quality

Every genre determines its own norms; so too with the joke. Given the
conventions of the joke, and within the margins of hurtfulness, everyone
tends to think the same jokes are better or worse. Even joke haters can distinguish a good joke from a bad one, and they do this in the same way as
joke lovers. Thus, there exist quality criteria for the genre that go beyond
humor styles.

These criteria have to do primarily with the form of the joke. The length
of the joke is a – very simple – measure of quality that remarkably influenced the valuing of jokes: the longer the joke, the better it is liked, even by
people who do not care for the genre. Most differences in the way jokes are
valued have much to do with the content: with offensiveness or possibilities
for identification. However, within the margins of their sensitivities, people
all employed roughly the same criteria for a good joke. In order to be found
funny, a joke must be well built-up and extensively spun-out, and should

preferably refer to different sensitivities at once. If the build-up and punch line is no good, the joke will usually not be amusing; but, if someone doesn't think the joke's subject is funny, it can still be a funny joke. A good build-up may even get people to laugh at a joke they object to: tempting them to transgression.

Research in the social sciences into taste difference leads quite quickly to relativism. Often, a taste is viewed as a cultural phenomenon, a completely self-contained system of norms and criteria adhered to by a certain group of people. There is not really any place for a concept of quality in an analysis of this sort, or quality is only seen as the result of a specific cultural system. The complete lack of such a concept unavoidably leads to a detached relativism that often makes cultural sociology a bit sterile. Research into taste and style, liking and disliking, cannot really be done without a concept like quality. To research humor, and to understand the peculiar seductive effect of jokes, the question of what constitutes "good" humor has to be asked – even if the answer threatens to remain unsatisfactory.

The discovery that people with little appreciation for the genre use similar standards as people who like it, points out that quality does not have to escape completely from scientific exploration: even outside the domain of taste differences and socially determined tastes, people can point to a gauge for quality. And, indeed, for a relatively simple genre like the joke, it is possible to come to grips with this, at least in part. Quality in a joke lies in the possibility of amusing an audience, in successfully tempting people to laugh. In the exploration of this particular quality of jokes, this chapter has taken me closer to the mainstream of humor research: it is concerned more with the specific qualities of humor, and less with the particularities of groups of people.

So some jokes are better, more attractive and funnier than others, at least within the constraint of the genre. And yet, in spite of this consensus about joke form, not everyone thinks the same jokes are funny. There are, for instance, huge style differences between joke tellers, both in delivery and repertoire. And huge differences in where the boundaries are placed within which one may laugh. In the next chapter, the last one describing the Dutch study, I will look into differences in how separate persons and social categories appreciate jokes. Who laughs at what? Which jokes are valued by which types of people? I will no longer dealing be with form and hardly at all with style, but rather with content of a joke, which, in a complex interaction with form, delivery and social context is the thing that, in the end, makes a joke work. This successful mix of the right joke, about the right subject, told in the right atmosphere I will refer to here as identification.

Chapter 8
Sense and sociability

This chapter has to do with the importance of content: with the role a joke's subject and purport plays in how it is appreciated. In spite of the fact that everyone uses roughly the same criteria for joke quality, not everyone likes every joke equally well. Even though the content of humor plays a less important role than I originally assumed, whether or not someone has to laugh at a joke in the end depends on the joke's subject, intention and tone. In terms of content, the main challenge for a joke teller is not only to find the right balance between funny and offensive, as we saw in the previous chapter. In order to amuse, a joke has to be transgressive (but not too much) and at the same time provide opportunity for identification. This chapter will explore the balance between transgression and identification.

Preferences as to the content of jokes can be derived easily from someone's repertoire: joke tellers will, in principle, only tell jokes they like themselves, or (and this is not exactly the same thing) jokes they expect other people to like. Joke tellers' jokes therefore provide insight into what each considers a good joke. In this chapter, I will begin by considering joke tellers' repertoires. Following that, I will look into age, gender and class differences, as well as some other social characteristics, to see whether these may provide opportunities for, of barriers to, the appreciation of individual jokes. What do the old and the young, men and women, the college and non-college educated, consider good jokes – assuming, of course, that people in all these groups think that such a thing as a good joke exists?

Personal styles of joke tellers

Creating humor – telling jokes falls into this category – demands a larger personal involvement than appreciating it. Real joke tellers have invested a great deal of energy building up a joke repertoire they find funny enough to commit to memory, tell regularly, jot down on coasters, or even file in notebooks or databases. Jokes in their own repertoires mean much more to them personally than they do to the people who simply laugh at jokes they have heard or have read in a questionnaire. Preferences for humor content are thus much more pronounced among joke tellers.

Not everyone tells jokes for the same reasons. Although most joke tell-ers stressed that telling jokes was most of all "sociable", some joke tellers mentioned specific motives, varying from the possibility of expressing racist ideas to recalling memories of pre-war, Jewish Amsterdam, and from ways of flirting with women to stimulating sales. These motives influence the repertoire: someone who tells jokes to create a good atmosphere or to establish contact with clients has a broader range of jokes than someone whose jokes gave vent to a specific, personal preoccupation.

The diversity of the joke tellers' jokes corresponded to the diversity of their motives. Each of them had an individual style. The individuality lay in presentation and storytelling technique, as well as content and drift of their jokes. Based on these repertoires, I distinguish two dimensions in which the tellers differed. The first has to do with subcultural differences: some joke tellers did everything in their power not to transgress boundaries; opposite them were those perfecting their aim with hard jokes. A second dimension runs through this distinction into transgressors and avoiders. I spoke to joke tellers who restricted themselves to one or two types of jokes and to people with a much broader repertoire: specialists and generalists. Their identifica-tion with a joke's content characterizes specialized joke tellers: the subjects of their jokes are very dear to them. Content is less important to generalists; to them the social aspect of joke telling is most important.

To my surprise, a distinction considered important by my informants themselves was reflected hardly at all in their repertoires. Joke tellers often emphasized the specificity of jokes from their own region: humor typical of Groningen, Amsterdam or Rotterdam. Nevertheless, informants from dif-ferent regions told the same jokes in large part. The only difference was that local references were inserted. People want to believe that humor dif-fers from region to region, but in practice this happens very little.

Avoiding or transgressing boundaries

The joke tellers who took care that their jokes did not go too far were often the older informants. The jokes of these "old-fashioned" joke tellers were often "proper" sexual jokes in which not a single indelicate word is used. Not transgressing pain thresholds seemed to be – in the public domain at least – more an automatism for these old-fashioned joke tellers than a moral issue.

The jokes they did tell lacked the naughty tone I often heard during other interviews. I did not experience uneasy moments with these joke tellers while they told me a joke of which they were actually ashamed. Often they remarked, with some surprise, that nowadays "anything" could be said or done and was seen as ordinary. The retired entertainer who made the selection for *Moppentoppers* said: "What we used to call proper jokes, well, you don't hear them much at all anymore; I guess they aren't even considered funny these days. It always has to be about – and now I'm going to sound coarse, because that's part of it – it always has to be about cunts and fucking, you see. Everything is permitted nowadays. Just go ahead and scream fucking ten times in a row at the top of your lungs if you want to, people'll think that's the most ordinary thing in the world." While Fred Crooswijk was probably inured to some of this due to his involvement with *Moppentoppers*, his matter-of-fact, hardly moralizing tone was typical of the old-fashioned joke tellers.

Younger joke tellers, especially those under thirty, preferred "hard" or "coarse" jokes. They seldom attempted to clean up language or consider propriety. This distinction between young and old-fashioned joke-tellers mirrors the historical changes described in Chapter 7. This distinction doesn't only show in the short, hard jokes discussed in the previous chapter. Young people also tell longer jokes incorporating the shock effect:

> A boy is walking along the beach, looking to see if there are interesting girls around but he doesn't see anyone much, except one. But she has no arms, she has no legs. So he goes over to her. He says: "Would you like me to rub you with sun tan lotion?" "Oh", she says, "no one's ever offered to do that before, you know. I have no arms, I have no legs." So he begins covering her with lotion and rubbing it in. At a certain point he says: "Would you like a kiss?" "Oh", she says, "I've never been kissed before, you know. I have no arms, I have no legs." So he begins to kiss her. At a certain point he says: "Shall we go for a swim together?" "Yes", she says, "I'd love to go swimming, but I have no arms, I have no legs. I can't swim at all." "Aw", he says, "that doesn't matter, I'll pick you up. And then we'll just move through the sea, whoosh." So she says: "A nice swim, hey?" At a certain point he says: "Shall I screw you?" "Oh", she says, "I've never been screwed before. I have no arms, I have no legs." "Okay", he says. And lets go of her. And this one was rejected [at the *Moppentoppers* selection]. And I think it's such a good one.
> *Because it's – not because it's off color is it?*
> No, it's not off color at all, because it's offensive. Because it's too offensive. (Jasper Bentinck)

However, many other joke tellers were younger than the old-fashioned joke tellers, usually between thirty and fifty, and also very keen not to transgress boundaries. The censure of these "decent" joke tellers was more emphatically expressed in moral terms. However, they enforced the bounds between private and public very strictly, between women and men and between "ladies" and "sluts".

> My background has always been not to tolerate coarse language. I'll give things double meanings, in the sense that a man – now this is going to sound a bit vulgar, right – if a man has a large prick, I'd never say that right out. A man with a large thing is what I would say. There was no question at all of using that sort of language at home. I don't want to upset women with that sort of thing. If you tell that type of really vulgar joke, using such extreme language, it's usually an attack on women, because it's almost always about cunt fucking screwing. I think that's a general tendency of your upbringing, you know: How should I approach a woman? Say it's a woman who, well, who goes traipsing around like a whore or a hussy with a neckline practically reaching her belly button, well you know that she's just asking for it, of course, asking to be approached like that. Someone with a bit of respect for women who – you just wouldn't do that that easily, would you, at least I'd use other words in any case. (Karel Vroon)

A moralistic approach to jokes is difficult to sustain consistently; the decent joke tellers contradicted themselves many times or went on to tell the jokes that they had to so recently fiercely condemned.

No matter whether the aim was to transgress or avoid boundaries, most jokes had to do with sex. Decent joke tellers were often much more daring with their jokes than the old-fashioned joke tellers, but tried at the same time to keep them respectable. That led to jokes full of euphemisms: "thing", "peter", "fulfilling fantasies", "going at it".

> A man comes home from work and hears his wife moaning wildly upstairs in the bedroom. So he runs up to the bedroom, and there's the neighbor and his wife madly going at it. Mad as can be, he pulls his neighbor off his wife, grabs him by his thing and drags him down the steps, outside and into the shed. In the shed, he sticks the neighbor's vital parts into the vice, tightens it as far as it will go and removes the pin. The neighbor's having a bird: "What do you think you're doing?" But the man runs back to the house and into the bathroom and when he comes back to the shed he's got a razor in his hand. Now the neighbor asks, totally horrified: "You're not planning to cut him off are you?" The man says: "No, you'll be doing that yourself as soon as I've set fire to the shed!" [Laughs] Yeah, I told that in Aalsmeer [at the *Moppentoppers* selection] too. Now that's what I call a great joke. You can tell it to anybody. It's not filthy. It's not crude. And it's fun. At least I think it's a lot of fun. (Matthieu Cnoops)

With all its euphemisms and self-censure, the repertoire of these "decent" joke tellers most closely resembled the standard joke repertoire. The decent joke tellers constituted the largest group, almost half of all the joke tellers interviewed. Their jokes also most closely resembled the repertoire of *Moppentoppers* and recent joke books. I would say that this is the "standard" joke teller, with a repertoire adapted to a public situation: the jokes cleaned up and censured for the benefit of the "university student" coming to interview them.

By no means everyone had as much consideration for me as the decent joke tellers did. The decent joke tellers' opposites are people perhaps best described as "direct". These joke tellers categorically refused to clean up their jokes, whether for the television or a well-behaved audience:

> I tell these jokes at birthdays too. You've got these people with two faces, at work they're different from how they are at home. Well, sorry for living, but I'm exactly the same at home as anyplace else and my kids wouldn't know any different than that we talk like that. And then I sometimes hear people saying, other people going something like: what a mouth on that guy that guy'll say anything. But I'm not saying anything strange, I'm just saying something absolutely normal. (Albert Reiziger)

These were "tracksuit types", to cite a *Moppentoppers* editor: types they tried to exclude from their show as much as possible. Their jokes differed significantly from the decent joke tellers: not only their choice of language, but also their repertoire was much more explicit. And yet it still differed from that of the adolescents, as they were not in it for the hardness or the shock effect but for a good, long, well-worked-out joke, one with a bit more "spice to it". They weren't aiming at shock effects but simply did not accept all sorts of limitations: the distinction between public and private, the idea that sex is not a respectable subject, that scatological jokes are not fitting, or that you aren't supposed to say that foreigners are good for nothing. Reiziger once more: "Look, I think Negroes are pigs too. Among ourselves we can say that without a problem but then all of a sudden we're not supposed to say it on television."

Direct joke tellers refuse to adapt their jokes to a more respectable audience. They often call others' standards of decency hypocritical:

> There was this alderman in Rotterdam and he was so la-di-da affected, hard to believe. Well okay, right, you come from a certain class I guess. And then one evening you're on about a little shit and a bit of a fart and sometimes I'll be talking about a prick and then he goes: "You just can't do

that." And it turns out later that that horse's ass has tickets, three tickets no less, for Paul de Leeuw. So I run into this same guy a few weeks later and I go: "You know what I don't get?" I say "Remember you attacking me about my use of language? And then you've gone and bought tickets for Paul de Leeuw. Everybody knows the minute that guy opens his mouth all that comes out is cunt and prick and sucking and licking." So what I think is: Take a look when you're wiping your ass and when your finger pops through the toilet paper – there'll be shit on it, you can bet on that. So they shouldn't pretend that they can't stand a bit of a dirty joke. (Jozef Loosduinen, 43, bartender)

I seldom heard these direct joke tellers' jokes from other joke lovers. The big difference was their graphic language, the masculine atmosphere, the numerous jokes about gays, the jokes rooted in bodily functions and secretions of all kinds, and the spontaneous and uninhibited way presenting of smuttiness as in Reiziger's "best joke" (actually two jokes glued together):

That was my best joke: Mothers and daughters get to talking to each other once in a while, and then one evening a daughter says to her mother, she says: "Well mom, it's going to happen tonight, for sure", she says, "tonight I'm going to become a woman." And then her mother says: "Well, make something nice of it, dear, go out to eat, buy some candles", she says, "because the first time is always a disappointment." So the girl goes out that evening and she doesn't come back home till three in the morning. And her mother's sitting at the kitchen table waiting, of course. So she says to her daughter: "And? How'd it go?" She says: "Well, it was wonderful, so delicious, we had great things to eat, we lit candles, she says, it was fantastic." The mother says: "Oh, I'm really relieved to hear that." She asks: "Was it the first time for the boy too?" She says: "It must've been cuz it was completely wrapped in plastic." Then about three months goes by. The mother says, "Wouldn't you like to bring your boyfriend around one of these days and introduce him to us – we like to know who you're going out with." The girl says: "Yeah, but I've got this problem, see, because I've got two boyfriends actually." She says: "The one's got a long thin one and the other's got, well, he's got a short fat one. I can't choose because I like both such a lot." The mother says: "Well that's easy, you'd better choose the boy with the long thin one because your father's got a short fat one and if he coughs it just keeps flipping back out."

The direct joke tellers are the opposite of the decent joke tellers. The decent joke teller, Vroon, would call this joke "vulgar"; Reiziger would call Vroon "two-faced". These two types of joke tellers differ hardly at all in educational level or income but markedly in presentation, behavior, and lifestyle:

the extent of their embourgeoisement. The classical distinction between blue and white-collar workers plays a role here. Direct joke tellers included a longshoreman, showman, garbage man, bartender, owner of a demolition firm and a production employee (the modern word for factory worker). Decent joke tellers included an entrepreneur, a group leader, technician, representative (more than once), chauffeur or administrative employee, all of them white-collar workers in professions bringing them into contact with many people (Collins 1992). The "direct" joke tellers were more often than not *backstage* workers: manual laborers working "behind the scenes" and thus less subject to the demand to be representative. They therefore can pay less attention to decency. Decency is a preoccupation of laborers with a more bourgeois lifestyle and the lower middle class. Candor and "not pretending to be any better than you are" is a central value for "real" laborers.

Differences between decent and direct, hard and old-fashioned joke tellers clearly have to do with the content of their jokes. However, they are more often found in the tone and tenor of their jokes than in their subjects. This difference can best be seen in sexual jokes, everyone's favorite category. Old-fashioned joke tellers' sexual jokes had to make do with innuendo, a humorous technique seldom employed by young people. The decent, the hard and the direct joke tellers more often told jokes revolving around the regulation of feelings of lust. These feelings were clothed in euphemisms by the decent joke tellers, but beneath the palliative language lay a completely sexualized universe. The jokes of younger joke tellers seemed very similar but were formulated more graphically. And they told jokes in which references to sex were combined with (other) shock effects, as in the joke by Bentinck, where his sexual references served to introduce the cruel dénouement. The direct joke tellers had still another repertoire: just as graphic but without shock effects. A surprising lack of secrecy was noticeable in their case. Sex was presented casually, not as something particularly naughty, or as something that had to be camouflaged, but as "something absolutely normal", be it something with enormous entertainment value. These joke tellers did not show off the unseemliness of their jokes, they just told them. Thus, with different groups of joke tellers, the subject was the same, the tenor very different.

Specialists and generalists

A second dimension in which the styles of the joke tellers varied is once again the question of content: generalism versus specialism. The specialists, approximately a quarter of all joke tellers, primarily told jokes of one specific type or with one specific theme with which they strongly identified. The generalists, the majority of the joke tellers, had a much broader repertoire.

The specialists' repertoire was connected to the specific function fulfilled by telling these jokes. The youngest informant, a 15-year-old girl, told me that she had entered her name for *Moppentoppers* because telling jokes was "at least something that she could do". The fact that she mainly told jokes about stupidity is probably no coincidence. For a Jewish man who told mainly classical Jewish jokes, these were strongly connected to pre-war Jewish culture: jokes were the vehicle for his nostalgia. The man who told the most ethnic jokes effortlessly switched from his joke telling to holding forth on foreigners who didn't want to work. He said the best joke he knew was also the shortest: "Ali's working". This man's type most upsets opponents of ethnic humor: he is someone for whom the tenor of his jokes completely coincides with his serious point of view. I also spoke to someone who told me that he always focuses on "one or two ladies in the audience". His jokes were mainly about sex, but his off color jokes showed remarkably little hostility to women. He seemed to use joke telling (in any case, with me) as a flirtation technique. I also spoke to a descendent of farm laborers who delighted in telling jokes about rich farmers.

Personal styles have to do with identification: people tell jokes about a subject that means a lot to them. For the lovers of farm jokes and the racist joke teller, this has to do with animosity. The man telling the Jewish jokes was, instead, dealing with something for which he had huge affinity. Stupidity, for the girl who told so many jokes about stupid Belgians, farmers and blondes, was a sensitive point. The charmer-joke teller used his jokes more as a social signal. Not all repertoires were this easy to define: I was not able to understand, for instance, why one jovial, sociable man told almost only crude jokes filled with blood, violence and animal abuse.

Personal styles can best be interpreted psychologically: individual specializations correspond to personal preoccupations. What makes interesting is that these joke tellers apparently felt the need to translate their preoccupations into performance. For that matter, this is something many humorists, from amateur joke tellers to the most renowned comedians, share: they make personal sensibilities public (Fisher and Fisher 1981; Fry and Allen 1999). How someone converts his or her experience into a humorous performance is a question of talent and personality. It is, however, also connected with certain roles and social backgrounds: in other circles one would choose not jokes but some other form.

Obviously it is more difficult to find a common denominator for the repertoire of the generalists, about three-quarters of all joke tellers. The function of telling jokes seems to be less personal for them. When asked, they usually mentioned "sociability" and "attention" as reasons for telling jokes. Sociability is, as has already become apparent, the central requirement of the popular humor style, the style of most joke tellers. They were trying to aspire to this ideal of "good" humor with their jokes.

In answer to the question why they themselves told jokes, and why enjoying another's jokes was not enough, joke tellers usually answered that they really wanted people to laugh at what they did. Somewhat reluctantly they admitted to that it was a "really great feeling" if people laughed at their jokes. As Reiziger said: "You start telling a joke and: Wow! All ears and eyes are focused on Bertie. I do it because it's really, yeah, a really good feeling. You've got all the laughers in the palm of your hand, everyone's having a ball." They are quite aware that in doing this they left a mark on the conversation: "It's simply my character to be pretty humorous and then I, well, I just simply influence the atmosphere" said Jasper Bentinck. The fact, too, that they gained a "reputation" as a joke teller was appreciated. As Hans Wagenaar explained: "I think that you just want a little bit more attention than other people might. I always really like it that you're being appreciated. If I go someplace, a reception or whatnot, there they go: "Hey Hans! Got a couple of jokes for us?""

For the majority of joke tellers, the first thing they said when asked why they told jokes was: it is sociable (*gezellig*; noun: *gezelligheid*). To understand joke teller's motivations, as well as the underlying logic of their humor style, it is worthwhile to take a closer look at this concept. Until now, "*gezellig*" has been translated as "sociable", but it is considered one of the untranslatable words of the Dutch language. It refers first and foremost to a pleasant atmosphere whenever people get together. However, the meaning can be extended to all other things that exude or suggest a pleasant social atmosphere, such as interiors of houses and other buildings (esp. bars, cafes, etc.), when it approximates the English word "cozy", but it can also refer to social events and activities (shopping, having coffee together, parties, excursions and outings, family get-togethers, sports events etc), people, or even objects.

The meaning of the word *gezellig* spills over, as it were, from sociable events and people into other things that may conjure up similar associations of togetherness. This spilling over has been hilariously parodied by cabaret artist Maarten van Roozendaal in a song listing things that are *gezellig*, including cubes of cheese with mustard, the election of the sportsman of the year, home-knit sweaters, a rabbit, a car mirror with a funny figurine, or Beatles songs played on a panflute.[21]

This suggests that *gezellig* may have negative connotations of oppressiveness, forced joviality, and cluttered living spaces. However, although it may occasionally be used derogatorily to denounce "bourgeois" behavior, it definitely is a word that everyone in the Netherlands, in all social circles, uses as a positive term. However, people with a popular humor style, such as the joke tellers, were much more likely to use the word to describe someone with a good sense of humor or good humor in general. To people with a highbrow humor style, humor may be more ambivalent: it does not have to be *gezellig*.

Gezellig clearly has to do with identification: *gezelligheid* defines a situation where you feel part of a social group and a social atmosphere. *Gezelligheid* has clear boundaries, too: a hurtful or offensive joke, or anything that spoils the feeling of togetherness, is not sociable anymore. On the other hand, transgressing boundaries together can lead to strong feelings of connection and togetherness and thus, *gezelligheid*.

All joke tellers, by telling jokes, are aiming at the combination of "attention" and "sociability". Specialists are usually looking for a specific sort of attention and sociability, or they are looking for attention, sociability and one more ingredient: proving they are right, rebelling, revising their self-image, convincing themselves of their courage, angling for allies. Joke tellers and probably everyone who develops into the joker, the humorist or the life and soul of the party, feel the need to attract attention, to win prestige and to be liked. The message that generalists want to convey is not so much the joke's content as the fact *that* they are telling a joke: this telling on its own is a social signal.

However, the content of jokes often is geared to generating the identification and solidarity that joke tellers are aiming for. Many jokes appeal to a group feeling: they create a feeling of fellowship that contributes to the sociability. Most jokes, for instance, draw a boundary line between one's own group and deviating, or inferior "others" who are dumb, lazy, aggressive, filthy or uncivilized. Laughing at others is one of the very best binding agents. It even works if you have nothing against this particular other – although it helps if you do. Another way to bring about the feeling of solidarity is to make a joke about something not permitted or not done. This feeling of being "naughty" together strongly enhances sociability. Also, jokes can emphasize shared feelings, preoccupations and cares, ranging from nostalgia for the good old days to political discomfort. Feelings are thus both revealed and shared at one and the same time and this too leads to a feeling of fellowship.

The joke teller issues an "invitation" to identification, both by the telling of the joke, and in the joke's content. This identification is contained in definition of ingroups and outgroups, in the nature of boundaries transgressed, and in the revelation of shared preoccupations – or inversely, in the absence of themes that one can identify with. In jokes, as in most humor, many of the feelings revealed are forbidden or loaded. Slightly exaggerated, the tenor of the Dutch joke repertoire could be summarized as "we all think about sex all the time, would like to have an affair with a twenty-year-old blonde, don't take religion very seriously, we all feel uneasy about Turks and gays, we all loath child rapists and terrorists, and we all feel superior to Belgians, drunks, and women." And while there is no reason to assume that all joke tellers agree with all of these statements, my interviews did leave me with the impression that many of them have, at times, agreed with some of them.

The solidarity evoked by sharing a joke, in combination with the exuberant and friendly atmosphere generated by telling jokes and the feeling of fellowship brought about by the joke's content certainly contributes to a sociable evening. Humor that increases the distance among those present quickly becomes unsocial. Sociable humor, instead, emphasizes points of agreement and diminishes social distance. In its combination of sociability, identification, and shared transgression, the telling of jokes in this way becomes a "tiny conspiracy" of the joke teller and his audience.

Transgression, identification, and the Dutch joke culture(s)

This, in fact, is a formula for a good joke: creating a "tiny conspiracy" by balancing transgression and identification. This formula offers signposts in our search for the role played by a joke's content in its appreciation. After all, not everyone has the same boundaries, and not everyone can identify with the same joke.

In the remainder of this chapter, I will explore what jokes are sociable for whom, or: who laughs at what. Using both the survey and the interview data, I will look again at the three social categories that have played the most important role in this book: age, gender, and educational level. The survey results and the interviews show how the appreciation of individual jokes is related to social background factors. Moreover, I will attempt to connect the preferences of each of these social categories with the joke repertoire, in an attempt to gauge what opportunities for identification this offers for each of these social categories.

Young and old

Of the three social categories, age is by far the easiest to connect to differences in appreciation of individual jokes. Age differences in the appreciation of humor have been addressed several times. The same pattern emerged again and again: the older people are, the more issues they find painful or coarse. Table 5 in Chapter 7 shows the factor loadings for the age-related "innocuousness" factor: appreciation of jokes loading positive on this factor correlated positively with age, while jokes with inverse correlations were liked better by younger people. This makes apparent that older people were less able to appreciate the "harder" jokes: this includes all ethnic jokes except for the classical Jewish jokes, all sick jokes, as well as the more explicit sexual jokes and the nastier jokes about religion. Thus, some themes seem to be too transgressive altogether, whereas with other themes it depends on the joke. One of the jokes that showed the largest differences of opinion between old and young was a joke about religion:

> This advertising man gets to make an advertisement for Trevor's Nail Factory. A week later he visits the factory's managing director, carrying a large roll of paper with him. He rolls it out and there's an image of Jesus on the cross, with the following text underneath: "THANKS TO NAILS FROM TREVOR, I'VE BEEN HANGING HERE FOREVER."
> The managing director is aghast and says: "We couldn't accept that, sir. No, we just couldn't. Have another try, and then without Jesus on the cross."
> A week later, the advertising man returns, carrying a large roll of paper with him. This time there's an image of Jesus lying face down in the dirt under the cross, with the following text: "NOW I'M FLAT ON MY FACE. WITH TREVOR'S NAILS I'D STILL BE IN PLACE."

This joke is appreciably more blasphemous than the joke about the stuttering Bible salesman, which everyone liked and which was at most blasphemous in suggesting that it would be unpleasant to have the Bible in its entirety read to one.

There were also jokes that older people appreciated more than others: decent sexual jokes, jokes about mothers-in-law, and the more absurd jokes. These connections are not related to sensitivity alone. Most absurd jokes have nothing at all to do with boundary transgressions. Young people love shock effects often missing in more absurd jokes. There was, for instance, a significant positive correlation between age and the appreciation of the joke about the half-deaf man ("Says the doctor: eighty-eight. Says the man: forty-four"). This joke is not more hurtful for the elderly but young people expect a boundary transgression and its lack makes the joke less interesting for them.

The preference for shock effects is a question of style that can also be recognized in other cultural manifestations. Shocking, hard or upsetting humor, previously appreciated by the cultural vanguard, is becoming more and more widely appreciated and therefore in lower and lower social classes too. And meanwhile it has trickled down to one of the humorous genres with the lowest status: the joke. This continuous status devaluation of cultural goods is also a process through time; taste difference is thus also phase difference. Therefore it does not just appear as class difference but also as age difference: younger people grow up with this humor that for the elderly, sharing the same environment, is still unusual and unsuitable. Additionally, the preference for shock effects perhaps has something to do with age (McGhee 1983). A desire for shock effects is probably most pronounced in adolescents, and something they grow out of with time.

The jokes, however, do not only differ in their hardness; the jokes of older and younger people also differ in their subjects. Older joke tellers told jokes about bosses and servants, farmers, pastors, ministers and rabbis, men who have had too much to drink, women wearing the pants, ill-tempered mothers-in-law and other negative aspects of the wedded state. Another favorite theme was visits to the pub and drinking habits; telling jokes was strongly linked to the act and the ambience of drinking. Jokes of people under fifty were more likely to be about Belgians and blondes, about shortcomings of all sorts, about foreigners, illnesses and misery but primarily about sex.

The increased space for jokes does not seem to have led to a broader repertoire. On the contrary: my impression is that the joke repertoire over time has instead become more limited. Comparisons through time remain difficult to make, but the older joke tellers seemed to have a larger diversity of subjects at their disposal than the younger. It could be that a society with more restrictions and sensibilities favored humor. The necessity of telling decent jokes perhaps forced people to be more creative.

These different repertoires mean that older and younger joke tellers have difficulty identifying with each other's jokes. The somewhat surprised tone – "anything's possible nowadays" – of the older about the jokes of the younger has already been mentioned. This surprise is caused more by tone than by theme. One of the old-fashioned joke tellers who was emphatically negative about foreigners said that he did not tell jokes about foreigners because he thought them "too stark". He did not object in principle to the jokes' intent; he thought the jokes too coarse. This is an unexpected contribution to the discussion about ethnic jokes. The esthetic argument weighs more heavily than the moral one, not in the usual way: the joke's intent is appreciated but the joke itself is simply not to one's taste.

Not only do they have a different tone, they refer to a different world of experience. A good example of this is the joke category "marriage as a mistake". These jokes address irritating side effects of marriage such as mothers-in-law, monogamy, aging, bossy or garrulous wives. But in many jokes, without any further explanation, marriage is presented as a mistake, such as this joke from a 1953 joke book:

> "No," sighed Moos. "I didn't have any luck with either of my wives! The first went off with someone else after a year..." "And the second!" "The second stayed!" (Tailleur 1953:58)

Marriage is at present no longer taken the inescapable fact of life it was thirty years ago, certainly not in the form taken in these jokes.

Classical Jewish jokes about Sam, Moos, and Saar constitute the most poignant example of disappearing jokes. The joke from the questionnaire most strongly correlated with age was of this sort:

> Moos goes skiing. He gets caught in an avalanche while he's out on the slopes. A search team is formed to go look for him. As soon as they see him, they start calling: "Mr. Cohen, Mr. Cohen, we're on our way. We're from the Red Cross!' Moos calls back: "I gave at the office!"

With the disappearance of the pre-war Jewish culture, the substrate for these jokes disappeared. Many of the references are no longer understood (I myself, for instance, only discovered during my research that a specific accent was used in telling these jokes). Moreover, emphatically pointing out stereotypes of Jews is very quickly experienced as painful. References to classical Jewish themes in jokes – miserliness, business acumen, sharp-wittedness, kosher food – no longer say anything to young people. To simply intone the names Sam and Moos, a world depicted with the accompanying nostalgia, was to evoke an entire world for older informants.

An important part of the we-feeling of older joke tellers was based in nostalgia: "You could still laugh in the old days". As a 72-year-old former manager of a campsite told me: "There used to be a whole lot of manual labor and lots and lots of people all together. Even in the little companies. A whole lot more contact. Back then there was more humor." And a 62-year-old longshoreman, Max Jongejans: "But in the port of Rotterdam harbor, I worked there for 35 years, you know, and back then you could really laugh. That was really something. But that's all gone now." The retired entertainer, Crooswijk, even performed in a program called "old time toppers". Nostalgia stirred into humor is an exceptionally powerful mixture contributed importantly to the older people's appreciation of their jokes; and this was doubtlessly a we-feeling with which young people could scarcely identify. On the off chance that they liked the joke and recognized the references, it still evokes an atmosphere where they don't belong.

Age difference in humor is thus a consequence of cultural change. It would seem that sense of humor is for the most part formed during the period in which someone grows up. This means that the jokes, and more generally the humor style of older people, reflect the world in which they grew up. It means that each generation shakes its head at the humor of the generation that follows, and that this new generation in turn is filled with disbelief at hearing the preceding generation's humor. In so doing, they distinguish themselves, intentionally or unintentionally, from one another.

Men and women

Men think jokes are funnier and more sociable than women do; all informants agreed on this. Gender differences are differences in sense of humor of which one is most aware, and for which there exist the most standards, rules, generally shared and contested kernels of wisdom: "Women can't really stand that kind of thing", "you've got to watch out with women", "women can't tell jokes", "women are more serious than men" and even: "women have no sense of humor".

Differences between men and women are often connected with the sensitivity of women. Most joke tellers were convinced that women were less able to stand shocking, hurtful, and particularly sexual jokes. Not only the joke tellers but also the women whom I interviewed often said: "Women get embarrassed more quickly". And, indeed, on average, women thought the jokes in the questionnaire more offensive than men did. This comes, to some extent, of their appreciating the genre less. If they think the joke less funny, the boundary transgression emerges more clearly. "We women reflect more seriously on jokes", said Claire van Kampen, a woman married to a representative with a huge joke repertoire. "And then we see much more as hurtful." And Maria Romein, who worked "as one of the guys" in an architect's bureau, said: "My idea is that women are quicker to see how pitiful a joke is. Women are more serious and more emotional and more easily offended, aren't they?" And Claudia van Leer, mother of a number of sons: "I think that my thresholds are lower than men's. I was living pretty exclusively in a men's world and when the boys started a round of joke telling, my husband joined in too, naturally. So you've got to listen to what's going on, of course. But sometimes it got pretty sordid or offensive. And then I didn't like it anymore."

However, women's objections were often not aimed at the sexual jokes for which joke tellers thought women to be too respectable. Women had more problems with aggressive, ethnic, and sick humor. The avoidance of sexual jokes in the company of women often arose, in my view, from the joke tellers' feelings of shame rather than from the women's feelings of aversion. The presence of women when these jokes are told too seriously sullies the atmosphere of "a man's world".

The pleasure of both sexual and hurtful jokes has a lot to do with boundary transgression, with the "naughtiness" of clandestine humor. This specific form of sociability, based on joint transgressive behavior, seem to be more specific to men than to women. Louis Baldé called this "boyishness" characteristic of the humor of men: "Shock people a bit, take a good kick at things, up the ante. I don't think women can stand that sort of behavior much." This "boyish" form of being together is once again connected with a combination of status seeking, competition, and sociability, already the focus of attention in Chapter 3. "Yeah, you tell jokes like that, you've gotta be a bit crass, because after all, it is a man's world", said Harm Arends about his work in the wharf. "You've got to play the tough guy, of course. You can't show up with your knitting."

The feeling of fellowship and conspiracy joke tellers, and men generally, seem to be seeking when using coarse language or sexual jokes to transgress boundaries together is sought instead by women in other forms of interaction: confidentiality, gossip and shared secrets are different strategies for achieving the clandestine. Various interviewees, both men and women, called gossip the female equivalent of joke telling. When I asked Maria Romein what female humor was, she said, somewhat hesitantly:

I'm not sure I should be saying this, you know. When women are on their own – yeah, it sounds pretty stupid, but that's the way it is – I've got quite a lot of women friends, and if we're together, an awful lot of gossiping goes on. Last night I was at a friend's birthday party. A great evening, really. And there was a party in a village and all that really got talked about was what this one or that one was up to, who was with whom and what and how and I was really surprised. Jesus. You'd practically have to work full-time to keep track of it, wouldn't you? [laughs] Unbelievable. And we are making jokes about this kind of thing, naturally. Lots and lots of jokes, even. [laughs] But then *that* sort of joke, you know. It's maybe a bit, could be a bit, it really sounds a bit like talking behind people's backs, doesn't it?

But if jokes are men's humor, what is women's humor in your opinion?
Well, gossiping, eh? That's my guess. It can actually be humorous, because women laugh a whole lot about other women, about their relationships with others and so on. What I think is simply that it's a lot more communicative. I think that women, that they're much more involved in social life, aren't they, in what they see around them, and then they see the funny side of all that kind of thing. (Vincent Zwagerman)

Women tend toward other sorts of conspiracies than men: more personal, more based in relationships. Women choose not only for conspiracies with a different tone, but also for conspiracies with more "content": conspiracies with a more personal slant. Telling a joke, while a social message, is not very personal.

The "tiny conspiracy" of the joke's humorous boundary transgression is thus less appealing to women. However, the joke repertoire has little to offer women through its content either. The identification in jokes is usually with men: the subjects, the perspectives and the points of view are male. Women play roles in jokes practically only if the joke makes a woman's presence absolutely necessary – and, in fact, this always has to do with sex or family relationships. Women are never neutral joke personages; they are always horrible mothers-in-law, women lurking behind doors with rolling pins at the ready, seductive secretaries, and other male dream and dread images. If a woman appears at the doctor's, or in a bar, it is bound to be a sexual joke.

Women's roles in jokes appeal to a masculine feeling of solidarity with which women have very few things in common, unless they are prepared to accept a male perspective on women. Identification does not by definition have to take place with the group to which one belongs. Certainly in groups with low social status, it is imaginable that someone will identify with the more powerful group. One of the first studies into ethnic humor showed that American blacks laughed harder at jokes about blacks than at jokes about whites (Middleton 1959). Other studies showed this to be true of women too: groups with low social status amuse themselves with jokes at their own group's expense rather than jokes at the dominant group's expense (Henkin and Fish 1986; Herzog 1999; Nevo 1985). The male perspective, or open animosity to women, found in many jokes does not therefore have to form an absolute impediment. Men, however, can probably enjoy jokes about wicked wives and seductive secretaries more fully and less ambiguously.

A relatively innocent example of this male perspective is the joke about Johnny and his teacher ("That's good, but I meant chewing gum"), one of the few jokes in the questionnaire very highly valued as highly by women as by men. While I don't want to present this as a joke hugely hostile to women, Johnny, young as he is, is quite able to stalemate the female protagonist: he strips her of her authority by addressing her in sexual terms.

The ascendancy of blond jokes, from the mid-1990s, can perhaps be seen as a form of progress: the woman is handed a role until recently allocated to (male) Belgians. These jokes always have to do with the backward version of one's own group, as set forth in Chapter 6. The fact that a specific type of woman is given this role indicates a certain emancipation within the joke. Despite not much female-friendly content, the dumb blond joke is one of the few joke categories with which women can identify. Women regularly tell these jokes. There is even a "rule" that primarily blond women have the right to tell these jokes. After all, for hurtful jokes the adage is: jokes about your own group are always allowed. This (self-) mockery of a certain female type may indicate a growing (self-)respect.

Even if jokes are not at the expense of women, their objects are frequently not gender-neutral: often groups men prefer to women as foils are the butt, as in the many jokes about homosexuals. Jokes about sex are not only expressly masculine, they are also rabidly heterosexual: (male) homosexuality is always describes as deviant in jokes. Male homosexuals are, moreover, continuously presented as obsessed by (anal) sex:

This gay guy goes to the doctor. He says: "Doctor, you've got to check me out because things aren't good." Says the doctor: "What's the matter then?" "Well", he says, "Doctor, my friend and I are right in the middle of our wedding night, my friend is chasing me across the top of the bed under the bed sideways hanging off the edge of the bed." He says: "Doctor, the fun we had! Oh, how we laughed!" He says: "Doctor, but then my friend falls and his glass eye rolls out, so I grab hold of that eye and head off with it and he's hot on my heels and we're killing ourselves laughing across the top of the bed under the bed sideways hanging off the edge of the bed." He says: "Doctor, then I tripped and fell but I didn't want to give up the eye so I stuck it in my mouth." "Oh", says the doctor, he goes: "that sounds serious." He says: "Yeah, turns out I swallowed that eye." "Oh", says the doctor, "that's not such a huge problem", he says, "just go on home and you'll see that everything that goes in at the top comes back out the bottom a couple of days later." "Well", says the guy: "Doctor, now you're talking about a couple of days but what I'm talking about is three weeks back already." "Oh", says the doctor, "then you'd better lower your trousers." So this fairy undoes his belt, lets his trousers fall down around his ankles and the doctor says: "Bend over then." So he bends over, the doctor's right behind him with a funnel and a penlight, searching, searching, searching. "Well", says the doctor, "it's really strange but I can't see a thing." "Well, that is strange," says the gay. "Because I can see you perfectly." (Egbert van Kaam)

During my interviews, I heard many degrading remarks about homosexuals even outside the jokes. "Homo" was even used regularly as invective, without further qualification, for instance by those who didn't make it through the *Moppentoppers* selection ("those homos at Endemol..."). Homosexuals form the one group for which serious remarks and hostile jokes were closely connected. Moreover, in this case, joke tellers made no attempt to hide between the excuse that is was "just a joke". The masculine slant of the Dutch joke repertoire is also made apparent by these jokes about male homosexuals.

There are, of course, preoccupations and aversions shared by men and women: jokes about shortcomings and abnormalities, jokes about dumbness, and ethnic jokes are really only masculine because these are continuously told about male prototypes in the groups concerned. The one joke with which women could identify somewhat better referred to a traditional women's domain, children. This was the only one more highly valued by women than men:

Whispering child's voice on the telephone: "Hello?"
"Hello, is your mother there?"
"Yeah, she's here, but she's very very busy!"
"Well, is your father there then?"
"Yeah, he's here too, but he's very very busy!"
"Are there any other adults there?"
"Yeah. The police' s here. And the fire department."
"Can I speak to one of them?"
"No, they're really really busy too."
"What's everyone doing there then?"
"Looking for me!"

In general, women value a joke most if it verges on the unrealistic: if it's very clear that no identification points exist within the joke, if no shock affect is aimed for, and if no one is hurt or excluded. Jokes women valued as highly as men were often lightly absurd: the skeletons in a bar, the mule going to the doctor, the man talking to his dog, and the Belgian thief identifying his jeweler.

Gender difference is a social boundary kept intact expressly and consciously in jokes, both by their content and the rules surrounding them. And yet not every joke teller, not every joke and not every circumstance in which jokes are told demonstrates machismo. There is sufficient repertoire for birthdays and other mixed functions. The emphasis on masculinity does more than solely create a feeling of "a man's world". It can also be used to amuse women. Jokes emphasize not only one's own and others' manliness; they also emphasize gender roles in mixed company. When men tell jokes, women are ideal audiences.

Non-college and college educated

People are very aware of the taste difference between men and women. This is much less so for class difference. Within the genre, no identification is made with class background either: I do not know any jokes about, for instance, laborers versus college graduates. Up till the 1960s, there were jokes connected to differences in social status: jokes about bosses and servants, ladies and maids, and also about the impossibility of understanding modern art, for example. These have, however, died out: class distinctions no longer play a visible role in Dutch jokes.

Since jokes are told and appreciated more by the less highly educated, the question arises whether this is in some other way reflected in the joke repertoire. Do Dutch jokes reflect the values, worldview, of lifestyle of the working or lower middle classes? Is something included in the content of jokes making them less funny for the college educated?

One thing that would mark the Dutch joke repertoire as being class-based is its explicit masculinity, described earlier in this chapter. The separation of gender roles and gender domains is generally stronger in the working and lower middle classes. Both the depiction of women, and of homosexuals, in jokes is very different from the way these groups are generally portrayed in more highbrow humor. Several of the educated interviewees commented on the stereotyping of women and gays in some of the jokes in the survey, as well in jokes more generally.

There is one joke category that was, on the basis of content, unanimously and categorically dismissed by highly educated respondents: jokes about migrants. Both in the survey and the interviews, this was the type of jokes that came out as the category leading to the widest divergence in opinions in this already contentious genre. The highly educated categorically rejected ethnic or "racist" jokes, without any of the exceptions joke tellers make for private situations and people who "can take it". References to ethnic difference are generally very loaded in the Netherlands; but this weighs most heavily for intellectuals (Vuijsje 1997). Joke tellers too saw "foreigners" as being a sensitive subject for jokes but experienced this more as an order not to make too many critical remarks or jokes about foreigners in public situations. In private situations, different rules applied.

Both a difference in identification and a difference in establishing taboos play roles here. The larger tolerance for ethnic jokes among joke lovers can partly be traced back to their view of minorities. Negative conceptions about foreigners are more wide-spread among the non-college educated (Sociaal en cultureel planbureau 1999: 46-47). Moreover, the ethnic taboo is stronger among the highly educated. Thus, less educated people are more likely to (openly) agree with stereotypes about minorities. However, jokes about foreigners are significantly more widespread than negative opinions about foreigners. More than 70 percent of a group of schoolchildren I researched in 1995 knew a joke about Turks but research into opinions about ethnic minorities show that the percentage of schoolchildren having a negative opinion about Turks is significantly lower than 70 percent (Kuipers 1995, 2000). Negative ideas in the background can thus never be the only reason for why jokes about certain groups are popular.

It is not only differing ideas about these themes that account for the differing opinion of jokes about minorities. A more general difference plays a role here: the meaning ascribed to transgressing pain thresholds, and to what "hurtfulness" in jokes entails. As apparent in the first part of this book, a joke at the expense of others is not by definition wrong for those with a highbrow style: sharpness was, indeed, appreciated. Jokes about foreigners are the exception here, for reasons which will be explained below. Otherwise "hurtfulness" is less absolutely censured by the college educated, particularly those with a highbrow humor style, than it is by the non-college educated. Provided they are presented in a suitable way, jokes at someone else's expense are, indeed, acceptable.

This differs for the non-college educated for whom "hurting" is not an absolute category. It is the most serious transgression within the popular humor style, but it means something else than it does to the college educated. For joke lovers, a joke is not hurtful on its own, but only if it is at the expense of someone who is likely to be directly hurt: someone who is present – a Turk, a woman, a gay man, someone suffering from certain illnesses – and then only if the person "cannot defend him or herself properly". This is why the difference between public and private, between men's and women's domains is so important for joke tellers.

According to joke tellers, and other people with a popular humor style, whether someone can be hurt or not always depends upon his or her position of power. Joke tellers were very precise in this: it is hurtful to make jokes about someone "who can't fight back" and that is often someone with lower status. Someone "who can take it" – a friend, a colleague, an equal – can always counter insulting jokes. If that person is indeed hurt by this joke, "he's being a spoilsport'. In this case, the target of the joke and not the joke teller loses face. An equal, who "can stand it", is expected to take part in the "horsing around" even if this is someone who could possibly be put in a tight spot by the joke.

Hans Wagenaar told ethnic jokes to his migrant colleagues as a sign that they belonged:

> I work with foreign employees, Surinamers, Turks, Moroccans, and I'd be just as likely to tell a Surinam joke, no matter how hard it is, to a Surinamese or a Turk or a Moroccan. Straight to their faces. Otherwise you get the problem – yeah, he's like that, he only tells a joke like that when we're not around. So you'd pretty quickly get the idea that I'm actually discriminating, that the moment he's around, I wouldn't dare to tell it to him. What I think is: just tell them the same jokes as you'd tell anybody.

College educated respondents looked at hurtfulness more in the context of the whole society: even if a particular woman, gay or foreigner counts as an equal, that is not so from a social viewpoint. For the highly educated interviewees, "hurtfulness" had to do with absolute boundaries; for the non-college educated it was contextual and situational. This is, apart from the "ethnic taboo" a second reason why the college educated are so sensitive to jokes about ethnic minorities: social groups with the lowest social status are being targeted.

This situational logic is directly related to notions of decency and respect. Joke tellers, as well as interviewees with a popular humor style, repeatedly connected hurtfulness with "decency". For them, "respect" dictated that you do not tell hurtful jokes to people who could feel attacked by them. *Not* because a subject on its own is too serious or too vulgar. Sexual jokes are not wrong on their own; decency simply requires that you do not use certain terms in the presence of ladies or the elderly. In some cases, it can instead be a sign of more respect to go ahead and tell vulgar or dirty jokes. For Wagenaar, not telling a joke to a Turkish colleague indicated less respect than actually coming right out with it. Decency and respect are linked to persons in situations.

This idea about what "hurting" means has influenced the content of jokes. In the case of ethnic jokes, or jokes about women and homosexuals, jokes sometimes go further than the absolute boundaries that the college educated attempt to enforce. But at the same time, many more boundaries are respected in jokes and many more taboos are maintained than in the humor of the college educated, where the search for "sharpness" often has priority. The shorter "hard" jokes of teenagers aim at shock effects, but outside that a very watchful eye is kept on certain boundaries related to respect and decency. This is visible, for instance, in the euphemisms and evasion of vulgar language by the "decent" joke tellers. In this respect, jokes reflect the class culture of the "respectable" working and lower middle classes.

The emphasis on respect, decency, and not hurting is connected to the main demand made of jokes in the lowbrow humor style: sociability. Humor has to benefit the atmosphere: no one should feel insulted, held in contempt, or attacked. This tone of decency, respect and not-wanting-to-hurt is also expressed in the content of many jokes. While jokes sometimes transgress boundaries that the college educated would prefer to have respected, it more often seems that jokes attempt too emphatically to maintain these boundaries instead. The many euphemisms, the caution and the naughtiness incorporated into the jokes to ensure sociability for the joke tellers are quite quickly seen as "self-consciously daring" by the college educated. They expect shocking, upsetting an unexpected feats of humor and not jokes finely tuned to the boundaries of decency.

In their content and phrasing, jokes reflect the standards for good humor as dictated by the logic of the popular humor style: sociability, a pleasant atmosphere, but also a certain exuberant masculinity. This exuberance is enhanced by competition and (controlled) transgression, the combination of which leads to a particular, very masculine, form of sociability, that many highly educated informants objected to. The joke repertoire is influenced by these standards: it is geared to generating a rather boisterous, male, irreverent-but-decent, at times conspiratorial, tone.

By degrees, the distinction into style and content begins to crumble in this connection. After all, if "not hurting" is a much more important criterion for good humor within one humor style than within another, and if, moreover, people mean so many different things when they say "hurting" – then subject choice also becomes a question of style.

The same goes for sociability as a criterion of good humor. The joke repertoire does reflect the demands for "sociability". Most joke subjects are sociable in and of themselves, because they have obvious and immediate humorous appeal: drinking, sex, wives, mothers in law, the shortcomings of others, ethnic stereotypes. Measured by highbrow humor style criteria, these subjects, however, very quickly become too "easy": they remain subjects that are too transparently and obviously funny. Jokes not only make something funny by their design or their joking technique, but also often deal with subjects already having a great deal of humorous potential anyway. And so it is true here as well: the humor style partially determines suitable subjects for a good joke.

Interactions of style, content, form, and subject are essential to the cultural differences, which are also class differences. Culture determines not only criteria by which humor is judged, but even suitable subjects for a good joke. Sociability is not the appropriate criterion for the college educated. Class difference, therefore, of the three social distinctions, has the most far-reaching effect on sense of humor. At the same time, it is the most difficult to recognize and to identify. Class difference is neither consciously articulated in jokes nor a subject of jokes. No conscious craving for distinction on the part of the joke tellers was at work here, only a difference in taste, linked to culture but largely unconscious. Still, the Dutch joke repertoire, in the end, has higher entertainment value for the less highly educated: it offers them more opportunities for identification, it respects their boundaries, and it creates a social atmosphere to their liking.

Conclusion: Mechanisms of taste and the sense of sociability

In this final chapter of the Dutch study, we have seen a variety of ways in which taste is connected with social background. In the personal styles of joke tellers, taste in jokes is connected with personal preoccupations or with more general identifications. Personal styles were also connected with broader social distinctions within their social stratum: age difference; the "respectable" working class versus the self-consciously unpolished blue-collar workers. These differences resulted in very different joke repertoires, with different topics, vocabularies, and styles.

In the second part of this chapter, the relation between joke repertoires and wider social categories were investigated: age, gender, and class. In the case of age difference, taste difference was found to be primarily *phase* difference. Gender difference is mostly a result of role differences between men and women and to the existence of separate men's and women's domains. But class difference is clearly cultural difference: differences in taste between classes are so strongly connected to style that it is barely possible to determine the influence of content in differences in appreciation. However, it was easy to see the reverse: how joke content was the result of differences in appreciation of the genre as whole. Dutch joke culture is a reflection of the people who tell and appreciate the genre most: men of working class and lower middle class background.

Each of these social categories thus seems to have its own dynamics and logic. And yet the same mechanisms occur again and again. Both age differences and class differences showed trickle-down effects: cultural tastes and preferences tend to diffuse toward lower social strata. Another mechanism that was visible throughout this chapter was a striving to distinguish oneself from other groups: old and young, men and women, people from different regions, decent and direct joke tellers, consciously attempt to show their distinctiveness in their use of humor. However, the greatest and most far-reaching difference was the one that were least consciously enacted: class. The most important mechanism operative in all these differences though, be they style differences between persons or groups, cultural, phase or role differences, is the need to belong to a certain group, an with this the automatic corollary: the need not to belong somewhere else. The craving for distinction energizing this trickle-down effect is the flip side, and more often still, the unintended side effect of the need to express feelings of fellowship.

For all preferences that have been reviewed in this chapter, the need to share something predominates above everything else: the need to identify with others, and to invite others to identify with you. People who tell jokes take something personal and transform it into a public performance, in order to laugh collectively about something. This is played out in the tiny conspiracies of humor. Sometimes emphatic outer boundaries are defined in doing this: by laughing at others, by shocking or insulting people, by transgressing boundaries. But more often the distinction from others is a side effect of the fellowship and solidarity. And this is perhaps most pronounced for class difference: the joke tellers would not have been at all displeased if the college educated had deigned to laugh at their jokes, and thus contribute to the feeling of sociability and sharing.

Part III. Comparing humor styles

Chapter 9
National humor styles: Joke telling and social background in the United States

Five years after I conducted my interviews in the Netherlands, I set up a similar, though much smaller, study in the United States. This study involved distributing a questionnaire that 143 persons in the Philadelphia area filled out, and interviewing twenty-eight Americans about their sense of humor. This enabled me to compare Dutch patterns of humor styles and social background with American humor styles: do Americans have humor styles similar to the Dutch, or are there national differences in sense of humor? Are American humor styles connected with social background in ways similar to what I found in the Netherlands? The American study also functioned as a cross-cultural validation of the approach to humor I had developed in the Dutch study: do the approach and the concepts described in previous chapters still work in a different cultural context, where social distinctions and classifications may be markedly different?

Before I started doing the American study, I was aware that joke telling did not have the strong, lower-class connotation in the United States that it has in the Netherlands. For instance, American academics (not just humor scholars) had regularly told me jokes – something Dutch, or European, academics would be highly unlikely to do. When, during presentations at international meetings, I said that jokes were not considered particularly intellectual and were, in fact, "not done" in academic circles, Europeans would usually nod, while Americans would be surprised, or misunderstand me, thinking I meant that, generally, highly educated Dutch people didn't have much of a sense of humor.

This made me expect that jokes would not be the strong social marker they were in the Netherlands. The aim of this study, therefore, was not to compare solely opinions on joke telling, but, more generally, to detect sociological patterns in the use and appreciation of humor. For this reason, I broadened the scope of my research somewhat. I included cartoons as well as jokes in the questionnaire, and I focused more on television comedy and other forms of standardized humor in the interviews and the questionnaire.

Even though I expected humor to demarcate symbolic boundaries between social groups, I wasn't completely sure which boundaries would be most prominent in the United States. Comparative sociological studies, such as those of Michèle Lamont (1992, 2000; Lamont and Thévenot 2000) that compare the US and France, suggest that the dynamics of social distinctions may differ significantly between countries. If the strong high-low distinctions had been something of a surprise in the Netherlands, in the US, I expected class differences to be even less marked (cf. Holt 1997; Levine 1985; Peterson 1997). I was not sure either what roles age, gender, or ethnic differences would play in American humor styles.

Clearly, it is not possible to discuss all the results of this American study in a single chapter. Therefore I will focus once more on the joke, and ways in which Americans view this genre, by asking three related questions. Firstly: I will ask to what extent patterns of appreciation of the joke in the United States resemble patterns of appreciation of this genre in the Netherlands. Secondly, I will look at the social status of the joke in the United States: does it have the same gender-related and low-class connotations it has in the Netherlands? Finally, I will explore how jokes relate to broader humor styles in the United States by looking at the way American interviewees define and describe "a good sense of humor".

As I hope to show, to compare opinions about joke telling and sense of humor is to point to more general differences in the way the Americans and the Dutch think about humor: Dutch opinions of humor revolve around notions of sociability and intellect while American s see humor in a greater variety of ways. Most notably, Americans tend to talk of humor more in terms of morality and playfulness. This leads to different views on jokes and joke telling, and also: to different processes of inclusion and distinction through humor.

Researching humor styles in America

The American study was smaller then the Dutch, consisting of twenty-eight interviews and a survey involving 143 Americans in the Philadelphia area. The first twenty-four interviewees were selected to represent maximum spread across social backgrounds in terms of age, gender, education, and humor appreciation. Four additional interviews with African-Americans were carried out because of the low response from minority groups.[22]

The survey in the American study was designed in a similar way to the Dutch one, but adapted to the American situation. This implied more than just translating questions and jokes. First of all, a number of the jokes could not be translated because they were based on wordplay or highly specific Dutch references, the monarchy for instance. Also, I changed the list of jokes to include not only jokes but also a number of cartoons, in order to allow a wider variation in humor styles to emerge from the survey. In terms of content, however, I had to settle for less variation even though the jokes in the American survey were more varied in form and genre. It turned out that a number of the ethnic and sexual jokes I had previously used in the Dutch study could not be used in the American one due to restrictions imposed by the University of Pennsylvania's Internal Review Board.

This means that, in many ways, the American study is not a strict replication of the Dutch study. Ten of the jokes in the questionnaire were translations or adaptations of jokes in the Dutch questionnaire.[23] The rest were American jokes, cartoons from the *New Yorker* magazine, political cartoons from the *International Herald Tribune* and Dutch cartoons about a duck and canary called Fokke and Sukke (less offensive in Dutch than in English, but with sexual connotations in both languages). These cartoons, which appear daily at the back of the Netherlands' most prestigious newspaper *NRC Handelsblad*, are very popular in the Netherlands (but, it turned out, less so in the US); they are also typical of the Dutch highbrow humor style. Even though this survey does not enable the strict cross-cultural comparison favored by psychologists, it does constitute a research instrument more sensitive to cultural specificities.

It is also somewhat harder in the US than it is in the Netherlands to measure educational or class differences. The formal structure of American education is not as stratified as the Netherlands.[24] In America, the main high-low distinction presumably does not lie in whether you have some form of college or university education, but in which college you attended. While in the Netherlands most highly educated people will have (upper) middle-class jobs, I spoke in the US to a bank teller and an emergency dispatcher – jobs I would describe as lower middle class – who had college degrees. Educational level is not the clear-cut predictor of job type or class position that it is in the Netherlands. Thus, in analyzing the interviews, I have focused on education and class position: upper middle class (professionals or higher, white-collar work), lower middle class (routine white-collar work), and working class (manual labor).

Jokes and humor styles in the United States: Survey results

The survey is once more the starting point for this exploration of American humor styles and joke telling. In contrast with the Dutch results, the American survey does not suggest as strongly that the joke is evaluated or appreciated *as a genre*. There is no relation between the overall liking for the jokes in the questionnaire and age, class, educational level, or income. Even the gender difference is marginal: women liked the jokes slightly less overall, but this difference is barely significant (p = .058).

As in the Dutch research, I subjected the ratings of the 37 jokes and cartoons to a factor analysis. Table 6 demonstrates that this resulted in a three-factor solution, showing a relationship between educational background, gender, and humor. Given my expectation that class would not be as important as in the Netherlands, and the complexity of operationalizing educational level in the United States, it was actually something of a surprise that even with a this simple measure of educational background – the highest level of education completed[25] – the analysis shows this relationship between humor and social background. Neither income nor class position was significantly related to any of the factors. Ethnicity was not significantly related either, but this was hardly to be expected when 92 percent of the respondents were white. In contrast with the Netherlands, gender seems more significant than age in the evaluation of more offensive humor.

The first factor can best be described as "intellectual" humor. However, the nature of American intellectual humor is rather different from the Dutch version. First of all, the notion of intellectual humor seems to be more a matter of content than form: this factor includes all the political jokes on the list. The most popular of these was:

A woman in a hot air balloon realizes she's lost. She lowers altitude and spots a man below. She shouts to him, "Excuse me, can you help me? I promised a friend I would meet him an hour ago, but I don't know where I am." The man consults his portable GPS and replies, "You're in a hot air balloon approximately 30 feet above a ground elevation of 2346 feet above sea level. You are 31 degrees, 14.97 minutes north latitude and 100 degrees, 49.09 minutes west longitude."

She rolls her eyes and says, "You must be a Republican." "I am," replies the man. "How did you know?" "Well," answers the balloonist, "Everything you told me is technically correct, but I have no idea what to make of your information, and I'm still lost. Frankly, you've not been much help to me."

The man smiles and responds, "You must be a Democrat." "I am," replies the balloonist. "But, how did you know?" "Well," says the man, "you don't know where you are or where you're going. You've risen to where you are due to a large quantity of hot air. You made a promise that you have no idea how to keep, and you expect ME to solve your problem. You're in EXACTLY the same position you were in before we met, but somehow now, it's MY fault."

Table 6. Joke appreciation and social background in the United States (Factor analysis of 37 jokes in survey).[26]

	Factor 1 Intellectual Humor	Factor 2 Transgressive humor	Factor 3 Ethnic and sexual jokes	Jokes not in factor
Mean appreciation	2.68	2.37	2.77	3.11
Mean offensiveness	1.67	2.22	2.05	1.78
Correlation with:				
Appreciation of all jokes	.51**	.42**	.44*	
Offensiveness of all jokes	.13	-.28**	-.41**	
Educational level	.22**	-.04	-.07	
Education father	.19*	.07	-.04	
Education mother	.18*	.14	-.005	
Gender	n.s.	M > F *	M > F**	
Age	.04	-.19*	.07	
Class position (ANOVA)	n.s.	n.s.	n.s.	
Income (ANOVA)	n.s.	n.s.	n.s.	
Ethnicity (ANOVA)	n.s.	n.s.	n.s.	
Favorite TV shows & comedians	John Cleese *Daily show*	*Jackass South park* Dice Clay H. Stern	L. Nielsen Drew Carey	

** $p < 0.01$.
* $p < 0.05$.

I found this joke on the website of Rush Limbaugh, a controversial (though witty) right-wing radio host. It ranked sixth in overall appreciation and also loaded very high on the first factor. In the interviews, too, political humor came up time and again as the clearest, and most conscious, distinction between the humor of the highly and less highly educated.

A number of other jokes, best described as *clever* jokes, based on word-play or complex references, loaded on (i.e. correlated with) this factor too, like the following:

What do you call an insomniac dyslexic agnostic? Someone who stays up all night wondering if there is a dog.

"Clever", incidentally, was a word that many of the more highly educated interviewees used to describe good humor.

Finally, this factor points to something of a genre distinction: only a small proportion of the jokes but most of the American cartoons loaded on this factor: *New Yorker* cartoons as well as cartoons from the *International Herald Tribune*. This could mean that jokes may not be a favorite genre of the more highly educated in the US either. However, the factor analysis does not indicate that Americans have a very pronounced view of the genre as a whole. Clearly, this analysis shows no evidence of certain groups dismissing all jokes outright.

The second factor I have dubbed "transgressive" humor. This factor included a number of rather tasteless ethnic and sexual jokes such as two jokes included in the Dutch survey: the blonde with two brain cells and the racist driver. This factor also included a cartoon about the attacks on the World Trade Center on 9/11. The attacks had taken place about a year before the survey was done and this topic was still felt to be too serious to joke about. This cartoon was considered most offensive overall.

All *Fokke and Sukke* cartoons loaded on this factor. These cartoons, with their combination of shock effect and intellectual complexity, are typical of Dutch highbrow humor style described in earlier chapters. Example can be seen in Figure 3 and 4. American respondents mainly considered these jokes offensive and not particularly funny. Only one of these cartoons loaded on the intellectual factor in the US. This cartoon was relatively inoffensive and contained an explicit reference to intelligence: "Fokke and Sukke are card-carrying Mensa Members. Fokke: 'Ordinary men think of sex every six seconds.' Sukke: 'We think of it once every three and a half.'"

All jokes and cartoons loading on the second factor were judged on average as being less humorous and more offensive than other items in the survey. Men liked these jokes better than women did; younger respondents appreciated them too. The scale was also correlated with a liking for American comics using shock effects, such as "shock jock" Howard Stern or the controversial comedian Andrew Dice Clay.

This factor is best interpreted as the sort of humor that most Americans reject: explicit sexual humor, strong language, and violent ethnic jokes. Most of my interviewees denounced this as "bad humor": offensive, demeaning, hurtful, lacking empathy, "gross", and far removed from the American mainstream. It was often referred to as "adolescent", something that seems to be corroborated by the correlation with age and gender. This factor highlights the distance between Dutch and American conceptions of

FOKKE & SUKKE
TAKE A STAND

Figure 3. Failed humor import; Average rating for funniness 1.94 (35th out of
37 jokes); Average rating for offensiveness 2.16 (eighth out of 37)

moral boundaries in humor. Fokke and Sukke, so typical of Dutch
highbrow "hard humor", were lumped together with the humor highly educated Dutch are most likely to reject: attitude jokes about racist murder.

The third factor, which I have named "ethnic and sexual jokes" is also related to gender, but the jokes loading on this factor were much better liked.
These were more mainstream ethnic and sexual jokes: the sort for which
parents might admonish their children, but still jokes that could be aired on
a late-night talk show, such as these:

A German, an American, and a Polack are travelling in the Amazon, and
they get captured by some natives. The head of the tribe says to the German: "What do you want on your back before you're whipped?" The German responds, "I'll take oil!" So they put oil on his back, and a large Amazon whips him 10 times. When he's finished, the German has these huge
welts on his back, and he can hardly move.

The Amazons haul the German away, and say to the Polack, "What do you
want on your back?" "I'll take nothing!" says the Polack, and he stands
there straight and takes his 10 lashings without a single flinch. "What do
you want on your back?" the Amazons ask the American. He responds, "I'll
take the Polack!"

FOKKE & SUKKE
HUNT FOR EASTER EGGS

© Reid, Geleijnse & Van Tol

Figure 4. Fokke and Sukke that was appreciated most. Average funniness 2.71
(19th out of 37). Average rating for offensiveness 1.94 (16th out of 37).

Another joke loading on the sexual and ethnic jokes factor was:

> Guy takes his wife to the doctor...
> The Doc says, "Well, it's either Alzheimer's disease or AIDS."
> "What do you mean," the guy says, "you can't tell the difference?"
> "Yeah, the two look a lot alike in the early stages... Tell you what. Drive her
> way out into the country, kick her out of the car, and if she finds her way
> back, don't have sex with her."

As Table 6 shows, appreciation of jokes loading on this factor is related to
gender. Age is not related to the appreciation of this mainstream form of
transgression, meaning that the relationship between age and offensiveness,
so clear in the Netherlands, was not very apparent in the US. Instead,
American women seem to have a lower threshold for offensiveness than
men, a distinction less clear in the Netherlands.

The third factor has to do with morality and offensiveness. Even though
patterns of joke appreciation were linked with morality in the Netherlands,
this theme was much more prominent in American interviews. The American discourse on humor is suffused with morality: I could easily get my
interviewees to talk at length about the humor they would allow their chil-

dren to watch, the humor they refused to watch themselves, and the humor that ought not to be allowed in public at all. As in the Netherlands, many interviewees expressed the belief that women were, on the whole, more sensitive to offensive humor than men. In the US, this was corroborated by both the interview and the survey results. Women generally expressed more concern about, and less appreciation of, ethnic and sexual jokes, as well as profane language in jokes.

Finally, some jokes in the American survey did not load on any of the factors. As a rule, these were jokes whose content could not be characterized easily, but ones that were most liked overall, and, as in the Dutch study, rather long jokes. I will return to these long and successful jokes later in this chapter.

The logic underlying this factor analysis differs from the logic underlying Dutch patterns of humor appreciation. The first two factors: both combine items that would be on opposite extremes of a scale in the Netherlands. Factor one includes jokes and political cartoons; factor two lumps together offensive jokes and intellectual cartoons using shock effects. The American pattern seems slightly more complicated as well compared to the Dutch highbrow-lowbrow and old-young pattern; it shows three factors, and a number of jokes falling outside these.

It is not likely that this more complex pattern merely results from including a wider variety of humor in the questionnaire than jokes alone. For one thing, there is no indication that the American respondents evaluate the joke *as a genre*. Social distinctions cut through genre boundaries, combining political cartoons and jokes, but separating jokes of various degrees of hurtfulness. Among American respondents, differences in humor appreciation are related to content rather than form or genre. These results not only contradict Dutch findings but also pose a cross-cultural challenge to the psychological studies by Ruch and Hehl (1998), who concluded that in humor appreciation, form was more important than content.

Based on the survey, we may conclude that humorous distinction in American seems more a matter of content than of form. Therefore, the strict separation of appreciation of the genre and individual jokes, which worked well in the Dutch study, seems much less valid for the American situation. For this reason, I will now first turn to patterns and mechanisms in appreciating individual jokes before moving on to the relationship between jokes and broader humor styles.

Transgression and identification in American jokes

When looking exclusively at the jokes that both the Americans and the Dutch informants were asked to rank, it is striking to see to which extent they agree on what they like and dislike (see note 23). The highest ranking jokes in the Netherlands were also among the American favorites: the priest in the flood, the stupid soccer players ("It's not your brother but your father's son"), adapted to an American setting, the vacuum salesman, and even more risqué jokes about Johnnie and his teacher, and the Bible salesman. The average ratings of these jokes were similar in both countries, too. These very popular jokes happen to be the jokes that did not load on any of the three factors in Table 6.

The most popular items were all long jokes with a clear build-up. They were mainly judged to be moderately offensive, ranking somewhere in the middle in terms of offensiveness. The Dutch finding of the effect of the number of words in a joke was replicated: correlation between the average appreciation of a joke and the number of words was even higher than in the Netherlands: .669 (p < .01), whereas it was .55 in the Netherlands. This suggests that the criteria for good joke form may be similar in the two countries. Indeed, it seems to support the conclusion of Chapter 7, that the joke genre implies standards for good quality, based mostly on joke form, which are not only similar across social groups, but also across nations.

Even though the most offensive jokes could not be included in the American survey, the Americans and the Dutch often agreed about the jokes they liked least too. The joke about the racist driver, who in the American version runs over blacks instead of Turks, was ranked most offensive. The Turkish woman who was spat at became an Italian (this was an existing American joke), and ranked second highest in offensiveness. Both these jokes also ranked low in humorousness: the racist driver ranked eighth lowest, the Italian woman eleventh. However, this was not as low as most of the Fokke and Sukke cartoons, and three of the political cartoons dealing with sensitive topics: the war in Iraq and the attacks on the World Trade Center on September 11, 2001.

The overall relation between funniness and offensiveness of jokes was less strongly negative in the US than in the Netherlands: -.293, whereas it was -.44 in the Netherlands. In contrast with the Dutch study, relations between appreciation and offensiveness for each individual joke and cartoon tended to be stronger. Thus: if people found a joke offensive, this was much more likely to negatively affect their appreciation. In this respect, Americans are most similar to the older respondents in the Dutch survey, or perhaps: quite dissimilar from the younger Dutch, for whom, as we saw in Chapter 7, offensiveness and joke quality are virtually unrelated.

The weaker overall correlation means there were items that American respondents, on average, liked even though they found them quite offensive (e.g. about Johnny and his teacher), and items they did not like even though inoffensive. Probably the latter caused this correlation to be lower than in the Dutch study. Items judged both inoffensive and funny were most notably the cartoons loading high on the intellectual factor, such as the less offensive political cartoons and the *New Yorker* cartoons.

One of these unfunny, inoffensive cartoons was based on a reference to the beginning of Charles Dickens' *A Tale of Two Cities*. It showed a publisher saying to a bearded man: "I wish you would make up your mind, Mr. Dickens. Was it the best of times or was it the worst of times? It could scarcely have been both." The attraction of this cartoon is definitely not its transgressiveness. Similarly, it most likely would be rejected through lack of understanding than offense. This goes for most American-style intellectual humor: its funniness is based on clever findings and witty references rather than boundary transgression or shock effects.

The correlation between humorousness and offensiveness for solely verbal jokes was -.472 (p < .05), markedly higher than for jokes and cartoons together. Thus, the difference between overall correlation in the Dutch and American studies is mainly due to including other genres, which rely less on boundary transgression for their effect than jokes do.

Within the genre of the joke, the dynamics of joke work and transgression seem quite similar in the Netherlands and the United States: all people prefer long jokes, with moderate transgressiveness and a clear build-up. Differences in joke appreciation, as in the Netherlands, are easily traced back to differences in sensitivities. Even the themes that work best are similar in the two studies: religious jokes, stupidity jokes (especially if they are not ethnic but about blondes or politicians) and mildly sexual jokes. However, the findings indicate that different genres, such as cartoons, may have completely different dynamics.

Even though the dynamics of appreciation are similar, the relation between appreciation and social background in the United States differs from the Dutch pattern. As Table 6 shows, age differences in appreciation and offensiveness weren't as clear in the American study as in the Dutch one. Instead, gender differences are very influential. While gender affected the appreciation of the genre as a whole in the Netherlands, American women only objected to specific types of jokes: they found both ethnic and sexual humor significantly more offensive than men, and tended to rate jokes and cartoons about these themes significantly lower.

American humorous identifications

Identification may mediate, enforce or mitigate the appreciation of jokes. I will not explore this too extensively here, since the mechanisms and dynamics appear mostly to corroborate the Dutch results. Also, I did not completely analyze the American joke repertoire, nor did I interview joke tellers, which makes it harder to explore how the culture would provide identification opportunities for various groups.[27]

Generally the strongest identification affecting humor appreciation in the United States is gender, as it was in the Netherlands. The American joke repertoire is as masculine as the Dutch, and many female interviewees commented on how they often felt jokes demeaned women. The questionnaire reflected the international joke repertoire, with the ensuing male bent: very likely this male perspective negatively affected women's liking for jokes and cartoons, especially sexual humor.

I will focus here on three group identifications that affect humor appreciation in the US much more than in the Netherlands: politics, ethnicity, and religion. The effect of political affiliation on humor is clearest in the appreciation of political humor. The joke cited above about the woman in the hot air balloon was liked significantly less by Democrats than by Republicans ($p < .01$). In America, politics, which hardly had any effect in the Dutch study, affected not only the appreciation of political cartoons, but also of ethnic humor, which Democrats found more offensive as well as less humorous.

Religion was another clearly pronounced group identification. The effect of religion was much stronger in the United States than in the more secularized Netherlands. The religious jokes, on average, were liked very well: the priest in the flood ("God will save me") was liked best overall, the joke about the stammering Bible salesman, and another that contained a reference to Jesus' resurrection. Christians actually liked these jokes significantly more than non-Christians. This effect was clearest for the joke about the Bible salesman, which Protestants liked better than non-believers, and Catholics liked even better than Protestants ($p < .05$). However, Christian background generally negatively affected the liking for sexual humor: Christians found this as a rule more offensive. Jewish respondents showed a rather different pattern, objecting more to ethnic humor.

Ethnicity was a final identification influencing humor appreciation.. Sadly, this cannot be analyzed properly using the survey results: there was not enough variety in ethnic background in the sample. Respondents from ethnic minorities tended to dislike ethnic jokes, but because of the low percentage of non-white respondents, this was hardly ever significant. What the survey does illustrate is further forms of identification: white respondents rarely were familiar with comedians or TV shows featuring people with different ethnicities. I included African-American and Latino comedies and comedians in the questionnaire, but white respondents generally only knew the very famous comedians Bill Cosby and Chris Rock. Most interviewees also mentioned spontaneously that they were not interested in "black comedy", which is clearly identified as a separate domain (cf. Coleman 2000; Jhally and Lewis 1992; Watkins 1994).

Interviews with African-Americans made clear that they were more oriented towards black comedy. These interviewees showed the typical pattern of a minority taste group: even though they did not like it, they were well aware of mainstream comedy. White respondents, on the other hand, were only vaguely and imprecisely, though dismissively, aware of the humor of minorities. In this respect, American white respondents were remarkably similar to the highly educated Dutch, who also dismissed popular humor without knowing much about it (Kuipers 2006a). While Americans were not very willing or likely to reject lowbrow tastes explicitly, they were quite comfortable stating their disinterest in the humor of ethnic groups (with the exception of Jewish humor).

My interviews, as well as more general observation of American culture and comedy, made clear to me how important a role humor plays in processes of ethnic distinction in America. Blacks, Latinos, and Jews are all very self-conscious about having their own brand of humor, which outsiders may not always understand. These humorous self-images are often shared outside these groups: there are popular stereotypes of witty Jews, and exuberant, though rather explicit, African-American humor. Other ethnic distinctions also appear to have connotations of specific humor styles tool: an informant of Italian descent explained to me at length how his humor differed from his wife's, whose roots were Irish.

However, in these processes of highly self-conscious boundary marking through humor, it is not always easy to separate identity politics from "actual" differences. Despite many of the Dutch interviewees' adamant belief in regional differences in humor, I could not identify differences in my data, no matter how hard I tried. In a similar vein, processes of ethnic distinction in the US may not always be related to clearly identifiable differences in humor style.

How ethnic identifications play out in liking jokes, or in broader humor styles, is hard to tell based on data collected for this study. Jewish informants often had a joke repertoire different from other respondents', and strongly identified with Jewish humor and Jewish comedians. Even based on a few interviews, it is clear that African-American interviewees generally have a style of humor and communication rather unlike most white respondents.[28] Both these groups have their own comic tradition, and African-American humor even has its own specialized outlet on the black television network, BET. Such institutionalization of ethnic humorous forms and tradition probably stimulates cultural differentiation and distinction in the domain of humor. However, a more extensive study may be needed of processes of ethnic "humorous distinction" and ethnic "boundary work" in American humor.

The social status of the joke in America

The survey results did not indicate that people tend to like or dislike jokes as a genre. The interviews gave me more opportunity to gauge people's opinions on jokes and joke telling, and, more generally, on how this genre lived up to the interviewees' standards for good humor.

American more highly educated interviewees generally did not dismiss jokes as radically as their Dutch counterparts did. Even though they usually professed to like humor that was "clever", "intelligent" or "meaningful", they did not link it to form or genre as strictly as my Dutch informants. Thus, a 54-year-old lawyer (Note: if ethnicity is not specified, the interviewee is white) described his sense of humor as "intellectual". But he also described his friend with a very good sense of humor as someone with an "excellent memory for jokes", which would amount to a complete disqualification for most Dutch lawyers. He also said he actively told jokes:

> I'm not great at jokes so I have to I have to try them out on people and I don't remember many of them. But you know it's a useful tool to break the ice with a crowd of strangers, when you're worried about getting their attention, so you get them to kind of lighten up.
> *Are you a good joke teller?*
> Not particularly. Only if I've told a joke many, many, many times and really rehearsed it. There's one I'll tell when we go off tape [he never did].

A college-educated, 56-year-old graphic designer professed a liking for "topical, intelligent humor", with a preference for political humor. But when asked to describe someone with a good sense of humor, she chose her ex-husband, whom she "admired for his sense of humor". "He can tell jokes very well. He could not only remember the punch line, which I never could, I can't even remember the jokes now and won't even attempt to try to tell them. But he could remember them and tell them and entertain people by telling them. He's a good speaker and I love that, his timing was fantastic."

In general, discussions between highly educated interviewees identified joke telling as part of a good sense of humor, one of the things that someone with a good sense of humor was likely to do:

Do you think joke tellers are usually people with a good sense of humor?
Not necessarily. But some are. I think a person with a good sense of humor is more likely to tell a joke well than a person who hasn't. (Retired professor of engineering and mathematics, M, 74)

Less educated interviewees were more likely to be true joke enthusiasts. For instance, I interviewed a 63-year-old building contractor who reminded me very much of the Dutch joke tellers: he told me many jokes during the interview, and his speech style and bearing, as well as the constant references to masculinity and gender, were very similar to the joke-lovers'. Male respondents with lower middle-class or working-class jobs (e.g. a database programmer, a police officer, a theatre technician, and a casino worker) usually told me at least one or two jokes during their interviews.

Some of the educated interviewees were more critical of jokes. One remark reminiscent of the Dutch highbrow attitude came from a 46-year-old female, bank employee, who was educated at one of the elite colleges in the Philadelphia area. She seemed mainly embarrassed by jokes:

A couple of my friends are joke-tellers. But, I always feel very nervous before they – I sometimes feel nervous when they start to joke because I'm afraid I'm not gonna think it's funny and then they'll just be there and I really can't fake the laugh, but I guess if I've been drinking, it's ok because as soon as they start telling me the joke, I'll start laughing because I just know it's gonna be good. And I'm usually just laughing so hard before he even gets to the punch line [laughs] and he's telling me to shut up, you know. But I do feel a little bit of anxiety because, you know, what if it isn't funny? But it's great when it is funny. And I'm really not a joke-teller myself. I can't remember them…

But she also says she has friends who tell jokes; whereas the highly educated Dutch usually said they hardly ever heard jokes in their milieu.

As in the Netherlands, upper middle-class Americans were more likely to speak of good humor in terms of fast wit and intellect, whereas those with lower-level jobs would evaluate humor in terms of sociability. However, such differences rarely led them to renounce other people's sense of humor. The few times this happened, it was a lowbrow dismissal of highbrow humor rather than the reverse. In none of the interviews did class differences in humor style lead to outright dismissal of an entire genre.

These tendencies to stress intellect versus sociability may be the effect of the working conditions of more and less educated people. Upper middle-class people have not only spent much time in educational institutions devoted to training the intellect, but their jobs also often consist of more intellectual (and more individualized) work, whereas routine white-collar and working-class jobs involve more team work, more standardization, and more gender separation (cf. Bourdieu 1984; Collins 1992; Willis 1977).

Such structural conditions are likely to translate into similar class cultures across different countries. However, such differences in class culture were less marked among Americans. From a Dutch perspective, at least, American (upper) middle-class informants did not behave as consistently "highbrow" as their Dutch counterparts. They could be very vocal about their enjoyment of more popular forms of humor, such as jokes or sitcoms. Moreover, differences that did exist generally were not articulated explicitly as markers of class differences. In other words: humor was less often used to demarcate *symbolically* or highlight class boundaries.

In the United States as in the Netherlands, joke telling definitely functions as a marker of gender distinctions – both explicitly and implicitly. Both educated women cited above state, in passing, that they can't tell jokes. Most women I spoke to said something similar: "I can't remember them"; "I often start with the punch line." These were exactly the same phrases their Dutch counterparts used. American women also would excuse themselves from telling jokes in a more typically American idiom: "I can't tell a joke to save my life". Most of the men I interviewed repeated the notion that joke telling was more of a "man thing". Two older men, the contractor cited above and a retired police officer, felt it wasn't "appropriate" for women to tell jokes.

However, unlike many Dutch women, the majority of American women I spoke to did not say they disliked jokes. They generally described their enjoyment of male joke tellers (boyfriend, husband, father), rather than their love of telling jokes themselves. I even interviewed one woman who, like her Dutch counterparts, had her husband tell her jokes for her: "If I hear a really really good one I'll tell my husband, and maybe tell him to relay it to someone else. But for me to tell it to anyone, that might have happened twice in my lifetime." (nurse, 32, F, African-American).

Although jokes are not similarly low in status, gender patterns in using and evaluating the genre are remarkably similar on both sides of the Atlantic: women may like jokes, but as spectators rather than performers. However, few of the interviewees spontaneously expressed particularly strong opinions about the genre as a whole. It was not as easy for me to provoke the rejections of the entire genre I had heard in the Netherlands ("spiritual poverty", "jokes – those aren't humor"), even from female interviewees. Clearly, in the United States, the joke does not conjure up the same connotations of boisterous men, working-class bars, and loud fun, an atmosphere excluding – or abhorring – both women and the highly educated.

American arguments against the joke

To understand this national difference in the status of the joke, I will now return to the arguments Dutch informants who disliked jokes or were indifferent to them formulated against the genre of the joke. I can explore in more detail how Americans perceive the genre by comparing theirs with Dutch views on the joke: to what extent are these shared by the Americans? Or do Americans use other arguments against the joke?

Chapter 3 dealt with these arguments against the joke, which can be summarized into the following, slightly overlapping, objections. Firstly, jokes are too impersonal. This point was made mainly by women. Secondly, and this is a highbrow variation on the objection to the inauthenticity of joke tellers: a joke teller is not creative since he is "merely passing something on". A third objection was the "attention seeking" and dominance implicit in joke telling. Fourthly, joke telling is too explicitly funny, too clearly framed. This explicit framing makes jokes either ambivalent or not very subtle. Some people said they felt cornered by this explicit funniness. This explicit framing also makes joke telling too loud, too exuberant; it shows a lack of restraint and control.

Several interviewees objected to the impersonal character of jokes; most of these were highly educated women. A 43-year-old male biochemist came closest to the Dutch highbrow style in explicitly describing his humor as:

Like, kind of more, not jokes. Not somebody who's going to go up there and just say, you know, a guy walked into a bar kind of a joke, just more somebody who can tell a story and, kind of be creative and make it funny.

This is a clear echo of the Dutch, educated, joke hater: he prefers creative storytelling to jokes. However, no other interviewee explicitly rejected the joke because it lacked creativity. The criterion of personal invention in humor, so important for Dutch highbrow humor lovers, was rarely found in the American interviews.

Women generally objected to the inauthentic nature of joke telling and framed this in terms of lack of personal involvement. When I asked the nurse who relayed jokes to her husband:

Do you think telling jokes is a sign of a good sense of humor?
No it is a sign of a lot of time on your hands [laugh]. I don't know I don't think the funniest people I know are joke tellers I think that they are more just naturally you know funny. They can find fun you know something humorous in the environment or just anywhere.

A 53-year-old woman working in a food coop described her friend with a good sense of humor:

She has a real good sense of the absurd. She can kind of hone in on like, the major personality characteristics of a person and exaggerate them a little bit to make a wonderful story or instructive story. Which also means that if she's aggravated, it can be kind of edgy and mean-spirited. And she has a wonderful sense of exaggeration . . . For example, she has a dog. And she's pretty; she's not ridiculous about this dog. And, then, sometimes she'll talk about the dog, like, that the dog's misbehaving and she's thinking of sending her to a boarding school in Connecticut. And then, you'll look at the dog and the dog's got like, staring off into space and she'll say, "Well, she's thinking about what to pack for boarding school" or, you know. Just kind of silly, exaggerated stuff like that. [silence] It's not a joke telling...
So, you don't like the joke-telling sense of humor?
[silence] I like, I like jokes. But that's probably not my favorite sense of humor. I find it a little off-putting in terms of relating to people, you know, if what they want to do is tell me jokes. I like more contextual humor. So I don't think I have any friends who mostly tell jokes as a way of having a sense of humor.

This is a typical example of the "shared humorous fantasies" that are described as typical for women's humor (see Chapter 3), also found among

many female Dutch respondents. Many of the American women I interviewed, both white and African-American, of various educational backgrounds, described this form of humorous storytelling. Clearly, this focus
on personal and contextual humor does not combine well with joke telling,
which is neither personal nor very contextual.

Objections against the impersonal nature of the joke were by far the
most prominent. One other argument that came up, mostly in interviews
with women, was the attention seeking and dominance implied in joke telling. The latter argument can be clearly discerned in the bank employee's
comments cited above: "I sometimes feel nervous when they start to joke."
Another woman told me, when I asked her if she liked jokes:

> It's OK, I mean some people really have a talent for it and they can do it,
> they can tell a joke with the best of them and you will sit and laugh at it even
> if you've heard it 20 times before. But other ones it is, oh, they just don't
> quite get the same spin on it so it is not clever when they do it. They just sort
> of hit you over the head with it, and if it is not funny, they just sort of pound
> you with it somehow. (Retired emergency dispatcher, 75, F)

This woman, too, stressed how the conversational event or "interaction
ritual" of telling a joke would make her feel uncomfortable.

A final objection, prominent in the Netherlands and shared by some
Americans, was the way joke telling tends to affect the atmosphere:

> *Working in a restaurant or a bar, you'd actually hear quite a lot of jokes like
> that?*
> I would probably just walk away from them, even when they try and tell
> jokes or whatever. There's a few people that just have to get on with the
> jokes you know. Plus if you tell jokes then you always get a joke in re-
> sponse, you know. And then it just becomes one up man kind of thing so I
> kind of, try and I try avoid that and whatever. (Hotel owner, M, 43)

However, I did not hear some other objections to the genre in the US. For
instance, the explicit humorous framing, as well as the loudness and exuberance of telling jokes, was not mentioned as a problem at all. Although I
am not sure how this could be corroborated in more systematic research, I
observed that Americans generally communicate more explicitly than the
Dutch. In everyday life, as in standardized humor, ironical, deadpan presentation is not as highly valued in the US as it is in the Netherlands. Instead,
people tend to be more outspoken both in their attempts to be humorous
and in their appreciation of such attempts; they will often verbally ac-

knowledge a joke, saying "That's so funny". Even when Americans are ironic or (more frequently) sarcastic, in forms of humor for which the framing may be rather vague, often the delivery still will be quite explicit.[29]

Dislike of loudness and exuberance is a strong marker of class difference in the Netherlands. Traditionally, restraint and self-control are at the center of class distinction (Elias 1978, 1982; Wouters 1990, 2004). Controlled body language and speech styles were among the main differences between joke tellers and Dutch interviewees with a highbrow style. In contrast, American educated interviewees did not seem very concerned with this sort of cultivated self-restraint (cf. Schalet 2000, 2001). In the United States, cultural refinement seems to be much less a marker of status. Even upper middle-class professionals tend towards informality (Collins 2004: 258-296; Kalberg 2000) and "cultural laissez-faire" (Lamont 1992: 100–110).

Most American respondents seemed to feel that "letting go" was one of the good things about humor, rather than a risky enterprise leading to potential status loss. Respondents of all social backgrounds linked humor with positive notions of release and the removal of self-restraint. They would comment how good humor not only provokes smiles and laughter but "belly laughs". Tellingly, in American English "hysterical" is a positive qualification in the context of humor, as is "crazy". The exuberance and physicality, which, as discussed in Chapter 2, has been one of the main objections to humor and laughter since early Modernity, has obtained a positive connotation in the late Modern American context.

American views on the joke genre differ from Dutch ones in two other important ways. The first is that objections to joke telling were, even more so than in the Netherlands, directly connected with interpersonal relations. For instance, the woman cited above felt that jokes are "off-putting in terms of relating to people". Another interviewee explained:

My oldest brother always has a joke and personality-wise we are very different. I kind of think I'm offended by a lot of his jokes.
Offended in what way?
I don't know I guess I'll find them racist or sexist or I guess they are dirty jokes. It is funny cause I don't think, if I read something I am not offended by it again, it is like if you have a personal relationship with someone and I will think in some subliminal way he is like my oldest brother he is not supposed to be telling me these you know jokes. . . He is a joke teller but he is not *the* joke teller of the family. I think he just knows how to get behind people's defences and make them you know, disarm. He is a really really good salesman like he has broken records and won awards and makes a lot

of money and everything and I think he is just very talented at making people disarm and getting them to trust him. And I think it is more in that than in like, I mean he does tell good jokes but I don't think of him as like a jokester. (marketing consultant, 39, F, Latina)

Note how joke telling is connected here with sales, as in the Netherlands. For this woman, however, her brother's use of humor in sales is almost a form of manipulation, a lack of authenticity in dealing with other people.

The second and main difference, however, between Dutch and American objections to jokes was that Americans, in denouncing jokes, often addressed the content of jokes. Chapter 3 shows that Dutch people who disliked jokes never objected to subject matter; they objected to jokes in terms of communication style. Only people who liked jokes referred to content to distinguish within the genre. In the American interviews, comments about communication styles were interspersed with comments about vulgar language, offensivenesss, or jokes demeaning to women:

Do you like jokes?
I try to keep an open mind, and people say well it is just a joke, don't take it seriously, so I take that into account. But in general I don't like racist, sexist, um, where the insult is demeaning a group of people or and I don't like. You had [in the survey] some jokes that bordered on violence, I don't like anything with like children being demeaned, or anything violent, pornographic. Free society, but I don't want to hear it. (freelance writer, 42, F)

The comparison between the Dutch and American objections to jokes suggests a divergence between the two countries. The more "sophisticated" or elite arguments against the genre, such as limited creativity in joke telling, lack of restraint, and emphatic humorousness, were mainly absent in American interviews. On the other hand, objections having to do with interpersonal relations and personal authenticity, that is, the more "feminine" objections, were voiced by various American interviewees, male *and* female, and in some respects more emphatically than by Dutch respondents.

American views on a good sense of humor

American opinions about the joke point to more generalized notions of good and bad humor among various social groups in the United States. However, it is also clear that the joke is not as fruitful a starting point for exploring American humor styles. As a genre, it is nowhere near as contested as it is in the Netherlands; it is not strongly connected with social categories either.

Therefore, I now turn to broader American humor styles: what is the cultural logic underlying American conceptualizations of good humor and bad taste? What sort of criteria do Americans use to distinguish good humor from bad? How is this related to social background? And why do opinions about the joke *not* function as a basis for social distinction?

As in the Dutch interviews, I asked everyone to describe someone they knew with a good sense of humor. American answers were much more diverse than the simple intellect-versus-sociability pattern found in the Netherlands. However, in the midst of this variety, there was one constant: a similarity in the way all American informants, regardless of education, ethnicity, gender or age, spoke about a good sense of humor: they spoke of humor in very moral terms. In the next sections, I will first explore the diversity, and then turn to this American commonality.

One social background factor came, again, to the fore: gender. Almost all Dutch interviewees chose to describe a man with a very good sense of humor. In the American sample, this was much more varied. Of the thirteen male respondents, only two named a woman as someone with a good sense of humor. But out of fifteen women, eight described a man they knew, and seven a woman. Thus, even though having a sense of humor is more associated with men in the US, too, American women are oriented more towards other women. One might say that, whereas in the Netherlands I found what looks like a sexual division of labor, what we see here is more like separate worlds: men joking primarily with men, but women joking with men and with other women.

Women's descriptions of someone with a good sense of humor, whether they were talking about a man or a woman, often were quite similar. Of the fifteen women, eight even used the same word, which only one of the male interviewees used: "silly".

I guess that's where I get the goofiness from. . . . She [mother] just, I don't know, all of a sudden does something just goofy, just a weird position or say something silly. (special education teacher, 47, F)

Kind of silly, clumsy you know like cutting up. Yeah, silly is a good way to put it: not afraid to embarrass herself by doing something kind of silly, kind of self-deprecating. (freelance writer, F, 42)

He [boyfriend] is just so silly that you just want to look at him and laugh . . . I think we are both silly. And we must, he makes me laugh all the time, I mean we laugh at each other. . . like giggling like laughing a lot in situations that I wouldn't. But when I am with him I am giggling too. It is almost like you know when you're a kid with your friends, like stealing your brother's underpants and putting them in the tree and like hahaha. I feel like I have that sense of humor with him but it's like I think I have to have like a certain level of personal intimacy with someone before I can be silly. (marketing consultant, 39, F, Latina)

Almost all female interviewees gave similar answers. I discovered a rich American vocabulary for humorous craziness: silly, goofy, off the wall, zany, kooky, loopy. The freelance writer cited earlier described herself (positively): "My kids think I am crazy, wacky, funny, childish."

These descriptions place humor firmly in the domain of playfulness and non-seriousness: humor as "sweet madness" (Fry 1963), associated with childishness and release. In this conception, humor is contrasted with seriousness and the domain of work. The nurse cited earlier:

As far as black men are in everyday life, I don't think they are humorous I think that they are faced with so much that the humor goes right out the door. And for me to tell my husband's colleagues at work that "he's funny" and they are like "no Eric, no". And for me I am like yeah and you know he's a really silly guy, but you know the people at work would never know it. Because he has I guess a standard to look up to and he doesn't have time to you know, to be humorous.

Thus, "silly" humor is located in the private domain, of the home, the children and the family, traditionally the domain of women.

These descriptions of silly humor often were combined with humor described earlier (see Chapter 3) as prevalent among Dutch women: shared humorous fantasies and funny stories about personal experiences. One example of this was cited earlier: the friend who wanted to send her dog to boarding school. Such stories fit well with this description of silliness: a combination of non-seriousness, exaggeration, and self-deprecation, often closely connected with specific relationships.

Men's descriptions of good humor were more diverse than women's. On the whole, men's answers revolved more around having fun and creating a good atmosphere. The building contractor described "a super joke teller". A database programmer characterized his co-worker as: "one of those brash you know like life-of-the-party kind of guys, warm and outgoing." The hotel owner mentioned his bartender because "he can make anybody laugh". And an architect lauded his wife's sense of humor: "She loves to have fun. Good clean fun, where nobody gets hurt or feels bad."

Prominent in male interviewees' descriptions of a good sense of humor were descriptions of insulting and transgressive humor: "Joking around, insulting each other all the time, always poking fun at others," the biochemist describing his co-worker. "We'll be sitting at the bar, and treat the waitresses abruptly, and anyone who comes in. Some of the guys are very witty, very fast. It's great fun but you have to be able to take it", a 73-year old retired police officer describing his favorite sort of humor. And a 28-year-old African-American who worked in a customer-service department (and occasionally as a model), called his friend with an excellent sense of humor: "A real idiot! He is such a sarcastic idiot. This guy, he is just so out there, things he finds funny are so ridiculous. He will watch an action movie and somebody will die and it will be really serious, and he will start laughing, and then I will laugh too. He has a sick sense of humor."

What these men describe is reminiscent of the "tiny conspiracy" of sharing transgressive humor, described in Chapter 8 as a pleasure more appealing to men. The factor analysis, too, indicates that men enjoy such (mildly) offensive humor better. However, most of the male informants expressed reservations about truly transgressive humor. Only three men professed to like the really "sharp" jokes comparable to Dutch "hard humor": a 43-year-old man working in a casino, a great admirer of Andrew Dice Clay (who also commented that Michael Moore "did not have enough viciousness"), the black customer-service worker cited above, and the biochemist who disliked jokes, but preferred African-American humor for its "edginess". Tentatively, I would say that sharp, transgressive humor is more typical of black humor, but there are not enough African-Americans in my sample to truly corroborate this.

The casino worker's perspective on humor, likening it to some sort of guerilla technique, illustrates the appeal of transgressive humor, but also the importance of being "able to take it":

> If I hear a joke, I love to retell it, yes. Usually my mother-in-law, of all people, I share a lot of the jokes with. She's a good joke-teller too. She's in her mid 60's. And, you really gotta go a ways before you can offend her too. You really can't be inhibited when you tell a joke, you gotta be able to fire it off to where you catch the people off guard. You know, when the punch line comes up, they gotta be astonished. They can't know it's coming at you. I think that's very, very important in how you tell a joke. Presentation is a hundred percent.
> *So, what makes your mother-in-law a good joke-teller?*
> She has no emotion. Like, she won't start laughing – you know, like some people, they can't get a joke out without laughing before the punch line's

out. She can sit there with a deadpan face and tell the whole thing and then burst out laughing. Same thing with me. I can do the same thing. You gotta be able to fire it off without any emotion. So they don't know what's coming at them. And then, when it hits them in the face, it's like: wow!

This man was one of the two interviewees who enjoyed Fokke and Sukke. He connected his love of offensive humor to his regional background: calling it "Jersey humor", referring to the urban, hard-hitting, lower-class image of New Jersey.

As mentioned in the section about joke telling, descriptions of good humor were related to educational and class background. This effect was more pronounced with men than with women. The female focus on playfulness and shared storytelling generally overshadowed not just educational differences, but race and ethnicity too.

Compared with others, upper middle-class interviewees often mentioned that people with a good sense of humor were intelligent and witty, and told "clever" jokes. In this sense, they were like Dutch lovers of highbrow humor: they favored complexity and intellectual challenge. However, they did not favor the emotional ambiguity, shock effects, or "hardness" described by Dutch educated informants. In the American interviews, people with a good sense of humor were always nice, likeable people, whereas in the Dutch, highbrow humor style, a person with a good sense of humor might be an unpleasant person. Thus, American criteria for good humor were primarily connected with sociability (and morality), not with the emotional detachment and intellectual stance of the "pure gaze".

Characteristic of the interviewees with upper middle-class professions – both men and women – is their focus on "topical" humor, especially political humor, which is probably the strongest, the most conscious, marker of highbrow humor I have encountered in the US. Generally, they expressed a preference for humor "with a meaning", or "underlying seriousness":

Well they laugh at themselves, they laugh at issues that other people take gravely serious and at the same time they make you think about the truth underlying the sarcasm. And I think that it takes an intelligent person to be able to make a serious message but at the same time get you to laugh. (lawyer, 56, M)

Finally, five interviewees described their friends with a good sense of humor in ways I had never heard in the Netherlands: someone with whom to share references to film and television comedy: "She's very funny. And she's got like this intense memory for movie references, comedy references", a 25-year-old grade-school teacher describing her friend. Similarly, this is a 28-year-old medical student describing his best friend's humor: "We watch the same shows, and we will always be referring to it, you know, *the Simpsons, Seinfeld*. . . I remember I saw *Caddyshack* [film] with him and it was so funny for me and I was only like fifteen at the time and it's just one of those movies where we will just repeat the lines and just laugh."

This answer was only given by interviewees under 35. Sharing film and TV references is not unlike highbrow snobbery: discussing cultural products, making arcane references. However, the references are transposed to the domain of popular culture, and the group boundaries involved are mostly age-related. These interviewees also flaunted their expertise: "*The Simpsons* is not as good as it was". "*Everybody loves Raymond* is clearly very well written but just not as original." In effect, this is the most explicit form of distinction based on humor I encountered in the US. It also has the same exclusionary effect, with references self-consciously inaccessible to others.

As probably is clear by now, it was not possible to isolate as clear-cut a pattern as the intellect-sociability pattern found in the Netherlands. Instead, American interviewees seemed to have at their disposal a wider variety of "repertoires of evaluation", to use the term Michèle Lamont (1992) coined. Moreover, these repertoires are not strictly separated from one another. In the course of one interview, a single person could talk about humor in a variety of ways.

Thus, very different criteria could be used to assess a person's good sense of humor and to describe the humor of a good television show, and this same interviewee might speak differently again of using humor in the workplace. I don't have the space or opportunity here to discuss the way Americans evaluated standardized humor such as television shows and comedians. But I found notably less continuity between standardized humor (television shows and comedians) and the humor of everyday life in American humor styles than in the Dutch.

In summary, this means that different social groups in America don't have the clearly distinguishable humor styles found in the Dutch study, with the clear underlying logic, leading to radically different interpretations and evaluations of the same humor. Instead, Americans of all backgrounds have a variety of criteria for good humor, which differ between domains and types of humor. This greater diversity in American descriptions and evaluations of "good humor" also accounts for the less frequent and less radical renunciations of other people's humor.

In the few instances that people explicitly rejected humor, this was more likely "upward" rejection:

> There's an intellectual humor, and there's the totally wacko abandoned kind of humor. Yeah I think there is different forms of humor, the thinking kind of humor is more satire, I mean you have to work harder to get it, and you gotta have a certain amount of intelligence in order for it to transfer to you or for you to prefer that kind of humor. And I think again that is where political humor falls, it sort of taunts the intellect, humor like MASH, it's intellectual. I don't prefer it as much, I'd rather it hit a funny bone other than up here [taps head], you know? . . . I'll get it. Intellectually I'll get it, I have enough smarts, I feel manipulated when it's kind of like given to me as one thing and then it turns out as something else. It is like a bad date. (theatre technician, 52, M)

As in the Netherlands, working-class or lower middle-class Americans often expressed the notion that their humor was better than the humor of "uptight" or "stiff" intellectuals with their "complicated" humor. However, in the Netherlands these rejections were symmetrical: educated people also believed *their* humor to be better.

This variety in repertoires seems to be greater for men than for women, who have a more strongly delineated understanding of humor as playfulness and silliness. This is a standard for good humor that excludes some forms of humor: transgression, explicit political references, brash jokes. People with more education also seem to have a wider variety of repertoires at their disposal: they enjoy both the sociable, joke telling humor, and the clever, topical wit.

Thus, in a roundabout way, this study supports the "omnivore" thesis (Peterson and Kern 1996; see also Chapter 4, esp. p. 80) in the American context: people with higher status have neither more specific tastes, nor more exclusively "legitimate" tastes; instead, they have broader tastes, including more inaccessible highbrow and popular tastes. These results also suggest that, in the domain of humor, men are more omnivorous than women. This is not very surprising since omnivorous cultural consumption is a marker of high status, which men are more likely to have than women.

Still, this means that in the US it would be harder than in the Netherlands to pinpoint social distinctions based on someone's humor. Even though omnivorous tastes mark high social status as exclusive and legitimate tastes do, they have different dynamics. Omnivorousness implies that high-status people have less to dislike, thus less to look down on and reject. The absence of a strong discontinuity between highbrow and lowbrow humor in the US also means there is no "legitimate" humor taste that is really inaccessible to less educated people.

Indeed, American interviewees very rarely explicitly rejected others' humor styles. Intellectual humor was occasionally refuted, as cited above. But generally, it was much harder to get Americans to draw explicit boundaries between themselves and people with bad taste in humor. If they expressed dislike of another's sense of humor (which eventually most of them did), they did not derive their criteria from the domain of sociability, sophistication, or intellect. All interviewees used the same standard to reject "bad humor": morality.

"You gotta have a sense of humor": Humor and the moral self

Despite the wide variety in American evaluations and descriptions of good humor, one element returned in most descriptions of someone with a good sense of humor. No matter whether people were talking about someone to share movie references with, whom they could playfully insult, or someone "witty", "kooky" or "the life of the party", virtually all interviewees also described this person as someone of moral quality: "a good person".

Specific phrases kept coming up when describing persons with a sense of humor. Someone with a sense of humor "can find the humor in everyday life"; "can look at bad things from a humorous perspective". He or she is "a person who can laugh at him/herself". Often, people with a good sense of humor were commended for their "self-deprecating humor", their use of humor to "relax" and "lighten up" themselves and others, their ability to "make light" of bad experiences. People with a sense of humor were not "hurtful" or "offensive", but used humor "in a positive way". For instance, the biochemist described someone who liked to tease but also:

> He's very self-deprecating, where he can make fun of himself, type of thing. He doesn't take life too seriously. That's kind of, when I think of somebody who's funny, that's kind of what I think of.
> *So that's your definition of a good sense of humor. Or are there other ways?*
> Yeah, I think being able to laugh at yourself. At the very same time, this person is very sensitive to other people. He doesn't go – doesn't make fun of other people but yet, only if, he would only do that if he knew you very well. Be joking, in a joking way. Not being mean about it.

Even though this is reminiscent of sociable Dutch humor, these phrases and descriptions strike me as much more moral in tone: by showing a good sense of humor, you are not just trying to be nice or create a good atmosphere; you are showing your moral worth.

Often, humor was connected very directly with personal quality. The freelance writer who described herself as "wacky" said:

Yes, I think a sense of humor would make you a good person, because to have a sense of humor you need to be able to relate to others, to empathize, sympathize, understand what it is like to be somebody else. Just relate in general.

And a 39-year-old technical, helpdesk operator (F, black/Latina) said:

If you don't have a sense of humor you are also kind of closed minded, 'cause you are not open to other people's opinions. You have to have a sense of humor when you are dealing with all types of people. And if you don't have a sense of humor and you get offended easily then you're in the wrong job.

Clearly, humor here means more than making sure that people are having a good time, and not taking offense or getting hurt. It is connected explicitly with the way in which you relate to other people, and it has personal authenticity, a criterion also prominent in people's objections to jokes.

This moral discourse surrounding humor was present in all interviews but one: the casino worker with the "Jersey humor". With this one exception, there was not only more talk of morality than in the Netherlands, but there was also a different sort of moral discourse. While Dutch interviewees focused on negative aspects of humor and morality – how not to go too far, how not to hurt others – the Americans spoke of humor as a positive moral force. I have never heard Dutch say things like:

I would say that someone that can keep his humor throughout life is you know is somebody that is like close to sainthood, because there are so many wrong things going on in the world which you would have to see if your eyes are open and have to talk about but, there is a medicine to about how to turn that around and be able to laugh at it. You know it just sort of floats, you float about all the turmoil and all the grief. (53, theatre technician, M)

I guess 'cause I'm very serious about humor. And in my life, my value about humor is to use humor to make people feel better, to bring people closer, to make something very difficult easier to bear, to give an insight or perspective that might be hard to get otherwise. To give a sense of proportion to troubling or difficult events. So it's sort of entwined with values for me. And there's no values [laughs] in *Seinfeld*. So, like, *Everybody Loves Raymond*, for example . . . when I come across it, I'll watch it. There are some significant underlying values being expressed there about family and intimacy and, uh, honesty and so forth. That, I mean, we're not talking Tolstoy, here, but, but it's both very funny and not offensive to me. Because there's something underpinning the humor. (53, works in food coop, F)

So do you think a sense of humour is important in life?
I mean you can get by without it but, to me personally, I think it's one of the best things, it helps you to relax, it's a good thing. I definitely have to have it in my life.
So could you live without humour?
Me personally, no. I'd curl up in a little hole and die somewhere, I think.
[laughs] Yeah, yeah, I definitely have to have it in my life. Besides God, that's one of the things that gets me by, definitely. (47, special education teacher, F)

So, good humor, even in the guise of a sitcom, "expresses values" about things like "intimacy" and "honesty". In some cases, this moral discourse on humor borders on the religious ("sainthood", "Besides God").

Two things were mentioned as especially important: being able to laugh at yourself, and being able to laugh at bad things. It is probably no coincidence that these are the two things in life people are most likely to take very seriously. Thus, this view of humor almost implies a moral imperative. Indeed, there is an American phrase, oft repeated when I explained my research project, which suggests such an imperative: "You gotta have a sense of humor".

In this perspective on humor, having a sense of humor means showing a "moral self". This moral understanding of humor in the United States eclipses all other conceptualizations of humor. Whether people preferred silly or meaningful, transgressive or more innocuous humor, they linked it with these notions of morality, selfhood, and personal authenticity.[31]

A moral view of humor sits uneasily with some of its other characteristics though, such as a proclivity to touch on moral boundaries. Transgressing boundaries, albeit in jest, is a risky way to express your moral self. And as described in Chapter 7, the humorous mode tends to temporarily shut off humor. It was already complicated for Dutch joke tellers to combine good humor with moral requirements; they grappled with the question of how to combine transgressive jokes and "hard humor" with their notion of sociable humor. For American interviewees, the inconsistencies were even greater.

This was a problem particularly for the male interviewees, who generally preferred more offensive jokes. The female preference for playful humor is more easily combined with morality. Perhaps unsurprisingly, the most outspoken "positive moralists" I spoke to were women. Typically, women are the guardians of morality (e.g. Bourdieu 1998). It is not surprising, therefore, that in the American moral conceptualization of humor, gender differences emerge more prominently than in the Netherlands.

The American focus on morality as a means of social distinction has emerged from other comparative studies, mostly comparing the US and France (Heinich 2000; Lamont 1992, 2000; Lamont and Thévenot 2000). Lamont shows extensively how both American upper middle-class men and blue-collar workers are much more likely than the French to evaluate others in terms of honesty, morality, and personal moral worth than cultural in terms of refinement or financial achievements. She has suggested adding "moral capital" to cultural and economic capital as a third form of symbolic capital, as the basis for drawing "symbolic boundaries".

In this respect, Lamont's work is an important addition to, and correction of, Bourdieu's and other sociologists' work studying social distinctions through money, education, and lifestyle. In *Distinction*, Bourdieu writes rather dismissively of morality: as a means of distinction for those who have nothing else to prove their worth (1984: 352–353, 367–368). However, within the American context, morality is very central to the way people judge themselves and others. Lamont's insights are confirmed by this study, which shows the important role morality plays in the American discourse on humor – not just in a negative sense, as the outer limit of good humor, but in a more positive sense. To Americans, good humor *is* moral humor.

The effects of this positive moral discourse on humor are discernable in the American humorous tradition, which is less edgy, transgressive, and controversial than Dutch humor, and European humor generally. American humor tends to be upbeat, inclusive, and often comes with a meaning, or a moral lesson. Even *The Simpsons*, a quintessentially American show that seems nihilistic and sarcastic at first, is generally recognized as portraying a family that is dysfunctional but nevertheless loving and close.[30] Americans who joke at the expense of others, in private and public settings, will generally make sure to joke about themselves first, a tactic especially important for late-night talk show hosts such as Jay Leno and David Letterman. The moral view of humor has also put more restrictions on humor in the public domain, especially on television, where certain words and topics are off limits.

In everyday life, too, Americans tend to be stern in judging offensive and transgressive humor. While interviewees were generally very careful when judging form and style of other people's humor, most interviewees commented explicitly on humor they felt was hurtful or offensive. They also voiced strong dismissals of the people enjoying or creating this humor.

Some of these, at times harsh, judgments of others are cited in this chapter, especially in the objections to jokes: "off-putting in terms of relating to others", "demeaning", "mean", "degrading".

Compared with Dutch rejections based more on culture, it is hard to establish exactly who is targeted by these rejections based on morality. I have no space here to analyze in detail the variety of ways in which my interviewees drew moral boundaries, but views on what constitutes good morality diverge tremendously in America. On the whole, American moral talk centered more around sexuality, language use, and was more religious in tone than in the Netherlands (cf. Kuipers 2006b). But, even within this small sample, I found a wide variety of moral views, and thus a wide variety of exclusions or judgments that something or someone was morally "bad", based on its humor.

In the US, differences in moral boundaries hardly resulted in age differences in humor style; I found almost no rejection by older interviewees of more offensive humor of the young (or vice versa). The social background factor most strongly connected with morality was gender: women tended to object more to offensive humor, and to engage more in "positive" moral talk. Moral distinctions also translated into distinctions based on politics and religion (which often converge in the United States).

In a more subtle and veiled way, moral boundaries were connected with distinctions based on race, class, and ethnicity. At times, there was a strong moral undercurrent in upward objections to "intellectual" people who were "uptight" or "took themselves too seriously". Also, intellectual humor was often equated with "sarcasm", a form of humor frowned upon, which one woman described as being "too much on the negative side".

Downward denunciations were even more veiled, and much harder to extract from interviewees. These would generally be about the more secure domain of television comedy, rather than the humor of everyday life. When asked if they could describe "lowbrow" humor, most people characterized it as "rude" or involving "crude" or "vulgar" language. People gave strikingly similar examples of "lowbrow" humor: *Roseanne* and *Married...with children*, two self-consciously working-class sitcoms, were disliked by many people for being "loud" and "offensive". One woman actually forbade her children to watch *Married... with children* (She did no want them to watch *Will and Grace* either, because the main character is gay).

African-American humor was also described similarly as more "explicit" or "crude" in language and subject matter, but even more reluctantly. The explicit nature of "ghetto humor", as it was referred to several times, was often mentioned as accounting for many white interviewees' disinterest in and lack of knowledge of it. However, such "downward" renunciations were frequently circumspect and hesitant. Most people tried to avoid stating explicit opinions, particularly on the racial issue.

On the whole, patterns of exclusion based on moral boundaries are harder to connect with "standard" sociological background variables. Morality is more variable and context-specific than cultural sophistication (or even sociable intent), making it harder to find out what exactly people are targeting with their objections. Further specifications of moral quality or the lack of it, such as "vulgar language" or "makes light of bad things" can have a wide range of meanings: one person's way of making light may be another's vulgar language. Moreover, morality is a frame of reference that everyone, regardless of class, ethnicity, age, gender, or political background, can employ to renounce, or applaud, other people. In this respect, morality is a form of capital that combines well with American egalitarianism and individualism. You do not need money, schooling or a pedigree to have moral standards. Everyone can be moral. Therefore, everyone can use moral logic to judge the quality of another's sense of humor.

Conclusion: Telling a joke to save your life

This comparison of American and Dutch humor styles leads to more observations than can be discussed within the limitation of a single chapter. Both the American and the Dutch study show clear relationships between humor and social background, but the patterning of these humor styles differed significantly cross-nationally. The impact of the specific social characteristics in the US was quite unlike the Netherlands, even though, contrary to my expectations, the American study showed a highbrow-lowbrow division in humor styles. Gender differences seem more pronounced in the US than in the Netherlands, whereas age differences are stronger in the Netherlands. Even though these subjects were only mentioned briefly, ethnic, political, and religious distinctions also seem more prominent in the United States.

Not only does the patterning differ, but also the underlying logic of these humor styles. American conceptualizations of good humor are more varied than Dutch ones: people use a variety of repertoires to describe a good sense of humor rather than employing a single encompassing humor style to judge all humor types. Americans were also less likely to reject other people's humor explicitly. This makes Americans, especially the men and the more highly educated, more "omnivorous" in appreciating and using humor.

The survey showed, most significantly, how judgments of good and bad humor in America are based more on content than on form and genre. American highbrow humor is political, intellectual, meaningful, and very unlike the distanced, form-based, Bourdieuian logic of the Dutch, highbrow style. Gender differences in humor styles too were more closely linked with differences in moral sensitivity and tolerance of transgression.

This sharper focus on content is related to the most prominent difference between Dutch and American humor styles: the strong moral discourse on humor in the United States. Americans tend to interpret good humor in terms of (positive) morality: sense of humor is a sign of being a good person, of having moral quality. This moral humor eclipsed all other views on humor by Americans. Obviously, a moral logic of this nature results in a stronger rejection of humor due to its content; and a positive evaluation of humor having "good" intention and content.

In this varied, but mostly moral, outlook on humor, many of the Dutch objections against the joke lose their validity. And indeed, the joke was not found to emphatically mark social class as it did in the Netherlands. Even though joke telling in the US is also an activity more favored by men than women, this did not lead to a strong denunciation of the genre as a whole. To Americans, the joke, as a *genre*, does not to conjure up the same set of connotations excluding – or abhorring – both women and highly educated.

These findings have a number of wider theoretical implications for understanding humor and the nature of social distinction and exclusion. In Bourdieu's theory, the fact that a genre is less popular in a specific group would automatically set in motion mechanisms of exclusion and distinction (cf. Lamont 1992: 181–188). However, in the US, it seems the joke may be appreciated differently in different groups without having become a true *marker* of difference.

This comparison also leads to questions about the more general theme of national comparisons and the explanation of national differences: how can these differences between the Netherlands and the US be interpreted and connected with wider characteristics of these two countries? It raises as well the more tantalizing (but slightly more ephemeral) question of what, exactly, such national differences in sense of humor mean, and what their consequences might be. In the next chapter, which is also the book's conclusion, I will address these more general questions on humor, difference, and distinction.

Chapter 10
Conclusion: Sociology and the joke

Why do some people laugh at jokes while others do not? This question has been prominent in the preceding nine chapters. Despite the limited breadth of the question – referring solely to one unpretentious, be it controversial genre – its answer fanned out in all directions. Attempts to interpret in how jokes are appreciated quickly led to more general questions about humor: what do people think is good and bad humor? What do people think is going too far or, instead, just stimulating enough to be funny? What does it mean if a joke "says nothing" to people? These questions also touched on themes beyond the domain of humor: the meaning of authenticity, the importance of style, the value of sociability, the relationship between form and content, between taste and quality, and the question of what people see as good and pleasant communication.

The sociology of the joke touched on more general questions of (cultural) sociology. In this epilogue I will comment briefly on some of these – all of which have been addressed already, some more explicitly than others. First of all, I will once again discuss the question of how the appreciation of humor works – the theme forming the leitmotif of the book. The next questions are less humorology and more sociology: what is the nature of the three social background characteristics connected to humor, namely gender, age and class? Which role do these play in the appreciation of humor? And how are these social background characteristics affected by cross-national differences? In concluding, I will look at the social consequences of these differences in the appreciation of jokes: what does it actually mean that tastes in the area of humor differ? Do differences in sense of humor necessarily lead to distinction and exclusion? How are taste differences in appreciating jokes (and other humor) related to taste differences in other areas?

The appreciation of jokes: Genre and individual jokes

In the chapters concerned with the Dutch study, I answered the question of why some people laugh at jokes and others do not in two parts: first I looked at the appreciation of the genre and subsequently at individual jokes. Both the interviews and the questionnaire made it apparent that in the Netherlands, people have an – often very decided – opinion of the genre in its entirety. Some, like the joke tellers I interviewed, were real joke lovers. Others reacted indifferently or even emphatically negatively to my question of what they thought of jokes. This judgment of the genre in its entirety always preceded the judgment of individual jokes.

Moreover, opinions about the joke as genre were strongly connected with social background factors. Thus, in the Netherlands, the joke symbolically highlights social boundaries, between men and women, highly educated and less highly educated. In the United States, in contrast, the joke as a genre hardly functioned as an explicit marker of social boundaries. Consequently, even though American informants recognized the joke as a specific genre, they did not have such explicit opinions about the genre as a whole. American humor styles and communication styles differed significantly from the Dutch. Not only did Americans have a very different view on jokes and joke telling; in the US I found a different interplay of humor and social background, and sometimes very different conceptualizations of good and bad humor. I will return to the American conceptualization of humor later, and first discuss Dutch humor styles and their relation to the joke.

Style: Evaluating a humorous genre

In the Netherlands, the question of why people think a certain joke is funny – or not – can only be answered if the judgment of the genre is first investigated. Taste judgments related to an entire genre must also be elucidated using the characteristics of this whole genre. Most of the usual explanations of taste differences in the area of humor offer no help here. These usually are more psychological than sociological, and have to do with characteristics of individual jokes, with their content, offensiveness, opportunity for identification, or with their form or humorous technique. Differences in the appreciation of genres are, as I have argued, primarily a question of *style*. In the case of jokes: a question of *communication style* and *humor style*.

Opinions about the joke as genre primarily had to do with *telling* jokes. Both the objections of joke haters and the enthusiastic descriptions of joke tellers often referred to telling jokes as a social activity. Joke lovers see this as a spontaneous, sociable form of communication whereas opponents tend to see telling jokes more as a conversation-disrupting, loud activity that evinces very little creativity and is lowbrow. These arguments for and against the joke are connected to differences in communication style: "joke telling" is a form of communication better suited to the communication styles of men than of women, and of non-college educated than the college educated. The objections of the highly educated and women at times seemed surprisingly similar: both groups preferred a more personal and cooperative form of humor to the joke that they saw as rather distant and attention-demanding, and that had not even been created by the joke teller. They appreciated humor that was less forced, that did not give them the feeling that they *had* to laugh.

These class differences came to light even more clearly when humor styles were compared. The way jokes were judged was connected not only to communication style but also to humor style: a broader taste or style in the area of humor. A surprisingly simple dichotomy emerged from analyzing the Dutch questionnaire. In addition to two age-connected tastes, primarily having to do with factors of content, I found two groups of humorists and television programs for which appreciation was primarily connected to education: popular and highbrow humor. These preferences were closely connected to the judgment of jokes: people with a popular humor style generally liked jokes while lovers of highbrow humor thought jokes had nothing to do with humor.

Dutch highly and less highly educated thus have different humor styles: lovers of lowbrow humor use different standards than lovers of highbrow humor in discerning good humor from bad humor. People with a highbrow humor style appreciate originality, absurdity, sharpness, and ambivalence. They expect humor to offer them an intellectual challenge. "Humor has to be complicated sometimes", as one informant formulated it. For people with a lowbrow humor style, humor does not so much have to arouse an intellectual sensation as to create a certain atmosphere: the atmosphere of the sociable evening. They tend to see humor in the light of sociability; performance, presentation, "how someone gets it across", is more important to them than content. They do not expect humor to challenge but to please.

Good humor and good interaction are extensions of one another for Dutch joke lovers – people with a popular humor style. Someone "with a sense of humor" is someone who can use humor effectively and pleasantly to communicate. This could very easily be a joke teller. For lovers of highbrow humor, someone with a sense of humor is more likely to be quick-witted and sharp. Someone like this is not by definition good company – perhaps not even nice. Funniness or sense of humor is for Dutch highly educated not so much a social quality as it an individual characteristic. The authentic expression of "sense of humor" lies for people with a lowbrow style in its social, spontaneous intention: the intention to be sociable, the intention not to hurt anyone and the intention to create a good atmosphere. The highly educated are seeking "real humor" – authenticity – not in sociability but instead in creativity. This is why they do not particularly value jokes: jokes tend to be more of a social performance than an individual expression of a creative intellect.

Form and content: Evaluating individual jokes

The appreciation of individual jokes or joke categories is connected to the form and content of jokes. In this respect, the American and the Dutch study showed strikingly similar dynamics: even though people may not like and dislike the same jokes, they do like and dislike jokes them for similar reasons: transgression, identification, and humorous technique.

The joke's form, as became apparent in Chapter 7, leads to large differences in the appreciation of individual jokes, but hardly at all to differences between people in judging jokes. As far as the form of jokes goes, everyone, whether he or she loves jokes or can't stand them, uses pretty much the same criteria of quality. And at times quality turns out to be surprisingly measurable for a joke. The length of a joke appeared to strongly influence how it was appreciated: everyone, regardless of social background, seemed to prefer longer jokes. This finding was confirmed in the United States. This indicates that this criterion for joke quality is not only the same across social backgrounds, but even across national boundaries: the longer the joke, the better.

The content of jokes, conversely, elicited pointed differences of opinion. These were primarily connected to boundary transgressions: to the question of "how far" a joke went. Almost all jokes touch upon a social boundary. Not everything is equally sensitive or painful for everyone: what goes too far for the one does not even stimulate the other enough to be remotely humorous. In the Netherlands, these differences in sensitivity seemed primarily connected to age. Over the last fifty years, social and cultural boundaries have shifted significantly, and this has led to a coarsening of the humor. This development is reflected in the humor of different age groups: younger people prefer their humor to be more transgressive, or "harder". In the United States, these age differences were less pronounced.

Dutch highly and less highly educated did not always seem to have the same pain thresholds either – the college educated were more sensitive to ethnic humor while disrespectful jokes about religion, death or sickness shocked the non-college educated more quickly. Even within the group of joke lovers great variation existed: some clearly delighted in telling very hard or explicit jokes, but the majority of joke tellers did their utmost best to remain within the boundaries of decency.

This connection between humor and pain thresholds also plays an important role in talking *about* humor: the joke tellers I interviewed in the Netherlands often paid a lot of attention to the dosage in boundary transgressions and to the risk of going "too far" and "hurting" people. In this they paid particular attention to gender differences: joke tellers thought that women were "more quickly embarrassed". Talks with female joke lovers in the Netherlands showed that this was often exaggerated: much of the shame was on the part of the joke tellers themselves. Gender differences in the appreciation of jokes probably have more to do with the emphatic masculinity of jokes than the sensitivity of women. Jokes do not reflect the mentality of Dutch society as a whole as truly as they do the worldviews of those telling the most jokes. Individual jokes therefore appeal more to these groups. In a male genre like the joke, the perspective is always a man's perspective. This often makes jokes funnier for men: the masculine dream and dread images in jokes – often *dreaming of* and *dreading* women, women's roles and women's types – offer bitterly few identification possibilities to women.

In the United States, offensiveness and boundaries were even more prominent in discussions of humor. Americans looked at humor from a more moral perspective, and this led to strong denunciations of offensive, coarse, demeaning, or vulgar humor in the interviews. This moral discourse on humor was even more pronounced among female respondents. In the US, I found strong gender differences in the appreciation of individual jokes, which were connected with a higher sensitivity among women to sexual references, vulgar language, and ethnic jokes. As the American joke repertoire is as masculine as the Dutch, it contains much American women may take offense to. And it offers them equally little to identify with.

Identification always plays an important role in the appreciation of humor. Identification possibilities are linked to social background but differ per person: the personal styles of joke tellers often reflect their individual preoccupations. Identification is, however, more than anything a social process: it is not only about how intensely someone recognizes him or herself in the joke, but also how intensely someone identifies with the joke maker and the rest of the company. By laughing together at a certain joke, people show not only their involvement in the joke at which they are laughing, but also, and primarily, their involvement with the *people* with whom they are laughing.

A good joke is not only funny but also sociable: the content or the drift of the joke supports or creates a feeling of fellowship. When a joke is successful, the solidarity brought about by laughing together is strengthened by the joke's content: for instance by drawing a line between one's own group and outsiders like Belgians, Turks, women, or gays, by collectively transgressing a boundary through unsuitable or "naughty" references, by emphasizing someone else's shortcomings, or by referring to shared experiences. The analysis of the content of the Dutch joke repertoire made transparent how excellently suited it is to appeal to feelings like this: it is very appropriate for expressing and confirming the solidarity of men and, to a lesser extent, of the non-college educated.

A good joke is a "tiny conspiracy" of the joke teller with his public. The appreciation of a joke is a social process, not just a confrontation between one person and one joke. Even if the joke is in a joke book (or a questionnaire), broader identifications play a role. This is also why joke tellers have made *telling* the jokes the main issue: it is not only about the joke but also about those with whom the joke is shared. The fact *that* a joke is told is basically more important than what the joke is about. The content of a joke can beef up or lend support to a social message, but the telling *is* the message. Thus, not only are style differences in how humor is appreciated linked to the humor's social meaning; each individual joke also only ultimately realizes its meaning within a given social situation. "Joke telling" is, like all humor, an *exchange* of jokes and laughter.

Gender, age, class, and nationality: The dynamics of social differences

In the both the Netherlands and the United States, the appreciation of jokes – separately or as a genre – was found to be connected with three social categories: gender, age and educational level or class. Today, when time-honored social indications of place are said to be losing power and slowly making way for a multiplicity of lifestyles and value orientations, the explicative power of this simple sociological background variables turned out to be surprisingly large.

In the Netherlands, these social distinctions were directly related with the genre of the joke, as well as other forms of humor. In the US, in contrast, the joke did not function as a marker of class boundaries at all. While joke telling was related to gender in the US, too, the genre did not *symboli-*

cally demarcate gender differences as strongly, either. More generally, whereas age, gender, and class affected sense of humor in both countries, the nature of the relation between these social background factors and humor styles was very different.

Within each country, the dynamics of these variables – class, age, and gender – differed significantly. Class difference is primarily connected to style; age difference more to content variations. And in both countries, interviewees were strongly aware of gender difference, quite aware of age difference, but only a few realized how class-linked their humor was, especially in the Netherlands. These variations are connected to the heterogeneous social origin and operation of these categories.

Gender and role

Gender difference in the appreciation of jokes is primarily a question of role difference: a more or less consciously maintained social difference, supported by norms and roles. In this respect, American and Dutch interviewees were quite similar, although gender differences were actually more pronounced in the United States. In both countries, many generally accepted truths and conventional wisdoms exist about the humor of men and women: that women "have to watch out", that they are more quickly embarrassed than men, or even: that they have no humor. Gender differences are, however, more keenly evidenced in attempts to make others laugh – in the jokes that are made and whether or not a person makes jokes at all – than in how jokes are appreciated. In the appreciation of humorists and television programs, hardly any gender difference at all was found in the Dutch study. Men and women occupy different places in the same surroundings and humor reflects this fact.

This apportioning of roles leads to men and women using humor in different ways: men more often use humor as a means to power and competition while women often use humor in more personal and cooperative ways. In the case of jokes, this role difference expressed itself even in a division of labor, most clearly visible in the case of women who liked jokes but left the telling to their husbands. They were extreme examples of a role pattern visible in much humor: women laugh at the jokes men make.

The role of women, where humor is concerned, is seriously limited by considerations of honor, decency, and morality. A woman telling a joke, especially a sexual joke – and this category makes up half of the repertoire – quickly disgraces herself. This certainly is true of jokes, but to a lesser extent of all humor. The humor is often a boundary transgression and the making of a joke always a bid for power with a ready chance of failure. For women, social risks of this sort always weigh more heavily. In America, where people generally have a more moral perspective on humor, the risk may even be greater than in the Netherlands.

These role differences are intertwined with power difference. This is beginning, however, to founder more and more. Women's emancipation is a typical example of social trickle-down: a development that began in the higher classes and was only thereafter taken up in lower social strata. In the lower social classes, where jokes are most loved, there is more stress on gender differences than there is in the higher social classes. Men's and women's domains are more definitely delineated. The joke, my interviewees assured me, belongs to the "man's world" of bars and sports canteens, of work in ports and harbors and on building sites, of tradesmen and representatives, and of the little "circles" men form at parties. Masculinity, which in the Netherlands is especially emphasized by the non-college educated, is seen as an unambiguously positive qualification.

While differences between men and women are diminishing over the course of time, no one has an interest in letting these disappear completely. Gender differences can be indicated and played out using humor: men demonstrate their masculinity with humor and women show their femininity by laughing at men's jokes. The telling of jokes is not only something better *suited* to the communication style of men: it is often also a display of masculinity – a form of distinction, a gendered performance, and a display of "masculine" symbolic capital.

Age and phase

Age difference in appreciating humor is mainly a question of phase difference. Social-cultural changes are reflected in the norms, values and worldviews of different age groups – and in their humor as well. In the second half of the twentieth century, norms, values and boundaries shifted significantly in the Netherlands; with this shift, humor has "hardened". The various cultural revolutions of the second half of the twentieth century seem to have hit the Netherlands harder than other countries (Duyvendak and Hurenkamp 2004; Kennedy 1995). As a result of this, social change in the Netherlands has been faster and more extreme than in the US.

This accounts for the finding that age difference in the Netherlands are stronger than in the US, where age differences in humor were less marked and contrasts between generations were much smaller. Where American youngsters did show a predilection towards transgressive humor, this was a very specific form of "adolescent" humor (*South Park, Jackass*), especially popular among younger men. This is more is typical of a phase in individual development, rather than of generational difference as a result of cultural change.

In the Netherlands, not only the boundaries but also the meaning of boundary transgression has changed. The shock effect as style technique, the prerogative of young, progressive comedians in the 1960s, has meanwhile trickled down to all social layers. Age difference here is thus indirectly connected to class difference: what used to be avant-garde is now common property. This has resulted in the "hard" humor of the less highly educated youth in some ways more closely resembling the humor of highbrow seniors than of seniors from their own class.

Dutch informants were very aware of this age difference, just as they are of gender difference: the coarsening of the humor, the sensitivity of the elderly and the coarse jokes of the "youth of today" were often repeated themes in the interviews. And yet I did not get the impression that my informants saw humor similarly and emphatically marking age differences as it did gender difference. The shared humor of people of the same age is sooner connected to emphasizing a feeling of solidarity than to ostracizing others: it is very seldom used as a conscious, distinctive strategy. Jokes that appeal to specific age groups are about interior boundaries, or social inclusion. Here exterior boundaries are marked at most by happenstance.

Class and culture

In the Netherlands, class differences in sense of humor were unexpectedly strong. Class difference in humor is connected to cultural difference: the college and non-college educated turned out, in the field of humor, to be employing different cultural logics. People at different educational levels not only disagree about what is funny and what goes too far but also about the atmosphere pertaining to humor, about subjects suited or unsuited for jokes, and even about how people should interact with each other pleasantly. Informants realized very seldom how strongly their sense of humor was connected to their educational level – in this research the most effective measure of class difference. This is typical of culture: it is largely unconscious. Culture feels "natural".

That it is cultural difference we are discussing also became apparent from the fact that often the knowledge my informants had of the humor of other social levels was severely limited. Jokes lovers often did not know that jokes implied "bad taste" in other classes. But they did quickly derive from hearing this that the highly educated did not like humor at all – a clear illustration of the very different opinions people had of what constitutes humor.

This knowledge was however – as is often the case with knowledge – not completely fairly distributed. Upper middle class Dutch often knew lowbrow genres and humorists but rejected them, while Dutch from working and lower middle classes often knew too little about highbrow humor to be able to reject it. While the image the highly educated had of popular humor was more accurate than vice versa, those on either side often had a very unflattering image of the others' humor: opposite the highbrow rejection of the loud joke teller and the "obvious" humor of the "Van Duin-like genre" was an equally negative image of the stiff intellectual who never laughs and a huge incapacity to understand why anyone could laugh with someone as "weird", "difficult" and even "hurtful" as Freek de Jonge.

In the American study, a relation between sense of humor and educational level was found, too, even though class differences were less pronounced than in the Netherlands. However, I found no strong divide between the cultural logics of upper middle class Americans and the working or lower middle classes. Instead, all interviewees employed a variety of "repertoires of evaluation" (Lamont 1992). At the same time, they all shared one underlying perspective on humor: all informants spoke of humor in moral terms. This moral logic caused judgments of good and bad humor, in all social layers, to be based more on content than on form and genre. Thus, American highbrow humor is political, intellectual, meaningful: completely unlike the distanced, form-based, ambiguous, Bourdieuian logic of the Dutch highbrow style. This means that American highbrow humor is nowhere near as inaccessible or exclusive as Dutch highbrow humor. Indeed, upper middle class Americans were less exclusive and more "omnivorous" in appreciating and using humor.

Thus, American class differences are probably best described as divergent subcultural differences within one overarching moral perspective on humor. These subcultural differences are generally not very self-consciously exclusive or inaccessible, even though the complexity of some intellectual humor of course does not appeal to everyone, as can be concluded from the mixed reactions to the *New Yorker* cartoons in the American questionnaire. However, American class differences in humor hardly ever led to the explicitly voiced rejections, dismissals, or to the puzzled incomprehension so common in the Dutch interviews. The few instances of explicit class distinction in the US were "upward", well informed, dismissals of intellectual humor, never "downward" denouncement of low-class humor.[32]

Thus, as many other authors have noted (cf. Holt 1997; Lamont 1992, 2000), Americans present an interesting challenge to Bourdieu's theory of class distinction. Whereas class differences in taste, culture, and refinement do exist, they don't automatically lead to processes of distinction, exclusion, or rejection. When Americans judge and reject others on the basis of their humor, they are more inclined to do so in moral, rather than cultural terms. While moral judgments may be veiled forms of class (or ethnic and racial) distinction, morality is more context-specific and more democratic: everyone can be moral. You do not need money, schooling or a pedigree to have moral standards. Therefore, everyone can employ a moral logic to judge the quality of another's sense of humor.

National differences and cultural logics

Both the American and the Dutch study showed clear relationships between humor and social background, but the patterning of these humor styles differed significantly cross-nationally. American conceptualizations of good humor are more varied, less exclusive, and more moral than any of the humor styles found in the Netherlands. As a result of these different views of humor, the impact of specific social characteristics on humor styles had a distinctly different pattern in these two countries.

Unlike taste differences within society, national differences cannot, be interpreted in terms of distinction and emulation. Instead, they are the result of a complex interplay of cultural traditions; and of structural factors such as the influence of institutions like government, education, or church, and the relations between various groups within one society. Since explaining cross-national differences is a rather daunting task. I will only briefly point out some factors that may explain the more moral perspective of Americans, versus the more cultural and social logics of Dutch informants.

Cultural hierarchies are traditionally more pronounced in Europe than in the United States, with its strong tradition of egalitarianism (cf. Lamont and Thévenot 2000; Lipset 1990). This study corroborates this general pattern. Even though the Netherlands is nowhere near as highbrow or stratified as France (we like to think), the Dutch findings are probably indicative of a wider divergence between European and American views on social hierarchy and personal worth.

Like the French, Dutch humor styles show a cultural hierarchy based on cultural capital: taste, intellect, restraint, and cultural sophistication. This study also shows how cultural distinction and emulation is a driving force behind changes in the field of humor: both the status decline of the joke and the diffusion of "hard humor" throughout Dutch society are instances of cultural forms trickling down. The starkly different logics of highbrow and lowbrow humor styles are embedded in, and reproduced by the relatively strong stratification of the Dutch educational system. This became especially clear in the stories of the upwardly mobile, who had to adapt to a whole new humor style, because "university had spoilt jokes for them".

The strong tradition of egalitarianism in the United States not only resulted in a less formally stratified educational system, but also in anti-intellectualism and a distrust of cultural sophistication and highbrow styles and institutions. Informality is highly valued even among highly educated Americans (Collins 2004: 258–296; Kalberg 2000; Lamont 1992: 117). This was reflected in their omnivorous tastes, and the reluctance of upper middle class Americans to denounce the humor of others.

Not only does American egalitarianism result in a more exuberant humor, it appears to have given humor a high status generally. Humor itself tends to create and atmosphere of informality and effervescence sought by most Americans (who even believe that having a sense of humor is one of the main qualifications for becoming a president, see Billig 2005: 214). Actually, humor is an excellent way of dealing with one of the contradictions of American culture: how to excel and be unpretentious at the same time. In making others laugh, you can show off, and at the same time prove yourself to be "a regular guy" who doesn't consider him or herself above others. Thus, humor is a way to be egalitarian and individualistic at the same time.

The American moral view on humor may be interpreted as a "democratic" alternative for drawing social boundaries. However, this does not mean that morality is just a "default" means of distinction for those who have no other route to status, as Bourdieu (1984: 352–353) seems to imply. Morality is a form of capital that combines well with American egalitarianism and individualism. America's specific brand of individualism not only stresses success and personal achievement ("the American dream"), but also personal authenticity (Bellah et al. 1996). This, of course, is very clear in the way American interviewees connected humor with personal worth and self-deprecation, as a way of showing a "moral self".

Finally, the American moral logic is likely to be related to the strong and lasting influence of religion in American society. As we saw in Chapter 9, the moral discourse on humor sometimes borders on the religious. American religion, moreover, is rather personalized, leading to a focus on the "moral self" in other domains than humor as well. Dutch culture has been strongly influenced by religion, especially Calvinism, but in the second half of the twentieth century, this influence has waned quickly.

Instead, Dutch humor is affected more by another long-standing Dutch tradition: tolerance and individualization (Goudsblom 1967, 1988), which has caused Dutch humor to be more transgressive than American humor, even among the "decent" joke tellers. Even though this varies between humor styles, Dutch humor is decidedly amoral at times. Especially for the young, and for lovers of highbrow humor, morality is almost an antithesis to humor.

A comparative study has a tendency to highlight differences rather than similarities. However, in comparison with other European countries, the Netherlands is relatively egalitarian, informal, and individualistic. In this respect, the country probably resembles the US more than neighboring countries like Germany, Belgium, or France. In the Netherlands, too, humor is valued very highly, and is more present both in the public and the private domain. The transgressiveness and directness of Dutch humor (and Dutch manners generally) are probably related to a similar mixture of individualism and egalitarianism. By being direct, honest, straightforward you show yourself "as you are", that is: not elevating yourself above others.

A comparison of American and Dutch humor styles thus shows how similar ingredients can lead to very different cultural logics. Even though they use different standards, in both countries, people employ related frameworks of individualism and egalitarianism. And in both countries, people look at humor to evaluate personal worth and status. But as a result of cultural traditions and structural conditions, the same frameworks lead to different cultural logics.

Distinction and difference

What are the social consequences of differences in the appreciation of humor found in this research? What does it mean, that tastes in the area of humor differ? The point of departure for this study was that taste difference in the area of humor, just as taste differences in other areas, marks and maintains social distinctions. Pierre Bourdieu described taste differences as "symbolic re-creations of actual differences". Esthetic judgments concern not only that which is tasteful or tasteless, but also the persons with or without taste. This entangles taste judgments inescapably with social distinctions. This distinctive effect is backed up by the nature of the humor itself. The ability to tell the most suitable jokes, to laugh at the perfect moment, is one of the most visible signs of "belonging". The laugh, more than any other means of communication, makes the boundaries of a group visible and palpable. Humor, just as taste, is an important means of establishing social boundaries.

Distinction is usually not a conscious strategy: people do not continuously emphasize the extent to which they differ from others. This was also clear from my talks with my informants: they saw humor as something they shared with others rather than something distinguishing them from others. The group one wanted to distinguish oneself from made a difference: in the case of gender, humor was consciously used to emphasize difference; this was much less so for age and class differences. However, taste and style difference seems, precisely for social distinctions of which people were less conscious, to be able to cause unbridgeable differences in sense of humor. Within the Netherlands, this is true of judgments of the joke as a genre, of the seriousness of ethnic jokes, of how hard Paul de Leeuw is or how old-fashioned Wim Kan. The clearest is how distinctive Dutch highbrow humor is in "saying nothing" to many people. Cross-national differences in sense of humor at times lead to even greater misunderstanding and miscommunication, leading not only to bafflement or confusion but even to outrage. In such instances, differences in sense of humor have the effect of marking a social distinction. But this may not have been its conscious aim.

The opposite, in fact, seems to be true: when people do consciously use humor to mark social distinctions, gender difference for instance, these are usually not particularly large differences. Remarkably few gender differences and the regional differences emphatically indicated when discussing humor seemed to exist in practice. While people were convinced of the regional specificity of their own sense of humor, from Groningen, Friesland, Limburg, Amsterdam or Rotterdam, or in the US, on the difference between Irish and Italian humor, they actually told the same jokes. Difference being exhibited to the outside world must, of course, be understandable for outsiders.

Humor more often emphasizes similarity and closeness than it does attempts to distinguish oneself from others. Distinction is more likely to be a chance side effect of attempts to underline equality and to emphasize feelings of fellowship. This calls into question the central thesis of

Bourdieu's *Distinction*, that all difference automatically leads to distinction, social exclusion, and the reproduction of social inequalities. In this study we have seen many ways in which sense of humor can differ, or be similar: some were exclusive, other inclusive, some consciously so, other much less. American interviewees even deemed the cultural standards, singled out by Bourdieu as the most influential in processes of distinction, relatively unimportant compared to criteria which may be almost unrelated to social and cultural hierarchies: moral criteria.

It is important to understand humor and humorous "boundary work" first and foremost as mechanisms of social inclusion and alliance. To quote Rose Coser again: humor is an "invitation to come closer". Of course, even an invitation implies a social boundary (as everyone who has ever made up a guest list knows): who will be invited and who will not? And in humor, this goes even further: it can happen that people do not completely understand the invitation or recognize it as such.

The results of the American study underlined this inclusive effect of humor even more than the Dutch study: American informants were very reluctant to actively renounce social groups on the basis of their humor. But even in the Dutch study, the reproductive effect of humorous distinction was less marked than may seem evident from the clear class differences. Even though highly and less highly educated had different humor styles, the less highly educated generally did not accept highbrow humor as legitimate taste. In this sense, even what may seem like a clear corroboration of Bourdieu's theory at first, calls into question one of the basis assumptions of *Distinction*: that people associate taste with status, and that they want to "move up" in their tastes.

In spite of the fact that the highly educated have more power to accept or reject others' humor, there does not seem to be such thing as "legitimate taste" in Dutch humor. A hierarchy of status of this type does exist for literature, art, or music: within these domains there are things which everyone suspects are of great value, even if they can't see it themselves. None of the joke tellers seemed to have been struck with the idea that Freek de Jonge must really be very good, even if they couldn't see anything in him. I did not find any intermediate layer like Bourdieu's *petit bourgeois* (Bourdieu 1984: 318–371) – a group that doesn't fare very well with Bourdieu – striving towards legitimate taste without succeeding. If there were people striving for legitimacy in a similar way in my sample, they were the decent joke tellers of Chapter 8. Their attempts at legitimacy were, however, focused on morality and avoiding boundaries, and certainly not on cultural refinement. The logic behind this striving was that of the lowbrow humor style: pleasing, not shocking.

The lack of status anxiety in the domain of the humor was apparent from the fact that all my informants had a positive image of their own humor. The direct jokes lovers, the more bourgeois, decent joke tellers and the intellectual lovers of Freek de Jonge all found their own humor the funniest. If a feeling did exist that there was "better" humor somewhere out there, this was not a question of educational level but of gender: women were often negative about their own sense of humor. The non-college educated definitely did not have the feeling that they were inadequate as far as humor went. They eagerly presented themselves as "real boys of the common folk" from "working-class neighborhoods" with sociable "common humor".

Where humor is concerned, people trust their own taste. This has to do with the direct way in which judging humor works: laughing at a joke is almost automatic. This is, however, not the only thing that plays a role: people seem to have hardly any "upward aspirations" in the case of humor. Humor functions sooner as capital within one's own circle than as a means distinguishing classes. For joke lovers, it is certain that humor is more an extension of social interaction and daily. And, indeed, in these domains the paths of the college and non-college educated seldom intersect. Humor is, to extend Bourdieu's economic imagery, production for the internal market: people primarily share their humor with those close to them and that usually means: with those who resemble them.

The fact that there is very little question of aspirations upward in the area of humor prompts one to question how the humor cultures of the upper middle classes and the lower classes relate to one another. While highly educated do seem to be distinguishing themselves actively from the less highly educated – by calling their humor common or coarse, for instance – people on lower social levels do not seem particularly interested in co-opting highbrow humor. If I told my informants that very few jokes were told at the university, a certain note of pity was sounded rather than the notion that their taste should be improved. Some of the upwardly mobile had upgraded their taste but just as many complained of the humorless atmosphere at higher levels. Differences in class culture are therefore more than phase differences. Not only does the private character of most humor ensure that there is little question of status anxiety or competition – a necessary condition of trickle-down – but the logic underlying different humor styles also simply differs too greatly: perspective on humor differs markedly at the various levels.

Certain forms of humor have diffused downward to permeate all social levels. The process of the hardening of the humor is one example. The shock effect as style technique, popular in the 1960s with the youthful, cultural avant-garde, is at present common property. Sick, coarse and hard jokes have spread out from a left wing, progressive cabaret to all humor, including the joke. These hard jokes, however, still constitute a problem within the logic of the lowbrow humor style. Dutroux jokes or other sick jokes are difficult to merge with the idea that humor has to be sociable. Jokes lovers always saw these "hard" jokes from the logic of the popular humor style and thus chose a solution for them conforming to this logic: these jokes may be told only in private circles due to the risk of hurting people. In this way, telling jokes of this sort becomes a "tiny conspiracy": hard jokes become "sociable", clandestine boundary transgressions.

The type of joke has trickled down to lower strata, but not the perspective from which people with highbrow humor see these hard jokes – ironic, based in the conviction that a certain sharpness is a good thing. The same thing is seen in the way humorists or comical television programs appealing to several social levels are appreciated: people continue to see them from their own humor style and cultural logic. The trickling down of elements from the highbrow humor does not lead to a change in the popular humor style, but rather to the introduction of new elements into the popular humor without the perspective actually changing.

These differences in cultural logic are most clearly reflected in the ways in which people think about authenticity. In the course of previous centuries, different objections to the joke as genre have been voiced: there is no restraint in jokes and very little refinement or intellectual effort. These are criteria directly connected to social stratification and distinctive behavior. Today too, gradual differences taking place here can be seen among people at different educational levels. What definitively discredited the joke in the course of the twentieth century is the objection that the joke is not authentic – this objection is difficult to couple to a process of social descent. Authenticity – being yourself, showing something of yourself – was important to all informants in judging humor. The college educated, however, appeared to interpret this differently from the non-college educated: for lovers of lowbrow humor, humor had to be spontaneous and sincere; lovers of highbrow humor looked for authenticity instead in creativity and ingenuity. Only in this latter meaning is lack of authenticity a conclusive objection to the joke: it is, after all, regurgitated humor.

It is therefore not the same cultural tendency, weighing more heavily in higher than in lower circles, that we are concerned with here, but a different cultural logic. The non-college educated Dutch did not seem to be intending to trade their own notion of sincerity for the sharp wit of intellectuals. These different conceptions of authenticity are connected to cultural logic and class cultures. They touch upon ideas of how people relate to one another, how people should behave with one another, how individuals occupy their place in social surroundings. This is not only a difference in phase but also a difference in worldview, and this differs in more than a gradual way from the worldview of the college educated. This accounts for the alienation of the upwardly mobile: they are not only pressed into hastening an identical process and intensifying an existing tendency, they are also being confronted with a different social world.

One of the most unexpected result of a research into humor is how little is known about the nature, organization, and origin of class cultures, in the Netherlands but, with some notable exceptions, in other Western countries, too. More research into cultural difference in less legitimate domains would throw quite an interesting light on the role played by class in (late-) Modern societies. In the Netherlands, preferences of the college educated, as now demonstrated for humor, hardly translate at all into the logic of laborers and and the lower middle class, and vice versa. Even if civilizing offensives and rising educational levels are perhaps leading to refined jokes winning territory, this alone will not change ideas of what constitutes good humor and bad taste.

Good humor and bad taste

The fact that there is no legitimate taste singles out an important difference between humor and the taste differences described by Bourdieu. Art, beauty, literature, music and even dining are forms of enjoyment that can easily be savored alone. Humor, on the other hand, as theorist of laughter Henri Bergson (1999) put it, "needs an echo". Many of the distinctive and binding effects of humor are connected to this particular social characteristic: the joke issues an invitation and the laugh voices its answer; the humor's conspiracy is reiterated in the delimiting and linking effect of the laugh. This ensures that humor, more than other matters of taste, stresses points of agreement between people.

A point of departure – unvoiced until this point – for this research was the idea that taste in the area of humor *resembles* taste in the area of art, clothing, food, reading material, or furnishings. I assumed a connection between humor and (other forms of) esthetic appreciation. Taste is a broad concept. Bourdieu, for instance, includes in it not only classical esthetic domains such as music, art and photography, but also food and newspaper preferences – admittedly subject to taste, but certainly not the traditional domain of esthetics. For Bourdieu these domains are all intertwined because they are considered and experienced from one and the same habitus.

This assumed parallel between humor and esthetic appreciation was also found, especially in the Netherlands. Echoes of the esthetic disposition could be recognized in the Dutch highbrow humor style: an emphasis on restraint and refinement, the mixture of other, mainly negative emotions to which one could react in a distant way, helped by the humorous packaging. The appreciation of the non-college educated Dutch, was, indeed, connected to a more direct affective judgment, one less strongly filtered through intellectualism and distance. The findings of the American study confirmed other studies of American taste cultures. Americans generally tend towards a more popular esthetic, and to a more moral and less distanced view on art (Heinich 2000).

And yet, the appreciation of humor does not resemble the appreciation of beauty in all its respects. Despite the observed agreements between humor and esthetic appreciation, there are essential differences between appreciating literature, art, furnishings and food, on the one hand, and appreciating humor on the other. At the conclusion of this book, in which the agreements between humor and other matters subject to taste have repeatedly been dealt with, I still want to briefly discuss *differences* between humor and those other matters. Not only do these differences say something about the sociology of taste, they also elucidate the nature of humor. And so I come full circle to once again confront the question I deemed unanswerable in the introduction: what is humor?

The question as to "what something is" is much easier to answer by comparing that something to something else. I am concerned here with the question of where humor differs from other esthetic experiences. It is true that humor can be included in the domain of Art and High Culture, or more generally of beauty and cultural products, partially, but not in its entirety. To start with, appreciating humor, more so than appreciating other attractive, delicious, or pleasant things, is always a social process. The appreciation of the joke is always determined partially by the social situation in which the joke appears. Additionally, the success of the joke is also connected to its content and its subject, and to the social, cultural, moral boundaries brought to bear in the joke. Pure abstraction – the summit of art within the esthetic disposition – is hardly imaginable in the humor. Even the most absurd humor always has an external reference point. And that which comes closest – total nonsense, as in children's riddles – has such a simple structure that it as a consequence has very low status.

Differences between humor and esthetic appreciation do not lie solely in the thoroughly social character of humor. Humor and beauty have a different emotional value and a different structure. Arthur Koestler, in *The Act of Creation* (1963), extensively discussed these differences. According to Koestler, art, humor and a third expression of human creativity, science, are based on one and the same mechanism: bisociation – the ability to make new, unexpected connections between two different frames of reference. What differs is not the structure but the emotional value of these creative expressions. Science is neutral; art is connected with positive emotional states. Humor is connected to less beautiful and uplifting feelings; it always contains "a drop of adrenaline". That which is found to be beautiful is temporarily elevated above the ordinary, while that which causes a laugh is demoted: it is "not taken seriously".

To appreciate beauty (whether of the high or the low variety) is, indeed, to be in a different emotional state than to be amused, the emotion belonging to the appreciation of humor. The pleasure of beauty is more harmonious and often closely approaches poignancy. The exaltation of humor is more physical, more exuberant, less restrained, and distant. At the same time, the identification with that causing the laugh is often lacking in humor. Even the most refined, elitist, highly cultured humorist is always demoting, debunking, failing to take seriously, mocking and trivializing. Humor is at one and the same time more distant – with regard to the subject of the joke – and more involved – with regard to the persons with whom one is laughing.

The almost completely sublimated emotions so essential to "high esthetics" are practically unachievable in humor. To subordinate the emotional reaction, to emphasize a detached, more rational judgment, is impossible in humor. The reaction to humor is always visible, physical and to a certain extent, unrestrained. Humor, moreover, always deals with the lower things of life, or with similarities (expected or not) between higher and lower things.

This means that humor will never completely belong to great art, high culture or pure beauty: even the highest humor will always be a bit low. A common glint and tarnished glow, with all their positive and negative associations, will continue to emanate from all humor, even from genres many times more refined, restrained, sophisticated, witty and creative than the joke. Good humor always implies some bad taste.

Appendix 1
The jokes used in the Dutch survey

1. Trevor's nails
This advertising man gets to make an advertisement for Trevor's Nail Factory. A week later he visits the factory's managing director, carrying a large roll of paper with him. He rolls it out and there's an image of Jesus on the cross, with the following text underneath: "Thanks to the nails from Trevor, I've been hanging here forever." The managing director is aghast and says: "We couldn't accept that, sir. No, we just couldn't. Have another try, and then without Jesus on the cross."

A week later, the advertising man returns, carrying a large roll of paper with him. This time there's an image of Jesus lying face down in the dirt under the cross, with the following text: "NOW I'M FLAT ON MY FACE. WITH TREVOR'S NAILS I'D STILL BE IN PLACE."

2. Moos in restaurant
To his own surprise, Moos has already been working for a few weeks as a waiter in a restaurant. One day a client calls out to him: "Waiter! What a small steak! Last time I was here, it was a whole lot bigger." "Sir", says Mose, "that's an optical illusion. Since you were last here, the restaurant's been rebuilt and it's much larger now."

3. Last names
Madonna doesn't have one; the pope has one but doesn't use it. Bush has a short one and Wolfowitch a long one. What is it? A last name.

4. German and Jew
A German and a Jew are standing at the side of the water wondering if they'll take a swim. The German sticks his elbow into the water and says: "Brrr, too cold for me." The Jew then sticks his nose in and says: "It's not just cold; it's really deep too!"

5. Flood
There's been a huge flood. The water is still rising. All the people have fled to the roofs. After a while, a boat comes along with rescue workers who pull everyone off the roof. Only the priest refuses to go. He says: "God will save me." The rescue workers try to convince him but he stubbornly insists, saying: "God will save me." So the boat drifts away with everyone in the village on it except the priest.

After a while another boat comes along. The water has meanwhile risen even further; the priest is in it up to his waist. But he still doesn't want to go, saying: "God will save me."

Still later, the priest is standing on the roof of the house up to his neck in water. A helicopter arrives overhead and through the megaphone a voice says: "Father, we've come to save you! You've been saved!" But the priest refuses to go with them, saying: "God will save me." The water rises and rises, the house disappears under water and finally the priest disappears too.

At the heavenly gates, in a deeply offended voice, the priest says to Saint Peter: "I was so sure God would save me." Peter, who doesn't understand it either, answers: "Indeed sir, you have lived a life beyond reproach. You had every reason to expect to be saved." So he sends the priest through to the big boss. The priest stands in front of God's throne asking: "Why didn't you save me while I was standing on that roof waiting?" God says: "You know, I don't understand it either. Something must've gone wrong. I personally sent two boats and a helicopter to get you."

6. Skeletons

Two skeletons come into a bar. One says: "Give me two beers and a mop."

7. Johnny and teacher

A primary school teacher promises a surprise to the one who solves the riddle. Her first riddle is: it walks around on a farm, it's spotted and it gives milk. Johnny puts up his hand and says: "A cow." The teacher says: "That's good, but I meant a goat."

Her next riddle is: "It walks around on a farm, it's got feathers and it lays eggs." Johnny tries again, saying: "A chicken." The teacher says: "That's good, but I meant a goose."

Johnny's pretty sick of this by now and he says he's got a riddle for his teacher. He says: "It's hard and dry when you put it in your mouth and it comes back out all soft and damp." The teacher turns red and Johnny says: "That's good, but I meant chewing gum."

8. A bit hoarse

A mule goes to the doctor. The doctor looks up and says: "A bit hoarse, aren't you?"

9. Migrant hunting license

I'm walking with a friend around the red-light district in Amsterdam and all of a sudden he shoots three black men dead. I say: "What're you doing?" He says: "I've got an MHL, a migrant hunting license." So I buy one too.

A week later, we're walking on the wrong side of the tracks in The Hague and I shoot five black men. Along comes a police officer and says: "What do you think you're doing?" "I've got an MHL." The police officer says: "Yeah but that covers the inner cities, not the reservations."

10. Johnny as base

"Can Johnny come out and play baseball?" Johnny's mother: "But children, Johnny doesn't have any arms or legs." "Oh that's okay, we'll use him as a base!"

11. Bible salesman

There's this man with a bible store and he's looking for someone to sell bibles door-to-door. So he sticks a sign in his store window: WANTED – door-to-door bible salesman. A man comes in and says: "IIIII would llllllike to ssssssell bbbbbbi-bles." The storekeeper: "But Sir, with your speech defect, do you think you'd have any luck?" "IIIII'd rrrrrreally llllike to be gggggiven a cccchance." "Well then," says the storekeeper, "I like to give everyone a chance, so I guess I'd better give you a chance too. Come back Monday at 9 o'clock."

The stutterer returns Monday morning and gets a huge stack of bibles. At 12:00 he returns to the store empty-handed. He's sold all the bibles and goes off again with a new stack. At 4:00 he comes back again. His second load of bibles has been sold and he asks for more. "Okay by me", says the shopkeeper, "but I'd sure like to hear how you're managing it. You've sold a formidable number of bibles!" The man says: "Tttthat's easy. IIIIII rrring the bbbbell. Ssssssomeone ccccomes to the ddddoor. Ttthen I aaaask: "Wwwwould you llllike to bbbbuy a bbbible? Or ssshall I rrrread it ttttto you?"

12. Millionaire

"Would you love my daughter just as much if I didn't have a cent?" asks the millionaire of his only daughter's fiancé. "Of course I would!" answers the fiancé. "Get the hell out of here then," says the millionaire, "I don't need any idiots in my family."

13. Diana and Dodi

Diana and Dodi are sitting in the car arguing. Their dinner that evening was disappointing and they still want something to eat but can't agree on what. Diana wants to go get Chinese food and Dodi wants shoarma. The chauffeur is sitting there listening and he's just about had his bellyful of the bickering in the back seat. He turns around and says: "If you can't make a decision, why not the drive-in."

14. Belgian jeweler

At the police station, three men suspected of a stick-up at a jewelry store are standing in a line-up: a German, a Dutchman and a Belgian. The jeweler comes in to identify the suspect. The Belgian steps out of the line-up and says: "Yeah, that's him!"

15. Whore who can sing...

A man visits a whorehouse and says: "I've heard that you have something very special here, a whore who can sing while she does a blow job." "That's right", says the madame, "there's only one condition – she won't do it unless it's completely dark in the room." The man agrees; he goes into the room. He can't see anything at all but it is as rumored, she begins to give him a blow job and she sings at the same time. When it's done, he's still very curious about how she managed to do it. So he goes back one more time and takes a penlight with him. He goes into the room and she begins her blow job and her singing and when she's really busy, he very carefully clicks on his penlight. And what does he see there on the bedside table? A glass eye in the water glass.

16. Football[19]

Willem van Hanegem approaches Van Gaal and says: "I've heard that football's connected to intelligence. Have you ever heard that?" "Yes," says coach Van Gaal, "football has a lot to do with intelligence. Watch while I demonstrate." So he calls Kluivert over and asks: "It's your father's son but not your brother. Who is it?" "Dead easy," says Kluivert, "it's me." "See what I mean about intelligence?" says Van Gaal to Van Hanegem. So Van Hanegem tries it out for himself. He calls Ed de Goey over and says: "It's your father's son but not your brother. Who is it?" De Goey, who has to have a good think about that, walks around the field a bit. On his way, he asks Taument the same question and he says: "Yeah, of course! That's me." So Ed de Goey returns to Van Hanegem and says: "I know who it is. It's Taument!" No, it's not," says Van Hanegem, "it's Patrick Kluivert."

17. Black baby

A welfare worker and his wife decide to have a black child. They ask a Surinamer how he got his black children. "Simple, just by screwing", says the Surinamer. So the welfare worker and his wife screw a few times and nine months later their child is born. But it's white. "Now how could that have happened?" the new father asks the Surinamer the next day. "Is your prick a foot long?" asks the Surinamer. "No." "Is your prick five inches wide?" "No." "Then too much light got in."

18. Moos skiing

Moos goes skiing. He gets caught in an avalanche while he's out on the slopes. A search team is formed to go look for him. As soon as they see him, they start calling: "Mr. Cohen, Mr. Cohen, we're on our way. We're from the Red Cross!" Moos calls back: "I gave at the office!"

19. Drink with both hands

A farmer is out walking through his pastures and sees someone about to drink from a poisoned creek. He calls out: "Watch out, don't drink that, the water is poisoned!" The man at the creek calls back in German: "What'd you say?" The farmer says: "Always use both hands when drinking from a creek."

20. Half deaf

A man goes to the doctor and says: "Doctor, I'm half deaf." "What do you mean, half deaf?" "Well," says the man, "I always hear exactly half of what anyone says." "That's new to me," says the doctor, "I'll just take a look then. Go on over to the corner of the room and stand there with your back to me. I'll be in the other corner. You repeat everything I say." So the man goes and stands in the corner, his back to the doctor. The doctor says: "Eighty-eight." The man: "Forty-four."

21. At heaven's gate
A man arrives at the heavenly gates, is greeted by Saint Peter and given a tour. He gets to see all the ins and outs of heaven and it is very beautiful and brightly lit and dazzling, with clouds and cherubim and classical music everywhere. All of a sudden the man sees a really thick, heavy, velvet curtain. "What's back there?" asks the man. "Shush", says Peter, "the Dutch Reformed are behind that curtain. They think they're the only ones up here."

22. Jew and stew
What's the difference between a Jew and a stew?
A stew doesn't scream when it's put in the oven.

23. Man and dog
A man and a dog are sitting next to each other on a bench in the park looking at the pigeons. The man wants to light up a cigarette but sees that the package is empty. He turns to the dog and asks: "Say Carl, can you lend me a fag?" "No", says the dog, "but I saw a store just down the street." "Great," says the man, "here's ten bucks. Get me a pack, will you?" An hour later the dog has still not returned so the man goes to look for him. He finds him in a bar, nursing a large whiskey. "That's just great," says the man, "I've trusted you all this time and now you pull a fast one on me." The dog says: "Yeah, but you've never given me money before."

24. Child on phone
Whispering child's voice on the telephone: "Hello?"
"Hello, is your mother there?"
"Yeah, she's here, but she's very very busy!"
"Well, is your father there then?"
"Yeah, he's here too, but he's very very busy!"
"Are there any other adults there?"
"Yeah. The police's here. And the fire department."
"Can I speak to one of them?"
"No, they're really really busy too."
"What's everyone doing there then?"
"Looking for me!"

25. Turkish woman
When are you allowed to spit in a Turkish woman's face? When her mustache is on fire.

26. Mother in law

In a fit of anger, Sam has thrown his mother-in-law out the second-floor window and now he's standing in front of the judge. "I hope", thunders the judge, "that you have finally appreciated that what you have done just isn't kosher. You could have caused a tragedy."Sam nods. "You're right", he admits. "I could've hit an innocent passer-by."

27. Prince Bernhard

There's this man who parks his bike near Soestdijk Palace. Along comes a member of the Royal Constabulary and says: "Sir, don't you know you're not allowed to park your bike there? Not only that, but his Royal Highness Prince Bernhard is about to arrive." To which the man answers: "Oh that doesn't matter, I've already locked it"

28. Two blondes

Two friends are both going out with dumb blondes. One says to the other: "I'll just show you how dumb my girlfriend is, okay?" He calls his girlfriend over and says: "Listen, here's five euros; can you go and get five crates of beer for me at the supermarket?" "Okay", says the dumb blonde and off she goes to the supermarket with the five euros. "That's nothing", says the other. "Shall I show you how dumb my girlfriend is?" So he calls his girlfriend and says: "Hey Anita, would you go to my place and have a look if I'm there too?" "Yeah okay", the blonde says and off she goes. A little while later the two girls run into each other. The one says: "My boyfriend is so incredibly dumb. He gave me five euros to buy five crates of beer for him while he knows I could never carry five crates all by myself!" "That's nothing", says the other. "My boyfriend just sent me to his place to see if he was there. He could just as easily have phoned!"

29. Mother superior

A mother superior goes to the doctor and blushes while she whispers to him: "Doctor, I don't know what it is, but I have a blue spot between my legs and I've no idea where it came from." "Then I'll have to have a look", says the doctor. After a short inspection, the doctor says: "No need to worry, Mother Superior. It's only a Chiquita banana sticker."

30. Vacuum cleaner salesman

A salesman goes out into the country to sell vacuum cleaners. He arrives at a farm and a big, fat farmer's wife opens the door, blaring: "What do you want?" "Madam", says the man, "what I've got here is a vacuum that will clean up anything and everything." The salesman throws a pile of dust into the living room and says: "Anything this vacuum leaves behind, I will eat up personally." "Well then", says the farmer's wife, "better start now because we haven't got electricity out here."

31. Blonde with two brain cells
What do you call a dumb blonde with two brain cells?
Pregnant.

32. Racist driver
A racist in Amsterdam always gets into his car in the evenings and goes and runs down Turks. One evening he gets into his car and drives away. There goes a Turk. He puts his foot to the floor, looks in his rearview mirror, and bingo, one down. He does this another couple of times. Then he sees a minister trying to hitch a ride so he picks him up. The driver sees another Turk but thinks: "I won't run him down, I'll just drive right up next to him." He's already passed the guy when he looks in his rearview mirror by habit and sees the Turk lying there dead anyway. The minister says: "Good thing I opened my door, or you would have missed that one."

33. Fairy godfather
What do you call the gay brother who's been asked to be a witness at his nephew's baptism? The fairy godfather.

34. Drunk
A drunk is walking across the fairgrounds. He comes to a shooting gallery and slurs: "I wanna shoot." So he gets a rifle and shoots – bull's-eye. He gets a bullfrog as his prize, takes it, puts it in his pocket and walks away. After a while he returns, drunker then ever, and repeats: "I wanna shoot!" Again, a bull's-eye and so he's won another bullfrog. The drunk puts the bullfrog in his pocket and staggers away. He comes back later and wants to shoot again. Bull's-eye. Regrettably, the bullfrogs are all gone so he gets a teddy bear. The drunk looks at the teddy bear, looks at the man in the shooting gallery with disgust and says: "Haven't you got any more cream puffs?"

35. Plane crash
All sorts of people are sitting in an airplane. All of a sudden they hear a voice coming from the speaker: "If you look out of the window on your right, you will see the Atlantic Ocean and also that the motor on your right is on fire. If you look out of the window on your left, you will see the Atlantic Ocean and also that the motor on your left is on fire. If you look down, you will see a rubber boat in the Atlantic Ocean containing the crew of this aircraft. This was a tape recording."

Appendix 2
Dutch humorists and television programs

Note on Dutch television: At the time of the research, the Netherlands had three public channels, and three big commercial networks: RTL, SBS6, and Veronica. The programs for the public channels are produced and broadcast by a number of independent broadcasting corporations, which originally were based in the various "pillars" of Dutch society (see page 16). The connections with social groups have become weaker in the course of time. Of the ones mentioned in this appendix, VARA is socialist, KRO Catholic, NCRV is protestant, but VPRO today is no longer protestant, but intellectual and progressive. TROS, started in 1964, is a non-denominational popular broadcaster.

Bananasplit: Dutch Candid Camera show, based on an American format, which was broadcast intermittently by TROS from 1983 until the early 2000s.

Bijl, Martine (1948): Singer, actress, cabaret artist, and television personality. Bijl made several cabaret shows that were stylish and unexpectedly sharp after her early singing career. She has been one of the protagonists of the sitcom *Het zonnetje in huis* which was broadcast first by VARA, afterwards by RTL4.

Bloemendaal, Adèle (1933): Extravagant performer, who worked as singer, actress, comedian, and cabaret artist, covering a wide range of genres and styles, from literary chansons to lowbrow carnival songs, and from television comedy to satirical cabaret shows.

Brandsteder, Ron (1950): Television presenter who first worked for TROS, presenting shows and quizzes, afterwards for RTL4, where he presented various shows, among which several humorous programs such as *Moppentoppers.*

Carmiggelt, Simon (1913–1987): Writer, best known for his daily columns in the newspaper *Parool*, which were small sketches, portraits, or observations of his daily life (most of which apparently took place in cafés in Amsterdam), in a highly recognizable humorous, ironical, and somewhat melancholy style. He also had a television program is which he read these columns.

Deelder, Jules (1944): Poet, writer, performer, and self-proclaimed "night mayor" (which happens to be a pun in English but not in Dutch) of Rotterdam. His presentation, as well as his writing, is rather absurdist. He has a very distinctive presence and presentation, always wearing a black suit, black glasses, with waxed hair, and speaking in short clipped sentences in a strong Rotterdam accent.

Dorrestijn, Hans (1940): Poet, writer, songwriter, and cabaret artist. Known for his glum and depressed presentation, his texts are poetic, depressed, and humorous at the same time. He became known for his weekly satirical reports of "Dorrestijn's press agency", with absurd fake news items, first on radio, afterwards in his own show on VPRO television.

Duin, Andre van (1947): One the Netherlands' best-known comedians, and the favorite comedian of most of the joke lovers, van Duin has his roots in the vaudeville tradition. Van Duin made humorous radio programs, several revue shows, and film comedies; he had a number of hit songs, mostly carnivals songs and parodies of popular songs; and had long running television programs, first on TROS, later on RTL4. His humor is based mainly on sketch comedy, with van Duin in the role of the comical stupid character.

Ederveen, Arjan (1956): Comedian, actor, and cabaret artist. Co-starred with Tosca Niterink first in a VPRO children's program, then in *Borreltijd* [Time for a drink] and *Creatief met kurk* [Creative with cork], absurdist parodies of an afternoon talk show, and a home decorating and crafts show, respectively. In the 1990s, he made *Thirty Minutes*, a series of carefully acted fake documentaries, one of which, about a farmer who is made over into an African because he was "born in the wrong body" is described on page 77 of this book.

Finkers, Herman (1954): Cabaret artist with a dry, deadpan style. His humor is never topical or satirical, but instead based on wordplay, absurdist logic, and unexpected associations. He is from Twente, a rural region in the east of the Netherlands, and has a clear regional accent. His regional background is often mentioned as the reason for his (self-consciously) dry and slow presentation. He has worked together with Brigitte Kaandorp, whose style shows some resemblances to Finkers'.

Flodder: Originally a very successful 1986 film comedy about an extremely low-class family moving to a very rich neighbourhood. The film, which was a huge success, was followed by two sequels, then made into a sitcom aired by Veronica. The films and the series portray the Flodder [mess, riffraff] family, a dysfunctional family featuring, amongst others, a cigar-smoking mother, a swindling son named Johnny, a very stupid names Kees, and an oversexed daughter also named Kees. The humor of *Flodder* is described best as self-consciously and exaggeratedly vulgar.

van Gogh, Theo (1957–2004): Controversial film maker, TV presenter and columnist, who had a brief stints as presenter of a wilfully offensive satirical dating show on SBS6 called *De Hunkering* [The yearning], which lasted for one year (the year the Dutch survey was done). He has been the centre of public outrage various times because of his satirical columns. In 2004, a Muslim fundamentalist assassinated him because of his film *Submission* (which, incidentally, was not humorous or satirical at all).

Haenen, Paul (1946): Cabaret artist, writer, and playwright, who has a television shows on VPRO television at the time of the survey, *Haenen voor de nacht* [Haenen before/for the night]. Haenen is known for his mild irony – as himself – and his rather extrovert emotionality, as the various types he impersonates, the most famous of which are the high-strung, highly emotional, but warm female character Margreet Dolman, and the long-winded, well-meaning Reverend Gremdaat. He is also is the Dutch voice of Bert on Sesame Street.

van 't Hek, Youp (1954). Arguable the most popular Dutch cabaret artist of the 1990s and early 2000s, van 't Hek manages to appeal to a wide variety of people. The main theme of his shows is rebellion against the bourgeois and their lifestyle, with recurring pleas for a passionate life ("Live your life as if it were your very last day"). Ironically, his shows also have become very popular among the people whom he ridicules: bourgeois with pearl necklaces and chequered trousers; people who have forfeited their ideals; and people who drink malt beer – he is held responsible for the failure of Heineken's malt beer brand. He is also known for his straightforward language, and his harsh comments on others, including the members of his audience. Since 1989, he has done the traditional New Year's Eve monologue various times with great success. He also has a weekly column in *NRC Handelsblad.*

Hermans, Toon (1916–2000): Comedian, clown, entertainer, and poet who was extremely popular until very late in life. Hermans was known for his clownish humor, and his skits, which went on for a very long time, apparently about nothing but managing to have the audience weep with laugher. His performances ranged from the nonsensical to the poignant. Hermans was never interested in satire or topical humor, and for this reason, he was wary of the "cabaret" label.

De Hunkering. See Theo van Gogh

Jekkers, Harry (1951): Cabaret artist and singer, whose cabaret shows are witty, personal, and slightly nostalgic in tone, often referring to his youth in The Hague. The monologues are interspersed with songs, which are, for a cabaret artist, remarkably sung and written remarkably well.

Jiskefet. Sketch comedy program broadcast by VPRO television in the 1990s and 2000s, made by Herman Koch, Kees Prins, and Michiel Romein. The sketches of *Jiskefet* range from completely absurdist to exaggerated-but-lifelike, but their humor invariably has a slightly uncomfortable touch. Their greatest success was a series called *Debtors Creditors* (see also Chapter 4 of this book). This series was about people working in an office, who only spoke in stock phrases and made each other's lives miserable, and (yet) was felt to be very recognizable and true to life by many people.

de Jonge, Freek (1944): The most influential highbrow cabaret artist of the Netherlands, de Jonge started his career in the late 1960s as part of a duo, *Neerlands hoop* [The Netherlands' hope]. First with his partner, and on his own after 1979, de Jonge basically set the standard for Dutch cabaret for a long time with his high speed, chaotic presentation, recurrent use of shock effects, and his mixture of satirical and more poetic texts. Progressive and critical in the early years, more reflexive and at times almost clownish later in his career, de Jonge always remained something of a moralist (or "preachy" according to later generations of cabaret artists). He also wrote novels, made two films, was a television presenter, and did a more "alternative" New Year's Eve monologue on VPRO television several times.

Kaandorp, Brigitte (1962): Cabaret artist with a wilfully unpretentious, personal, sometimes disarmingly clumsy, but also dry and absurdist style; and a deadpan presentation. She is often mentioned, with Herman Finkers, as representatives of the anti-shock, anti-topical cabaret coming in vogue in the 1980s, but Kaandorp's absurdism is more personal and down-to-earth than Finkers' rather abstract absurdities.

Kan, Wim (1911–1983): Most prominent cabaret artist of the Netherlands for a long time. He did a traditional comic monologue on New Years Eve intermittently from 1954 to 1982, first on radio, later on television, which almost literally reached the entire country. He was especially known for his jokes about politicians, who would come to his shows to enjoy the jokes he was making at their expense.

van Kooten, Kees (1941) and Wim de Bie (1939), also known as Koot and Bie: Cabaret artists/ satirists, mainly known for the television programs which they made for intellectual VPRO television from 1974 till 1998. Before that, they worked together in various radio shows and other television programs. Their shows consisted of satirical sketches, based sometimes on impersonations of well-known people, especially politicians, but most often on their own types, often very lifelike characters, which kept returning over the years. A sing both of the popularity of their shows, and their keen eye for current events and cultural phenomena, is the lasting impact they have had on Dutch language: several of the words and phrased they minted are still widely used.

de Leeuw, Paul (1962): Comedian, television presenter, singer, who had a daily late night show during the survey, and has presented various talk shows and quiz shows since then. He is known for his direct and confrontational, though disarming, interviewing style and his general irreverence to everyone. His humor and language at times is coarse, and not appreciated by all (he was fired by NCRV because of his constant jokes about a popular singer). He also made a successful film about the exploits of two of his best-known characters.

Liberg, Hans (1954): Dutch cabaret artist, mostly known for his mingling of high and low cultural forms and references, and his use (or pastiche) of classical music.

Maassen, Theo (1966): Cabaret artist, not very well known at the time of the Dutch study, who has become very popular since then, especially among younger people.

Millecam, Sylvia (1956–2001): Comedian, actress, and presenter, known for her types and impersonations, for instance in the KRO program *Ook dat nog!*

Moppentoppers: Television joke telling contest aired by commercial network RTL 4, produced by Endemol, presented by Ron Brandsteder.

Ook dat nog! Highly popular television show broadcast by KRO, in which comedians enacted (true) conflicts about all forms of consumer conflicts, ranging from conversations with unhelpful help desks to more serious forms of swindle. One of the performers in *Ook dat nog!* was Sylvia Millecam.

Oppassen!! Rather traditional, long-running Dutch family sitcom, aired by VARA, the socialist public broadcasting corporation, featuring a family cared for by two grandfathers. The name is a pun on *opa's* [grandpas] and *oppassen* [babysitting].

Over de roooie: Reality show, broadcast by commercial network SBS6, in which people on the street were dared to do unpleasant or embarrassing tasks (e.g. biting other people's toe nails) in order to win 1,000 guilders (rooie is slang for 1,000 guilders; over de rooie means "over the edge"; and the three o-s are a reference to the amount of 1,000)

Reve, Gerard (1923–2006): One of the most important Dutch writers of the twentieth century. Even though he was primarily a "serious" novelist, he was appreciated by many people for his humorous and ironical style.

Schippers, Wim T. (1942): Artist, television writer, actor, and presenter. Schippers started as an artist (one of his art works was a peanut butter floor); he created a number of television variety shows for VPRO in the 1960s and 1970s, including the first show to feature a naked woman; had a weekly radio show for the VPRO; and wrote a comedy series for this broadcasting corporation. He also wrote a play for dogs (as actors). Schippers is known for his playful and absurd language, which is full of neologisms. His style and general outlook is absurd, anarchistic, and highly original. Schippers also does the voice of Ernie in the Dutch version of Sesame Street.

Schmidt, Annie M. G. (1911–1995): *Grande dame* of Dutch humor, who wrote cabaret texts, musicals, songs, plays, (humorous) poems, television series, and children's books and poetry, many of which were highly successful. It is hard to summarize Schmidt's sense of humor, but it generally characterized by a mildly rebellious tone, sharp observation, and witty and playful language use. She is well known for her motto, more controversial when first phrased than it is today, that "Laughter is allowed by God".

Schouten, Tineke (1954): Comedian (she decidedly does not consider herself a cabaret artist), who has been very successful with shows with punny titles like "all you need is lach" [lach=laughter] since the early 1980s. She is known for her impersonations and types, her strong Utrecht accent, and her parodies of popular songs and performers.

Sonneveld, Wim (1917–1974): Cabaret artist, actor, and singer, and one of the most prominent entertainers and performers of his time. Sonneveld did many cabaret shows, with others and by himself, has a long-standing slot on VARA radio in the 1950s, and played many roles in musicals (esp. *My fair lady*), films, and television programs. He is remembered most for some of his types and for his songs, both humorous and serious.

Tailleur, Max (1909–1990): Jewish entertainer and joke teller, who became known for his "Sam and Moos" jokes, which he published in his many joke books, and told, in a strong Amsterdam-Jewish accent, in his own theatre in Amsterdam, and on the *geinlijn*, a phone number one could call to hear a new joke every day.

Teeuwen, Hans (1967): Cabaret artist who was just getting known during the time of Dutch study, but has become extremely popular since then, especially among young people. Teeuwen's humor is a prime example of "hard" humor: confrontational, shocking, and at times distinctly (and self-consciously) unpleasant. However, Teeuwen's shows can also be absurdist, nihilistic, unexpectedly sensitive and reflexive, or, at times, experimental and outright weird.

van Vliet, Paul (1935): Cabaret artist and actor. While van Vliet has roots in the student cabaret of the 1960s, his style has always tended more towards to the romantic than to critical-progressive cabaret. His humor is based mainly on types, and he is also known for his poetic (especially by cabaret standards) songs.

van Waardenberg, Martin (1956) and Wilfried de Jong (1958): Cabaret artists whose performances were irreverent, rough, and very physical.

Notes

1. In the terminology of the sociology of emotions, laughing with someone is one of the strongest signals of interactional "attunement" (Scheff 1990), or "emotional energy" that marks a smooth and successful interaction ritual (Collins 2004). Thus, humor has a strong emotional component, which determines many of the important but ambivalent social functions and effects of humor.
2. There are some scattered studies on the humor of specific groups, varying from police officers and waitresses to court jesters and migrants to Israel (Powell and Paton 1988; Powell, Paton and Wagg 1996; Shifman and Katz 2005; Zijderveld 1982; Goldstein 2003 – a very good ethnography of humor, that came just too late for this book) as well the occasional general work on the sociology of humor, most recently by Peter Berger (1997). For the most recent, though rather old, overviews see Zijderveld (1983), Mulkay (1988) and Palmer (1994). There are a number of psychological comparative studies of humor, mostly aimed at cross-cultural validation of humor scales rather than exploration of cultural variations (e.g. Ruch and Forabosco 1996; Saroglou and Scariot 2002). The only sociological comparative work in this field is the work on ethnic humor by Davies (1990, 1998a, 1998b, 2000).
3. See Davies (1998); Dundes (1987a); Ellis (2001); Kuipers (2002, 2005); Morrow (1987); Oring (1987, 1992).
4. Marc Dutroux was apprehended by the Belgian police in 1996. When he was arrested, two young girls were found alive in his basement. In the next year, the bodies of four other young girls, as well as one of his accomplices, were found. In 1998, Dutroux escaped from prison, leading to the resignation of two government ministers. He was captured again later. In 2004, he was found guilty of kidnapping and murder, and sentenced to life. The Dutroux case caused much publicity both in Belgium and the Netherlands, and in Belgium led to much political unrest and mass popular protests called the "White Marches".
5. The joke was a pun on a song for Sinterklaas (Saint Nicolas), a holiday on December 5 when children get presents if they have been good in the past year. Bad children are threatened to get a beating with the rod. The text of one of the best-known Sinterklaas songs is "Who's sweet will get candy who's naughty the rod." The rod in Dutch is "*de roe*", hence the new text to this song: "Who's sweet will get candy, who's naughty Dutroux."
6. The questionnaire consisted of a series of personal questions, a list of 35 jokes that people were asked to rate for humorousness and offensiveness on a 5-point scale. It also contained a representative list of Dutch humorists, comedians and writers, as well as Dutch and international humorous television programs, of which people were asked to indicate whether they knew it, and if so, to rate it for humorousness on a five-point scale. This list was sent to 1500 randomly

chosen Netherlanders, along with an introductory letter explaining the aim of the study as well as warning people for possibly offensive content.

Thus, the response was not very high: 23 percent is low even in the Netherlands where questionnaire response is always lower than in other countries (de Leeuw and Hox 1996, 1998; Stoop 2005). The response was probably negatively influenced by the fact that people were completely randomly approached. The response will not have been aided by the nature of the jokes and the perception of the subject as "not being very useful". Non-response is a problem especially if as a consequence the sample strongly deviates from the population. A comparison with Netherlands population data proves that there was a relatively higher response from the more highly educated and from men and that the response of persons older than 65 was relatively low – both rather general biases in questionnaire research (de Leeuw and Hox 1998). Distributions of ages, family size, region, religion, political preference and income lay reasonably close to data for the Netherlands population. Demographic biases are, however, not so serious; what is important is differences between these groups and not their distribution throughout the Netherlands population. A larger danger is that the respondents differ from the Netherlands population in the area of humor, the so-called selection for the dependent variable.

There are, however, two reasons to assume that the questionnaire, in spite of the low response, is a valid instrument to measure the appreciation of jokes and humor. To start with, the different research methods show a high degree of agreement: the interviews corresponded significantly with the results from the questionnaire. Moreover, there was a great degree of variation in the answers: these large differences between respondents indicate that no selection for the dependent variable took place. The differences between respondents are rather large and, moreover, systematic. In other words, a certain pattern appears to exist, a pattern also demonstrated in other sources.

7. Eigenvalue factor 1 (joke appreciation): 9.266. Eigenvalue factor 2 (innocuousness): 3.389. Total explained variance of factor analysis: 36.16%. Measures for cultural and economic capital: see Ganzeboom, de Graaf, and Kalmijn (1987). Class is measure on a five-point scale based on the EGP-classification by Erickson, Goldthorpe and Portocarero (1979). Education appropriate for current profession is based a five-point scale (1 = elementary, 5 = university) developed by the Dutch Statistical Bureau (CBS 1992).

8. Of the joke tellers I interviewed, eight were approached through newspaper advertisements asking for "people who knew and told a lot of jokes", three regularly told jokes in a radio show, and nineteen were approached at the selection for *Moppentoppers*. Only three of them were women, two of whom were found through the grapevine. Almost all of these joke tellers will be cited in the text, when their age and profession is mentioned. The youngest was 15, the oldest was 89. Generally these joke tellers were not educated above secondary school (vocational or general): only two of them had higher vocational educa-

tion. They lived in all regions of the Netherlands, both in rural, urban and suburban surroundings.

9. These 32 people were selected from the people who had filled out the questionnaire, and who had indicated that they would be willing to be interviewed for the study. A selection was made to approach an even distribution of gender, education, and liking of the jokes in the questionnaire (high, average, low). The latter was not completely possible, since there weren't many women and highly educated with high liking, or men and less highly educated with low liking of the jokes. In the sample there were seventeen women and fifteen men; fifteen were highly educated and seventeen were educated below college-level. The oldest interviewee was 84, the youngest 22. They lived in all regions of the Netherlands, both in rural, urban, and suburban surroundings. Almost all these respondents will be cited in the text, when their age and profession is mentioned.

10. PRINCALS (non-linear principal component analysis) is a statistical method for non-linear factor analysis, e.g. factor analysis for categorical variables. Because most respondents did not know many of the humorists and television programs in the questionnaire, I have done this analysis as well as a regular factor analysis of the appreciation in Table 3. PRINCALS provided the opportunity to include awareness as well as appreciation in the clustering. This method is similar to (but not the same as) the correspondence analysis used by Bourdieu in *Distinction.* See van de Geer (1993).

11. Eigenvalues for factor analysis of appreciation: Popular humor: 5.91. Highbrow humor: 2.40. Veterans: 4.75. Celebrities: 1.86. Total variance explained by these four factors: 45.18%. Cronbach's α is a measure for internal consistency, based on the average inter-item correlation. α for highbrow taste was computed from the best-known 10 out of 14 items, because of the amount of unknowns. However, whereas adding or removing items lead to a large variation in the number of respondents used to compute α, it hardly caused any variation in the value of α, which remained above .70 in all cases.

12. This episode that caused the scandal contained a eulogy to "The Image", in biblical language, ending with a variation on Our Father addressing "The Image", with footage of people glued to the screen as well as images of roofs of houses crowded with television antennae which are, indeed, reminiscent of crosses. See the report by one of the makers of the program, Rinus Ferdinandusse (1966) and Ibo (1981: 79–82).

13. For psychological studies of humor appreciation and offensiveness, see Herzog and Anderson (2000); Martin (1998); Ruch (1988); Ruch and Hehl (1998).

14. For the effects of identification on humor see for instance Ford and Ferguson (2004); LaFave (1972); Martineau (1972); Middleton (1959); Nevo (1985); Zillman (1983).

15. For studies of gender representation and identification in humor, see for instance Greenwood and Isbell (2002); Herzog (1999); Herzog and Anderson

(2000); Moore, Griffiths and Payne (1987); Mundorf et al. (1988); Ryan and Kanjorski (1998).

16. In linguistics, various researchers are working on the development of inventories or classifications of humorous technique, mostly within the framework of the General Theory of Verbal Humor, see Raskin (1985); Attardo and Raskin (1991); Attardo (1994, 2004); Attardo, Hempelmann, and di Maio (2002). There have only been few attempts to combine this linguistic approach with studies of appreciation, see Ruch, Attardo, and Raskin (1993) and Hempelmann and Ruch (2005).

17. This approach has been used in various studies of humor appreciation, most notably in of Ruch (1988) and Ruch and Hehl (1998). See also Martin (1998).

18. For Eigenvalues of factor analysis, see note 7.

19. Willem van Hanegem and Louis van Gaal were coaches of, respectively, the Rotterdam and Amsterdam soccer teams at the time of the research. Patrick Kluivert played for Ajax, the club from Amsterdam. Ed de Goey and Gaston Taument played for Feyenoord, the Rotterdam club.

20. A long tradition of scholarly thought exists about the uses, meanings, functions and pleasures of non-serious transgression. Within social science, the two most influential traditions derive either from the work of Freud (on humor: 1905), see also Gay (1994), Oring (1992, 2003), which has found a more sociological incarnation in the work of Norbert Elias, especially in Elias and Dunning (1986); or to the work of Emile Durkheim on ritual and social solidarity, which has been applied to the study of humor by Mary Douglas (1966, 1975). For an excellent overview of both philosophical and social scientific approaches to transgression see Jenks (2003).

21. Maarten van Roozendaal, *Aan gezelligheid ten onder* [roughly translated as *Gezelligheid* will be our downfall]. Theatre show 2000–2002. A CD of this show was released in 2002 (Amsterdam: Dodo).

22. The survey was sent first to 750 people living in the city of Philadelphia, an affluent suburb of the same city, a village in South New Jersey, and a smaller city in eastern Pennsylvania. Because the response proved depressingly low (14%), 100 questionnaires were sent out later in another New Jersey suburb of the Philadelphia agglomeration, this time with the endorsement of the municipal council, sadly, not to much avail. This led to a final sample of 143 respondents, or an overall response rate of 16.8%. Spread of the respondents along age, gender, as well as religion and (for the area) political affiliation is a reasonable approximation of the population (as based on US Census data), but whites, college educated, and high income groups are overrepresented. Humor tastes, both in the ratings of jokes and comedians and TV shows show a large variation that is somewhat reassuring.

The first twenty-four interviewees were selected from the respondents on the basis of age, gender, education, and humor appreciation. Among these were thirteen men, eleven women. Five of the informants had a graduate degree, eleven had a bachelor's degree, five had some college but no degree and three had completed high school. On the basis of their jobs, three of these can be classified as working class, eight as lower middle class (routine white collar work), and thirteen can be classified as higher middle class (interpreted rather widely here to include anything from hotel manager to grade school teacher to management consultant and lawyer). Ages varied from twenty-five to eighty. It was not easy to get a good ethnic mix: of these twenty-four, one was African-American, one was Latina and two were Jewish (I am aware that there is some debate whether this would count as "ethnic"). In order to make up for the underrepresentation of African-Americans I did four additional interviews with African-American women during a stay in Ohio in 2004. These were all women, enrolled in a college course in African-American studies (which is where I recruited them), ranging in age from 25 to 48. In addition to going to college, they worked as a nurse, a phone operator, a Navy technician and a homemaker.

23. In some cases, the jokes were translated directly, but in jokes with culture-specific references (ethnic, names of soccer teams) an American version of the same joke was used. For instance, the Turkish woman who could be spat was Italian in the American version. The table shows the ratings for the ten jokes that were the same or similar in the Netherlands and the US.

	US		Netherlands	
	Humorous	Offensive	Humorous	Offensive
God will save me	3.51	1.50	3.76	1.62
not your brother..	3.42	1.76	3.55	1.51
vacuum clear	3.30	1.70	3.87	1.22
teacher and Johnny	3.24	2.19	3.86	1.67
Bible salesman	3.13	1.79	3.93	1.69
Phone conversation	3.06	1.35	3.43	1.26
Blonde with two ...	2.61	2.16	2.79	1.88
Half deaf	2.44	1.34	3.10	1.25
Woman w/moustache	2.41	2.62	2.32	3.43
Racist driver	2.24	2.91	2.69	3.53

24. Participation in tertiary education in the US is higher than in the Netherlands: in the US, 38% of the population from 25 to 64 has attained tertiary education, versus 24% in the Netherlands. However, the number of years spent in formal education in the Netherlands is not much lower than in the US: 12.9% versus 13.8% (OECD 2005). This reflects the strong stratification and early selection in the Dutch educational system. The variety in American college or university education is much higher than in the Netherlands, and the level of some American junior colleges would probably be more or less comparable with what in the Netherlands is called secondary or advanced vocational education (MBO).

25. The scale used for educational level in the US: 1. no formal education 2. less than high school 3. high school 4. one or more years in college without earning

a degree 5. bachelor's degree 6. graduate degree. Like the other demographic questions used in the survey, the scale was adapted from the social background questions in the US Census.

26. Eigenvalues for factor analysis: Intellectual humor: Eigenvalue 10.847. Transgressive humor: 2.337. Ethnic and sexual humor: 2.054. Total variance explained: 42.33%.

27. However, various authors have made extensive studies of (parts of) the American joke repertoire, most notably Alan Dundes (1987a, 1987b), Gershon Legman (1982), and Eliot Oring (1992, 2003).

28. This African-American humor style is reminiscent of the interaction and communication style described by Anderson (1999), who contrasts "street" style with the more restrained, less flaunting and self-consciously transgressive "decent" style. Anderson describes this "street" behavior, which is widely recognized, stereotyped, and imitated as "Black", as typical of only part of the African-American population.

29. The more explicit humorous framing in American humor, as compared with European humor, even in more highbrow forms, is very visible in two recent American remakes of successful British comedies, *Coupling* (2003) and *The Office* (2005). In both cases, the British originals were not very clearly framed as humorous. Especially *The Office*, with its gritty realist style, looked and sounded very unlike a sitcom, and was very unemphatic in its humor. The remakes not only looked slicker and more glamorous (which is typical of all American remakes) but also adhered more strictly to the conventions of the sitcom format, and both the overall framing and individual attempts at humor were much emphatically humorous.

30. There are some notable exceptions, such as Lenny Bruce, Woody Allen, or Eddy Murphy, but it is telling that these more transgressive or less upbeat comics are generally Jewish or African-American.

31. Wickberg (1998), in his history of the notion of a sense of humor in America, notes how this concept had strong moral connotations since its inception, which he dates in the nineteenth century. Incidentally, this moral outlook on humor has probably influenced the strong American "humor and health" movement, which has founded an entire industry of therapies, workshops, and laughter training programs on the belief that humor is good for you (Billig 2004: 15–33). Even though some of this movement now starts to catch on in Europe, this serious view on positive humor generally leaves Europeans rather baffled.

32. In terms of DiMaggio's dimension of cultural classification (1987), the Dutch constellation of humor styles is hierarchical and seems to have stronger boundary strength (i.e. stronger exclusion), whereas the American humor styles are more diverse and less hierarchical, and have weaker boundaries. The fourth dimension of classification DiMaggio mentions is universality: the degree to which people in a society all accept the same criteria for classification. In this respect the comparison of the Netherlands and the US leads to the rather unexpected conclusion that the Dutch constellation has rather limited universality,

as people with lowbrow tastes do not seem to feel that highbrow humor is better (see Chapter 10). In the US, on the other hand, everybody seems to accept a moral logic, which points to a greater degree of universality, despite the diversity and limited hierarchy of the system.

It is easy to see how such a constellation leads to a preference among American cultural sociologists for a "tool kit" approach (cf. Swidler 1986), stressing how people employ various "cultural repertoires", rather than the more deterministic "habitus" approach of Pierre Bourdieu. However, the comparison between Americans and Dutch, in my view, demonstrated clearly how diversity and the reluctance to exclude or judge others also can result in an embodied, almost-automatic style of behavior and communication – in other words, a habitus. Moreover, the American research showed that people with more status had considerable more aptitude and skill in switching between repertoires: the predominantly upper middle class male omnivores. Thus, the notion of habitus, or embodied culture, does not imply that people have to be the same all the time, or that they cannot choose how to behave. Rather, a specific habitus may entail a wider variety of repertoires, and a greater skill at handling them.

References

Anderson, Elijah
    1999   *The Code of the Street. Decency, Violence, and the Moral Life of the Inner City.* New York: Norton.

Apte, Mahadev L.
    1985   *Humor and Laughter: An Anthropological Approach.* Ithaca: Cornell University Press.

Archaïvarius (pseudonym of Rinus Ferdinandusse)
    1972   *De duizend slechtste grappen van de wereld* [The thousand worst jokes in the world]. Amsterdam: De arbeiderspers.

Attardo, Salvatore
    1994   *Linguistic Theories of Humor.* Berlin/ New York: Mouton de Gruyter.
    2001   *Humorous Texts: A Semantic and Pragmatic Analysis.* Berlin/ New York: Mouton de Gruyter.

Attardo, Salvatore and Victor Raskin
    1991   Script theory revis(it)ed: Joke similarity and joke representation model. *Humor* 4 (3): 293–347.

Attardo, Salvatore, Christian Hempelmann, and Sara di Maio
    2002   Script oppositions and logical mechanisms: Modeling incongruities and their resolutions. *Humor* 15 (1): 3–46.

Bailey, Peter
    1998   *Popular Culture and Performance in the Victorian City.* Cambridge: Cambridge University Press.

Bakhtin, Mikhail Mikhailovich
    1984   *Rabelais and his World.* Bloomington: Indiana University Press. Original Russian edition 1965.

Baldwin, Barry (ed.)
    1983   *The Philogelos or Laughter-Lover. Translated with an Introduction and Commentary by Barry Baldwin.* Amsterdam: J.C. Gieben.

Bateson, Gregory
    1972   *Steps to an Ecology of Mind.* New York: Ballantine Books.

Bauman, Richard
    1977   *Verbal Art as Performance.* Rowley, MA: Newbury House Publishers.
    1986   *Story, Performance, and Event: Contextual Studies of Oral Narrative.* Cambridge: Cambridge University Press.

Beck, Ulrich
    2002   The cosmopolitan society and its enemies. *Theory, Culture and Society* 19 (1/2): 17–44.

Bellah, Robert, Richard Madsen, Steve Tipton, William Sullivan, and Ann Swidler
  1996   *Habits of the Heart. Individualism and Commitment in American Life.*
          Berkeley: University of California Press. Original edition, Berkeley,
          University of California Press, 1985.
Berger, Peter
  1997   *Redeeming Laughter: The Comic Dimension of Human Experience.*
          Berlin: Walter de Gruyter.
Bergson, Henri
  1999   *Laughter: An Essay on the Meaning of the Comic.* Los Angeles: Green
          Integer. Original French Edition, Paris: Presse Universitaire de France,
          1900.
Bernstein, Basil
  1971   *Class, Codes and Control. Volume 1. Theoretical Studies towards a
          Sociology of Language.* London: Routledge and Kegan Paul.
Billig, Michael
  2005   *Laughter and Ridicule: Towards a Social Critique of Humor.* London:
          Sage.
Bilsen, Richard van
  1999   CabaretMail 2.11, November 1999. Electronic newsletter of the
          Nederlandse Cabaret Homepage.
Bourdieu, Pierre
  1977   The economics of linguistic exchanges. *Social Science Information* 16
          (6): 654–668.
  1984   *Distinction: A Social Critique of the Judgment of Taste.* London:
          Routledge. Original French edition, Paris: Les Editions de Minuit,
          1979.
  1990   *The Logic of Practice.* Cambridge: Polity Press. Original French
          edition, Paris: Les Editions de Minuit, 1980.
  1991   *Language and Symbolic Power.* Oxford: Polity Press. Original French
          edition, Paris: Fayard, 1982.
  2001   *Masculine Domination.* Stanford: Stanford University Press. Original
          French Edition, Paris: Seuil, 1998.
Brands, Jan
  1992   *Die hoeft nooit meer wat te leren. Levensverhalen van academici met
          laaggeschoolde ouders* [He'll never have to learn anything more. Life
          stories of academics with less educated parents]. Nijmegen: SUN.
Brandsteder, Ron
  1994   *Moppentoppers deel 1.* Baarn: Tirion.
Brewer, Derek
  1997   Prose jest-books mainly in the sixteenth to eighteenth centuries in
          England. In *A Cultural History of Humor,* Jan Bremmer and Herman
          Roodenburg (eds), 90–111. Cambridge: Polity Press.

Brinkgreve, Christien and Bram van Stolk
1997   *Van huis uit. Wat ouders aan hun kinderen willen meegeven.* [From the home. What parents want to transfer to their children.]. Amsterdam: Meulenhoff.

Brown, Penelope and Stephen Levinson
1983   *Politeness: Some Universals in Language Usage.* Cambridge: Cambridge University Press.

Burke, Peter
1978   *Popular Culture in Early Modern Europe.* London: Temple Smith.

CBS [Centraal Bureau voor de Statistiek/ Statistics Netherlands]
1992   *Standaard Beroepen Classificatie 1992* [Standard occupations classification 1992]. The Hague: Centraal Bureau voor de Statistiek.

Coleman, Robin R. Means
2000   *African American Viewers and the Black Situation Comedy: Situating Racial Humor.* New York: Garland

Collins, Randall
1975   *Conflict Sociology: Toward an Explanatory Science.* New York: Academic Press.
1981   On the microfoundations of macrosociology. *American Journal of Sociology* 86 (5): 984–1014.
1988   *Theoretical Sociology.* San Diego: Harcourt Brace Jovanovich.
1992   Women and the production of status cultures. In *Cultivating Boundaries,* Michèle Lamont and Marcel Fournier (eds.), 213–231.
2004   *Interaction Ritual Chains.* Princeton: Princeton University Press.

Collinson, D.
1988   Engineering humour: masculinity, joking and conflict in shop-floor relations. *Organization Studies* 9: 181–199.

Coser, Rose
1959   Some social functions of laughter: A study of humor in a hospital setting. *Human Relations* 12 (2): 171–182.
1960   Laughter among colleagues: A study of the social functions of humor among the staff of a mental hospital. *Psychiatry* 23 (1): 81–95

Crane, Diana
1992   High culture versus popular culture revisited: A reconceptualization of recorded cultures. In *Cultivating Boundaries,* Michèle Lamont and Marcel Fournier (eds.), 58–74.

Crawford, Mary
1989   Humor in conversational context: Beyond biases in the study of gender and humor. In *Representations: Social Constructions of Gender,* Rhoda K. Unger (ed.), 155–166. Amityville: Baywood Publishing Company.
1995   *Talking Difference. On Gender and Language.* London: Sage.

2003   Gender and humor in conversational context. *Journal of Pragmatics* 35 (9): 1413–1430.

Davies, Christie
1990   *Ethnic Humor around the World: A Comparative Analysis.* Bloomington: Indiana University Press.
1991   Ethnic humor, hostility and aggression: A reply to Eliott Oring. *Humor* 4 (4): 415–422
1998a   *Jokes and their Relations to Society.* Berlin/ New York: Mouton de Gruyter.
1998b   The dog that didn't bark in the night: A new sociological approach to the cross–Cultural Study of Humor. In *The Sense of Humor*, Willibald Ruch (ed.), 293–308.
1999   Jokes about the death of Diana, Princess of Wales. In *The Mourning for Diana,* Tony Walter (ed.), 253–268. Oxford: Berg.
2002   *The Mirth of Nations.* New Brunswick: Transaction.

Dekker, Rudolf
2001   *Humor in Dutch Culture of the Golden Age.* Basingstoke: Palgrave. Original Dutch Edition, Amsterdam: Wereldbibliotheek, 1997.

Dekker, Rudolf en Herman Roodenburg
1984   Humor in de zeventiende eeuw: opvoeding, huwelijk en seksualiteit in de moppen van Aernout van Overbeke (1632-1674) [Humor in the seventeenth century: education, marriage and sexuality in the jokes of Aernout van Overbeke]. *Tijdschrift voor sociale geschiedenis* 10: 243–266.

Derks, Peter, Rosemary E. Staley and Martie G. Haselton
1998   "Sense" of humor: perception, intelligence, or expertise. In *The Sense of Humor*, Willibald Ruch (ed.), 143–158.

DiMaggio, Paul
1987   Classification in art. *American Sociological Review* 52: 440–455

Dines-Levy, G and G. Smith
1988   Representation of women and men in "Playboy" sex cartoons. In *Humour in Society*, Chris Powell and George Paton (eds.), 234–259.

Douglas, Mary
1966   *Purity and Danger: An Analysis of the Concepts of Pollution and Taboo.* London: Routledge and Kegan Paul.
1975   Jokes. In *Implicit Meanings: Essays in Anthropology*, 90–114. London: Routledge and Kegan Paul

Dronkers, Jaap en Wout Ultee (eds)
1995   *Verschuivende ongelijkheid in Nederland. Sociale gelaagdheid en mobiliteit* [Shifting inequality in the Netherlands. Social stratification and mobility]. Assen: Van Gorcum.

Dundes, Alan
1987a   At ease, disease – AIDS jokes as sick humor. *American Behavioral Scientist* 30(3): 72–81.
1987b   *Cracking Jokes: Studies of Sick Humor Cycles and Stereotypes.* Berkeley: Ten Speed Press.

Dundes, Alan and Thomas Hauschild
1983   Auschwitz jokes. *Western Folklore* 42 (4), 249–260.

Durkheim, Emile
1964   *The Rules of Sociological Method.* New York: The Free Press. Original French edition, Paris: Alcan, 1895.

Duyvendak, Jan Willem, and Menno Hurenkamp (eds.)
2004.   *Kiezen voor de kudde. Lichte gemeenschappen en de nieuwe meerderheid.* [Choosing for the herd. Light communities and the new majority]. Utrecht: Tijdschrift voor de Sociale Sector.

Eijck, Koen van
1999   Socialization, education, and lifestyle: How social mobility increases the cultural heterogeneity of status groups'. *Poetics* 26: 309–328.
2001.   Social differentiation in musical taste patterns. *Social Forces* 79 (3): 1163–1185.

Eijck, Koen van and Kees van Rees
2000   Media orientation and media use: Television viewing behavior of specific reader types from 1975 to 1995. *Communication Research* 27: 574–616.

Elias, Norbert
1978   *The Civilizing Process: History of Manners.* Oxford: Blackwell. Original German edition, Basel: Haus zum Falken, 1939.
1982   *The Civilizing Process: State Formation and Civilization* .Oxford: Blackwell. Original German edition, Basel: Haus zum Falken, 1939.

Elias, Norbert and Eric Dunning
1986   *Quest for Excitement: Sports and Leisure in the Civilizing Process.* Oxford: Blackwell.

Ellis, Bill
2001   A model for collecting and interpreting world trade center disaster jokes. *New Directions in Folklore* (web journal) URL: http://astro.temple.edu/~camille/journal.html

Fallers, Lloyd A.
1954   A note on the "trickle effect". *Public Opinion Quarterly* 18 (5): 314–321.

Ferdinandusse, Rinus, Jan Blokker and Dimitri Frenkel Frank.
1966   *Zo is het toevallig ook nog 's een keer: drie seizoenen "Zo is het..." in teksten en foto's* [That was the week that was: three seasons in texts and photos]. Amsterdam: Polak en Van Gennep.

Fisher, Seymour and Rhoda L. Fisher
1981   *Pretend the World is Funny and Forever: A Psychological Analysis of Comedians, Clowns, and Actors.* Hillsdale: Erlbaum.
Fiske, John
1989   *Understanding Popular Culture.* Boston: Unwin Hyman.
Ford, Thomas and Ferguson, Mark
2004   Social consequences of disparagement humor: A prejudiced norm theory. *Personality and Social Psychology Review* 8 (1): 79–94.
Fry, William
1963   *Sweet Madness: A Study of Humor.* Palo Alto: Pacific.
Fry, William and Melanie Allen
1999   *Life Studies of Comedy Writers: Creating Humor.* New Brunswick: Transaction Publishers.
Freud, Sigmund
1976   *Jokes and their Relation to the Unconscious.* Harmondsworth: Penguin. Original German Edition, Leipzig: Deuticke, 1905.
Gans, Herbert
1962   *The Urban Villagers: Group and Class in the Life of Italian-Americans.* New York: Free Press of Glencoe
1999   *Popular Culture and High Culture: An Analysis and Evaluation of Taste.* Revised and Updated Edition. New York: Basic Books.
Ganzeboom, Harry
1988   *Leefstijlen in Nederland: een verkennende studie* [Lifestyles in the Netherlands: An explorative study]. Rijswijk: Sociaal en Cultureel Planbureau/ Alphen aan den Rijn: Samsom
Ganzeboom, Harry, Paul de Graaf and Matthijs Kalmijn
1987   De culturele en de economische dimensie van beroepsstatus [The cultural and economic dimension of professional status]. *Mens en maatschappij* 62 (2): 153–175.
Gay, Peter
1994   *The Bourgeois Experience: Victoria to Freud, Volume 3: The Cultivation of Hatred.* London: Harper Collins.
Geer, J. van de
1993   *Advanced Quantitative Techniques in the Social Sciences, Vol. 3: Multivariate Analysis of Categorical Data.* Thousand Oaks: Sage.
Giddens, Anthony
1991   *Modernity and Self–Identity. Self and Society in the Late Modern Age.* Cambridge: Polity Press.
Goffman, Erving
1959   *The Presentation of Self in Everyday Life.* New York: Doubleday.
1967   *Interaction Ritual: Essays on Face-to-face behavior.* New York: Pantheon Books.

1971   *Relations in Public: Microstudies of the Public Order.* New York: Basic Books.

1974   *Frame Analysis: An Essay in the Organization of Experience.* Boston: Northeastern University Press.

Goldstein, Donna

2003   *Laughter out of Place: Race, Class, Violence and Sexuality in a Rio Shantytown.* Berkeley: University of California Press.

Goudsblom, Johan

1967   *Dutch Society.* New York: Random House.

1988   De Nederlandse samenleving in een ontwikkelingsperspectief [Dutch society from a developmental perspective]. In *Taal en sociale werkelijkheid,* 30–68. Amsterdam: Meulenhoff.

1990   *Balans van de sociologie* [Sociology in the balance]. Nijmegen: SUN.

1998   *Reserves.* Amsterdam: Meulenhoff.

Greenwood D. and L. M. Isbell

2002   Ambivalent sexism and the dumb blonde: Men's and women's reactions to sexist jokes. *Psychology of Women Quarterly* 26 (4): 341–250.

Hall, Stuart

1980   Encoding/Decoding. In *Culture, Media, Language: Working Papers in Cultural Studies (1972–1979),* S. Hall, D. Hobson, A. Lowe, and P. Willis (eds), 128–138. Birmingham: Hutchinson/ CCCS.

Hanenberg, Patrick van den and Frank Verhallen

1996   *Het is weer tijd om te bepalen waar het allemaal op staat. Nederlands cabaret 1970–1995* [It's time again to decide where things are at. Dutch cabaret 1970–1995]. Amsterdam: Nijgh en Van Ditmar.

Hebdige, Dick

1979   *Subculture: The Meaning of Style.* London: Methuen.

Heinich, Nathalie

2000   From rejection of contemporary art to culture war. In *Rethinking Comparative Cultural Sociology,* Michèle Lamont and Laurent Thévenot (eds.), 170–209.

Hempelmann, Christian and Willibald Ruch

2005   3WD meets GTVH. Psychology and linguistics break the ground for interdisciplinary humor research. *Humor* 18 (4): 353–387.

Henkin, Barbara and Jefferson Fish

1986   Gender and personality differences in the appreciation of cartoon humor. *Journal of Psychology* 120 (2): 157–175.

Herzog, Thomas R.

1999   Gender differences in humor appreciation revisited. *Humor* 12 (4): 411–424.

Herzog, Thomas R. and Maegan Anderson

2000   Joke cruelty, emotional responsiveness, and joke appreciation. *Humor* 13 (3): 333–352.

Holmes, Janet
2006   Sharing a laugh: Pragmatic aspects of humor and gender in the workplace. *Journal of Pragmatics* 38 (1): 26–50.
Holt, Douglas
1997   Distinction in America? Recovering Bourdieu's theory of taste from its critics. *Poetics* 25: 1–25.
Hymes, Dell
1974   Ways of speaking. In *Explorations in the Ethnography of Speaking*, Richard Bauman and Joel Sherzer (eds.), 433–452. Cambridge: Cambridge University Press.
Ibo, Wim,
1981   *En nu de moraal…Geschiedenis van het Nederlands cabaret. Deel 1: 1885-1936* [History of Dutch cabaret. Part 1: 1885-1936]. Alphen aan den Rijn: A.W.Sijthoff.
Jamison, Kay Redfield
2004   *Exuberance: The Passion for Life.* New York: Knopf.
Jenks, Chris
2003   *Transgression.* London/ New York: Routledge.
Jhally, Sut and Justin Lewis
1992   *Enlightened Racism: The Cosby Show, Audiences, and the Myth of the American Dream.* Boulder: Westview Press.
Kalberg, Stephen
2000   Formen der Interaktion von Akademikern. Eine Ebene des Strukturierten Missverständnisses. In *Die Vermessung kultureller Unterschiede: USA und Deutschland im Vergleich*, Jürgen Gerhards (ed.), 127–137. Wiesbaden: Westdeutscher Verlag
Kapteyn, Paul
1985   *In de speeltuin Nederland. Over gezagsverhoudingen tussen ouderen en jongeren* [In playground Netherlands. About relations of authority between the old and the young]. Amsterdam: Arbeiderspers.
Katz-Gerro, Tally.
2002   Highbrow cultural consumption and class distinction in Italy, Israel, West Germany, Sweden, and the United States. *Social Forces* 81 (1): 207–229.
Kennedy, James
1995   *Nieuw Babylon in aanbouw: Nederland in de jaren zestig* [New Babylon under Construction: The Netherlands in the 1960s]. Amsterdam: Boom.
Koestler, Arthur
1964   *The Act of Creation.* London: Hutchinson.

Kotthoff, Helga
1986   Scherzen und Lachen in Gesprächen von Frauen und Männern. *Der Deutschunterricht–Beitrage zu seine Praxis und Wissenschaftliche Grundlegung* 38 (3): 16–28.
2006   Gender and humor: The state of the art. *Journal of Pragmatics* 38 (1): 4–25.

Kuipers, Giselinde
1995   Etnische humor. Een onderzoek naar de serieusheid van kwetsende humor. M.A. dissertation Cultural Anthropology, Utrecht University.
2000   The difference between a Surinamese and a Turk: Ethnic jokes and the position of ethnic minorities in the Netherlands. *Humor* 12 (2): 141–175.
2002   Media culture and Internet disaster jokes: Bin Laden and the attack on the World Trade Center. *European Journal of Cultural Studies* 5 (4): 451–471.
2005   "Where was King Kong when we needed him?" Public discourse, digital disaster jokes, and the functions of laughter after 9/11. *The Journal of American Culture* 28(1): 70–84.
2006a   Television and taste hierarchy: The case of Dutch television comedy. *Media, Culture and Society* 28 (3): 359–378.
2006b   The social construction of digital danger: Debating, defusing, and inflating the moral dangers of online humor and pornography in the Netherlands and the United States. *New Media and Society* 8 (3): 379–400

Lakoff, Robin.
1975   *Language and Woman's Place.* New York: Harper and Row.

Lafave, Lawrence K
1972   Humor judgments as a function of reference groups and identification classes. In *The Psychology of Humor*, Jeffrey Goldstein and Paul McGhee (eds), 195–210. New York: Academic Press.

Lamont, Michèle
1992   *Money, Morals and Manners: The Culture of the French and American Upper–middle Class.* Chicago: The University of Chicago Press.
2000   *The Dignity of Working Men: Morality and the Boundaries of Race, Class and Immigration.* New York: Russell Sage Foundation/ Cambridge: Harvard University Press.

Lamont, Michèle and Marcel Fournier (eds.)
1992   *Symbolic Boundaries and the Making of Inequality.* Chicago: University of Chicago Press.

Lamont, Michèle and Virag Molnar
2002   The study of boundaries across the social sciences. *Annual Review of Sociology* 28: 167–195.

Lamont, Michèle and Laurent Thévenot (eds.)
2000   *Rethinking Comparative Cultural Sociology: Repertoires of Evaluation in France and the United States.* Cambridge: Cambridge University Press.

Lampert, Martin D. and Susan Ervin-Tripp
1998   Exploring paradigms: The study of gender and sense of humor near the end of the 20th century. In *The Sense of Humor*, Willibald Ruch (ed.), 231–270.
2006   Risky laughter: Teasing and self-directed joking among male and female friends. *Journal of Pragmatics* 38: 51–72.

Leeuw, Edith de and Joop Hox
1996   A comparison of nonresponse in mail, telephone and face–to–face surveys. Applying multilevel modeling to meta-analysis. *Quality and Quantity* 28: 329–344.
1998   Nonrespons in surveys: Een overzicht [Nonresponse in surveys: An overview]. *Kwantitatieve Methoden* 19 (57): 31–54.

Legman, Gershon
1982   *No Laughing Matter: An Analysis of Sexual Humor.* Bloomington: Indiana University Press.

Levine, Lawrence
1988   *Highbrow/ Lowbrow. The Emergence of Cultural Hierarchy in America.* Cambridge: Harvard University Press.

Lewis, Paul (ed.)
1997   Debate: Humor and political correctness. *Humor* 10 (4): 453–513.

Lijphart, Arend
1968   *The Politics of Accommodation: Pluralism and Democracy in the Netherlands.* Berkeley: University of California Press.

Lipset, Seymour Martin
1990   *Continental Divide: The Values and Institutions of the United States.* New York: Routledge.

López–Sintas, Jordi and Tally Katz-Gerro
2005   From exclusive to inclusive elitists and further: Twenty years of omnivorousness and cultural diversity in arts participation in the USA . *Poetics* 33: 299–319.

Man, Jacqueline de
1993   De etiquette van het schertsen. Opvattingen over de lach in Nederlandse etiquetteboeken en spectators uit de achttiende eeuw. [The etiquette of banter: Opinions on laughter in the Dutch books of manners in the eighteenth century] *De achttiende eeuw* 25 (2): 93–136.

Martin, Rod A.
1998   Approaches to the sense of humor: A historical review. In *The Sense of Humor*, Willibald Ruch (ed.), 15–62.

Martineau, William H.
1972   A model of the social functions of humor. In *The Psychology of Humor,* Jeffrey Goldstein and Paul McGhee (eds.), 101–128. New York: Academic Press.

McGhee, Paul E.
1979   *Humor: Its Origin and Development.* San Francisco: W. H. Freeman and Company.
1983   Humor development: Toward a life span approach. In *Handbook of Humor Research,* Jeffrey Goldstein and Paul McGhee (eds.), 109–134. New York: Springer Verlag.

Meder, Theo
2000   *Vertelcultuur in Waterland. De volksverhalen uit de collectie Bakker (ca. 1900)* [Oral culture in Waterland. Folk tales from the Bakker collection]. Amsterdam: het Spinhuis.
2001   *"Er waren een Nederlander, een Turk en een Marokkaan...." Een multidisciplinaire benadering van moppen in een multiculturele wijk* ["There were a Dutchman, a Turk and a Moroccan..." A multidisciplinary approach to jokes in a multicultural neighborhood]. Amsterdam: Het Spinhuis.

Meder, Theo and Eric Venbrux
2000   Vertelcultuur. [Oral culture] In *Volkscultuur. Een inleiding in de Nederlandse etnologie,* Ton Dekker, Herman Roodenburg, and Gerard Rooijakkers (eds.), 282–336. Nijmegen: SUN.

Middleton, Russell
1959   Negro and white reactions to racial humor. *Sociometry* 22 (2): 175–183.

Moore, Timothy, Karen Griffiths and Barbara Payne
1987   Gender, attitudes toward women, and the appreciation of sexist humor. *Sex Roles* 16 (9–10): 521–531.

Morreall, John
1983   *Taking Laughter Seriously* Albany: State University of New York Press.

Morreall, John (ed.)
1987   *The Philosophy of Humor and Laughter.* Albany: State University of New York Press.

Morrow, P.D.
1987   Those sick challenger jokes. *Journal of Popular Culture* 20 (4): 175–184.

Mulkay, Michael
1988   *On Humour: Its Nature and Place in Modern Society.* Oxford: Polity Press.

Mundorf, Norbert, Azra Bhatia, Dolf Zillmann, Paul Lester and Susan Robertson
1988   Gender differences in humor appreciation. *Humor* 1–3, 231–243.

Nash, Walter
1985   *The Language of Humour. Style and Technique in Comic Discourse.*
        Londen: Longman.
Neumann, Norbert,
1986   *Vom Schwank zum Witz: zum Wandel der Pointe seit dem 16.*
        Jahrhundert. Frankfurt: Campus Verlag.
Nevo, Ofra
1985   Similarities between humor responses of men and women and Israeli
        Jews and Arabs. In *Women's Worlds*, Marylin Safir, M. T. Mednick,
        D. Israeli and J.Bernard (eds.), 135–141. New York: Prager.
Norrick, Neill
1993   *Conversational Joking: Humor in Everyday Talk.* Bloomington:
        Indiana University Press.
2001   On the conversational performance of narrative jokes: Toward an
        account of timing. *Humor* 14 (3): 255–274.
OECD (Organization for Economic Co-operation and Development)
2005   *Education at a Glance 2005.* URL: http://www.oecd.org/document/
        11/0,2340,en_2825_495609_35321099_1_1_1_1,00.html
Opie, Iona and Peter Opie
1959   *The Lore and Language of Schoolchildren.* Oxford: Oxford University
        Press.
Oring, Elliott
1987   Jokes and the discourse on disaster – The Challenger Shuttle explosion
        and its joke cycle. *Journal of American Folklore* 100 (397): 276–286.
1991   Review of "Ethnic Humor around the World". *Humor* 4 (1): 109–114.
1992   *Jokes and their Relations.* Lexington: the University Press of
        Kentucky.
2003   *Engaging Humor.* Champaign: University of Illinois Press.
Overbeke, Aernout van
1991   *Anecdota sive historiae jocosae: een zeventiende–eeuwse verzameling*
        moppen en anekdotes [A seventeenth century collection of jokes and
        anecdotes]. Edited by Rudolf Dekker and Herman Roodenburg.
        Amsterdam: P.J. Meertens-Instituut.
Pakulski, Jan and Malcolm Waters
1996   *The Death of Class.* London: Sage.
Palmer, Jerry
1994   *Taking Humour Seriously.* London: Routledge.
Paton, George and Ivan L. Filby
1996   Humour at work and the work of humour. In *The Social Faces of*
        Humour, Chris Powell, George Paton, and Stephen Wagg (eds.), 105–
        138.

Peterson, Richard and Albert Simkus
1992   How musical tastes mark occupational status groups. In *Cultivating Differences*, Michèle Lamont and Marcel Fournier, 52–186.
Peterson, Richard A. and Roger Kern.
1996.   Changing highbrow taste: From snob to omnivore. *American Sociological Review* 61: 900–907.
Peterson, Richard
1997   The rise and fall of highbrow snobbery as a status marker. *Poetics* 25 (2/3): 75–92.
Pleij, Herman
1979   *Het gilde van de Blauwe Schuit. Literatuur, volksfeest en burgermoraal in de late middeleeuwen* [The guild of the blue ship. Literature, popular festivity, and civil morality in the late middle ages]. Amsterdam: Meulenhoff.
1983   *Een nyeuwe clucht boeck: een zestiende–eeuwse anekdotenverzameling* [A new jest book: A sixteenth century collection of anecdotes]. Muiderberg: Coutinho
Powell, Chris and George Paton (eds.)
1988   *Humour in Society: Resistance and Control.* Basingstoke: MacMillan Press.
Powell, Chris, George Paton, and Stephen Wagg (eds.)
1996   *The Social Faces of Humour. Practices and Issues.* Aldershot: Arena.
Provine, Robert
2000   *Laughter: A Scientific Investigation.* New York: Viking.
Raskin, Victor
1985   *Semantic Mechanisms of Humor.* Dordrecht: Reidel.
1998   The sense of humor and the truth. In *The Sense of Humor*, Willibald Ruch (ed.), 95–108.
Reijnders, Stijn
2006   Holland op de helling: Televisie-amusement, volkscultuur en ritueel vermaak [Holland on the slide. Television entertainment, popular culture, and ritual amusement]. PhD dissertation, University of Amsterdam. Alphen: Veerhuis.
Robinson, Dawn and Lynn Smith-Lovin
2001   Getting a laugh: Gender, status, and humor in task discussions. *Social Forces* 80 (1): 123–158
Röhrich, Lutz
1980   *Der Witz: seine Formen und Funktionen: mit tausend Beispielen in Wort und Bild.* München : Deutscher Taschenbuch Verlag
1988   Erzählforschung. In *Grundriss der Volkskunde. Einführung in die Forschungsfelder der Europäischen Ethnologie*, Rolf Brednich (ed.), 353–380. Berlin: Reimer Verlag.

Roodenburg, Herman
1997   To converse agreeably: Civility and the telling of jokes in Seventeenth–Century Holland. In *A Cultural History of Humour*, Jan Bremmer and Herman Roodenburg (eds.), 112–133. Cambridge: Polity Pres.

Rubin, Lillian Breslow
1976   *Worlds of Pain: Life in the Working-class Family*. New York: Basic Books.

Ryan, Kathryn and Jeanne Kanjorski
1998   The enjoyment of sexist humor, rape attitudes, and relationship aggression in college students. *Sex Roles* 38 (9/10): 743–756.

Ruch, Willibald
1988   Sensation seeking and the enjoyment of structure and content of humor: Stability of findings across four samples. *Personality and Individual Differences* 9: 861–871.

Ruch, Willibald (ed.)
1998   *The Sense of Humor. Explorations of a Personality Characteristic.* Berlin/New York: Mouton de Gruyter.

Ruch, Willibald, Salvatore Attardo, and Victor Raskin
1993   Toward an empirical verification of the General Theory of Verbal Humor. *Humor* 6 (2): 123–136.

Ruch, Willibald and Giovannantonio Forabosco
1996   A cross-cultural study of humor appreciation: Italy and Germany. *Humor* 9 (1): 1–18.

Ruch, Willibald and Franz-Josef Hehl
1998   A two-mode model of humor appreciation: Its relation to aesthetic appreciation and simplicity-complexity of personality. In *The Sense of Humor*, Willibald Ruch (ed.), 109–142.

Saroglou, Vassilis and C. Scariot
2002   Humor Styles Questionnaire: Personality and educational correlates in Belgian high school and college students. *European Journal of Personality* 16: 43–54.

Schalet, Amy T.
2000   Raging hormones, regulated love: Adolescent sexuality and the constitution of the modern individual in the USA and Netherlands. *Body and Society* 6 (1): 75–106.

2001   Geciviliseerd of gestigmatiseerd? Afhankelijkheid en lichaamsbeheersing in de Nederlandse figuratiesociologie en Amerikaanse 'welfare'–debatten [Civilized or stigmatized? Dependence and bodily control in Dutch figurational sociology and American "welfare" debates]. *Amsterdams Sociologisch Tijdschrift* 28 (3): 321–349.

Senelick, Laurence
1981   *British Music Hall. A Bibliography and Guide to Sources with a Supplement on European Music Hall.* Hamden: The Shoe String Press.

Scheff, Thomas
1990   *Microsociology: Discourse, Emotion, and Social Structure.* Chicago: University of Chicago Press.

Slide, Anthony
1994   *The Encyclopedia of Vaudeville.* Westport: Greenwood Press.

Sociaal en Cultureel Planbureau
1999   *Sociale en culturele verkenningen 1999* [Social and cultural explorations 1999]. Rijswijk: Sociaal en Cultureel Planbureau

Stein, Charles W. (ed.)
1984   *American Vaudeville as seen by its Contemporaries.* New York: Knopf.

Stoop, Ineke
2005   *The Hunt for the Last Respondent: Nonresponse in Sample Surveys.* The Hague: Sociaal en cultureel planbureau.

Straver, Cees, Ab van der Heiden, and Ron van der Vliet
1994   *De huwelijkse logica: huwelijksmodel en inrichting van het samenleven bij arbeiders en anderen* [The marital logic: marriage model and management of living together among workers and others]. Leiden : DSWO Press.

Strating, Alex
1997   *De lijnrijders van Rijnsburg: een antropologische studie van bloemenhandel, verwantschap en identiteit* [An anthropological study of flower trade, kinship and identity in Rijnsburg]. Amsterdam: Universiteit van Amsterdam.

Swaan, Abram de
1985   *Kwaliteit is klasse: de sociale wording en werking van het cultureel smaakverschil* [Quality is class: The social development and workings of cultural taste difference]. Amsterdam: Bert Bakker.

1990   *The Management of Normality. Critical Essays in Health and Welfare.* London/New York: Routledge.

1995   Widening circles of identification: Emotional concerns in sociogenetic perspective. *Theory, Culture and Society* 12 (1): 25–39.

1997   Widening circles of disidentification. On the psycho– and sociogenesis of the hatred of distant strangers – Reflections on Rwanda. *Theory, Culture and Society* 14 (2): 105–122.

Swidler, Ann
1986   Culture in action: Symbols and strategies. *American Sociological Review* 51: 273–286.

Tallieur, Max
1953   *Langs m'n neus weg* [Off the cuff]. Blaricum: Bigot en Van Rossum.

Tannen, Deborah
1984   *Conversational Style: Analyzing Talk among Friends.* Norwood: Ablex.
1994   *Gender and Discourse.* Oxford: Oxford University Press.
Tannen, Deborah (ed.)
1993   *Gender and Conversational Interaction.* Oxford: Oxford University Press.
Thomas, Keith
1977   The place of laughter in Tudor and Stuart England. *Times Literary Supplement* 21–1–1977, 77–81.
Veblen, Thorstein
2001   *Theory of the Leisure Class.* New York: Modern Library. Original Edition, New York: MacMillan, 1899.
Verberckmoes, Johan
1999   *Laughter, Jestbooks and Society in the Spanish Netherlands.* Basingstoke: Macmillan. Original Dutch edition, Nijmegen: Sun, 1998.
Vuijsje, Herman
1997   *Correct: Weldenkend Nederland sinds de jaren zestig* [Correct: Well– thinking Netherlands since the 1960s]. Amsterdam: Contact.
Walker, Nancy
1988   *A Very Serious Thing. Women's Humor and American Culture.* Minneapolis: University of Minnesota Press
Watkins, Mel
1994   *On the Real Side: Laughing, Lying and Signifying: The Underground Tradition of African–American Humor That Transformed American Culture from Slavery to Richard Pryor.* New York: Simon and Schuster.
Wickberg, Daniel
1998   *The Senses of Humor: Self and Laughter in Modern America.* Ithaca: Cornell University Press.
Willis, Paul
1977   *Learning to Labour. How Working Class Kids get Working Class Jobs.* London: Saxon House.
Willis, Paul, Simon Jones and Joyce Canaan
1990   *Common Culture: Symbolic Work at Play in the Everyday Cultures of the Young.* Milton Keynes: Open University Press.
Wouters, Cas
1990   *Van minnen en sterven: informalisering van omgangsvormen rond seks en dood* [Of loving and dying: informalization of manners con- cerning sex and death]. Amsterdam: Bert Bakker.
1999   Changing patterns of social controls and self–controls. On the rise of crime since the 1950s and the sociogenesis of a 'third nature'. *British Journal of Criminology* 39: 416–432.

2004   *Sex and Manners: Female Emancipation in the West, 1980–2000.*
         London: Sage.
Zijderveld, Anton
   1982   *Reality in a Looking–glass: Rationality through an Analysis of Tradi-
            tional Folly.* London: Routledge and Kegan Paul.
   1983   Trend report on the sociology of humour and laughter. *Current Sociol-
            ogy* 31 (3): whole issue.
Zillman, Dolf
   1983   Disparagement humor. In *Handbook of Humor Research: Volume 1,*
            Paul McGhee and Jeffrey Goldstein (eds.), 85–108. New York:
            Springer Verlag.
Ziv, Avner
   1984   *Personality and Sense of Humor.* New York: Springer.

Index